The Art of Collecting

Cover illustration
Jan van Goyen
River Landscape, 1648 (detail)
Oil on panel
Gift of Bruce B. Dayton 83.84

The Art of Collecting

Acquisitions at The Minneapolis Institute of Arts   1980-1985

The Minneapolis Institute of Arts

Edited by Louise Lincoln and Elisabeth Sövik
Designed by Ruth Dean
Photographs by Gary Mortensen

Publication of this catalogue was made possible
by the generous support of the Dayton Hudson
Foundation, through the contributions of
B. Dalton Bookseller, Dayton's, and Target stores;
and the Andrew W. Mellon Foundation.

PREFACE

The reputation of an art museum is based primarily on the distinction of its permanent collection, the works of art it proudly possesses and exhibits and which give the museum its character and image. The collection is the heart of an art museum, the reason for its existence, the source of its status, and the basis upon which all other museum activities—conservation, exhibitions, education, public programs, research, and publication—are built. Excellent public collections come into existence, grow, and improve because of a sense of commitment on the part of civic-minded community leaders and art collectors who care deeply about the quality of the cultural life in their region. This concern, coupled with moral and financial support and the employment of a knowledgeable and discerning professional staff—art historians with "good eyes," a thorough knowledge of art history and the art market, and the courage of their convictions—are the necessary ingredients for a museum's success.

The Minneapolis Institute of Arts and the community it serves benefit from a tradition of intelligent art collecting and enlightened patronage which continues to this day, and from a tradition of connoisseur-directors and curators who have stressed quality and excellence in museum purchases. As a result the Institute's collection, with its world-renowned masterpieces and superb holdings in many fields, should be a matter of great pride to Twin Citians.

During the past five years the collection has grown and improved in a remarkable fashion. Spurred by the centennial celebration of The Minneapolis Society of Fine Arts in 1983, which resulted in a generous outpouring of financial support, the museum acquired an unusually large number of notable works of art, many of which are illustrated in this catalogue. Some of these objects have filled gaps in our holdings while others have added to existing strengths. The series of exhibitions documented by this catalogue celebrate the accomplishments of the past half-decade and report on these achievements: a blending of curatorial expertise and community support. The intention of this catalogue, however, is neither to sing our own praises, though we are certainly proud of our new acquisitions, nor to thank the generous donors who helped with the purchases listed here, though we are immensely grateful to the individuals, foundations, and corporations which made the acquisitions possible. Our main purpose is rather to examine the history of our collection and the motivation behind purchases, the philosophy of acquisition which governed or influenced the museum's decisions, and the reason for the enthusiasm of our staff for the kinds of art objects acquired. Each of our seven curators has contributed a short essay which describes his or her own aspirations for departmental collecting as well as guidelines for judging possible new additions to the collection. Taken together the essays demonstrate several things:

—that curators are motivated by a strong, almost overwhelming urge to obtain significant objects for the museum.

—that the curators have a clear sense of priorities and a clear image of what the ideal museum collection should be.

—that art museum purchases are not made haphazardly, but are based on standards of quality and a set of policies and objectives the museum staff and the trustee accessions committee hold in common.

—that our staff is committed to acquiring diverse objects that lead to a collection which is both historically complete and excellent in overall aesthetic quality.

—that in the inflated and competitive art market today, curators working for museums such as ours, with limited purchase funds, are inevitably frustrated at times in their endeavor to obtain the best possible art objects for Minnesota.

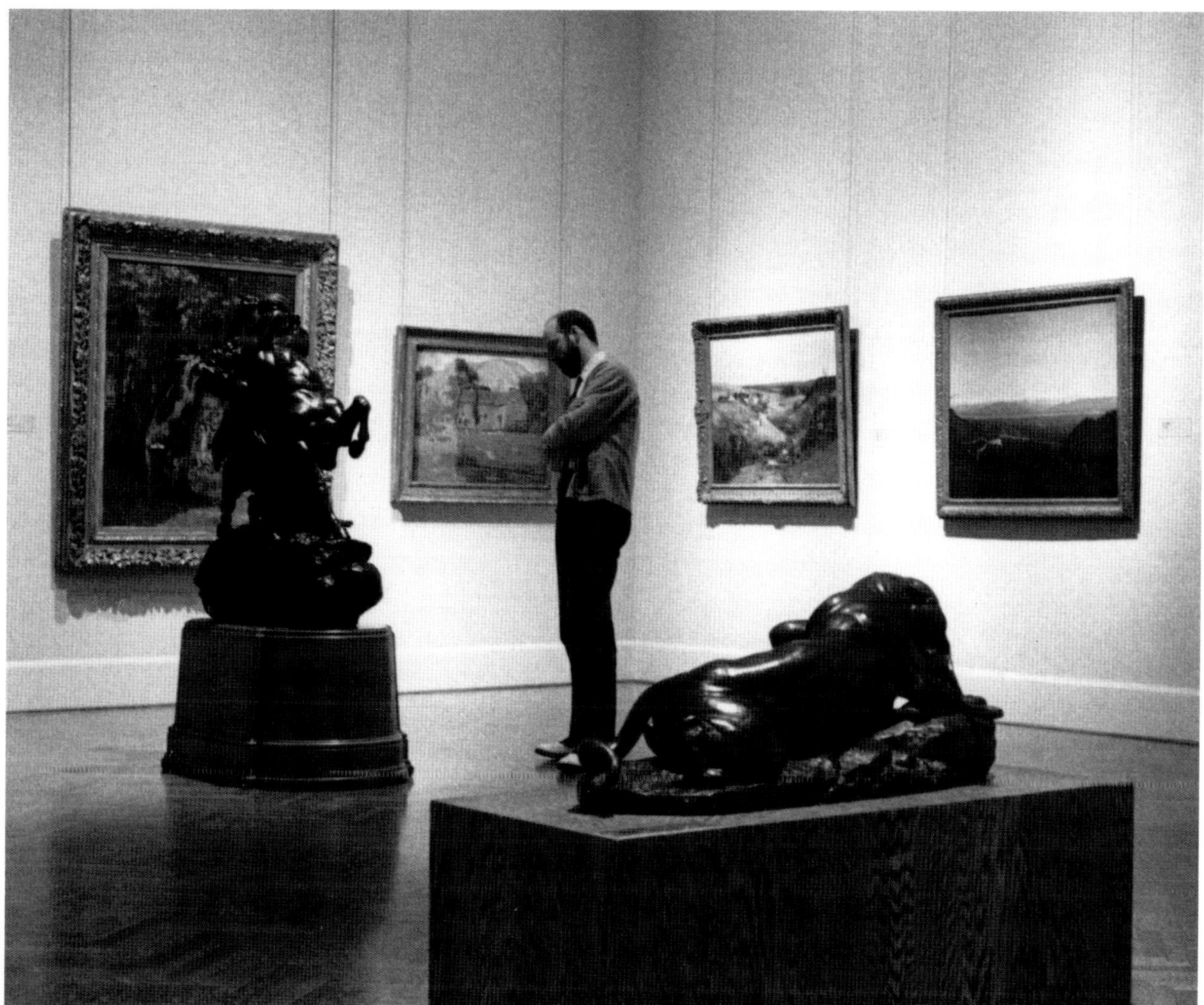

In the face of curatorial initiatives, it is the director's responsibility to keep in mind the overall objectives of the museum, to weigh each proposal against his own sense of the museum's priorities and ultimate goals, and to mediate as objectively as possible the interests and desires of the various departments to maintain a balanced program of accessions.

I am not aware of any other existing publication in which a group of curators, specialists in different fields, have articulated their attitudes toward museum collecting. The specific matters discussed in this book relate to The Minneapolis Institute of Arts and its recent history. The issues, however, are general and applicable to virtually all art museums. I hope this text will thus demystify the processes by which museums acquire art, and also provide the general reader with useful and informative insights into the problems and procedures of museum collecting.

Alan Shestack
Director

The Minneapolis Institute of Arts, designed by
McKim, Mead and White. (Photo taken shortly
after its 1915 completion.)

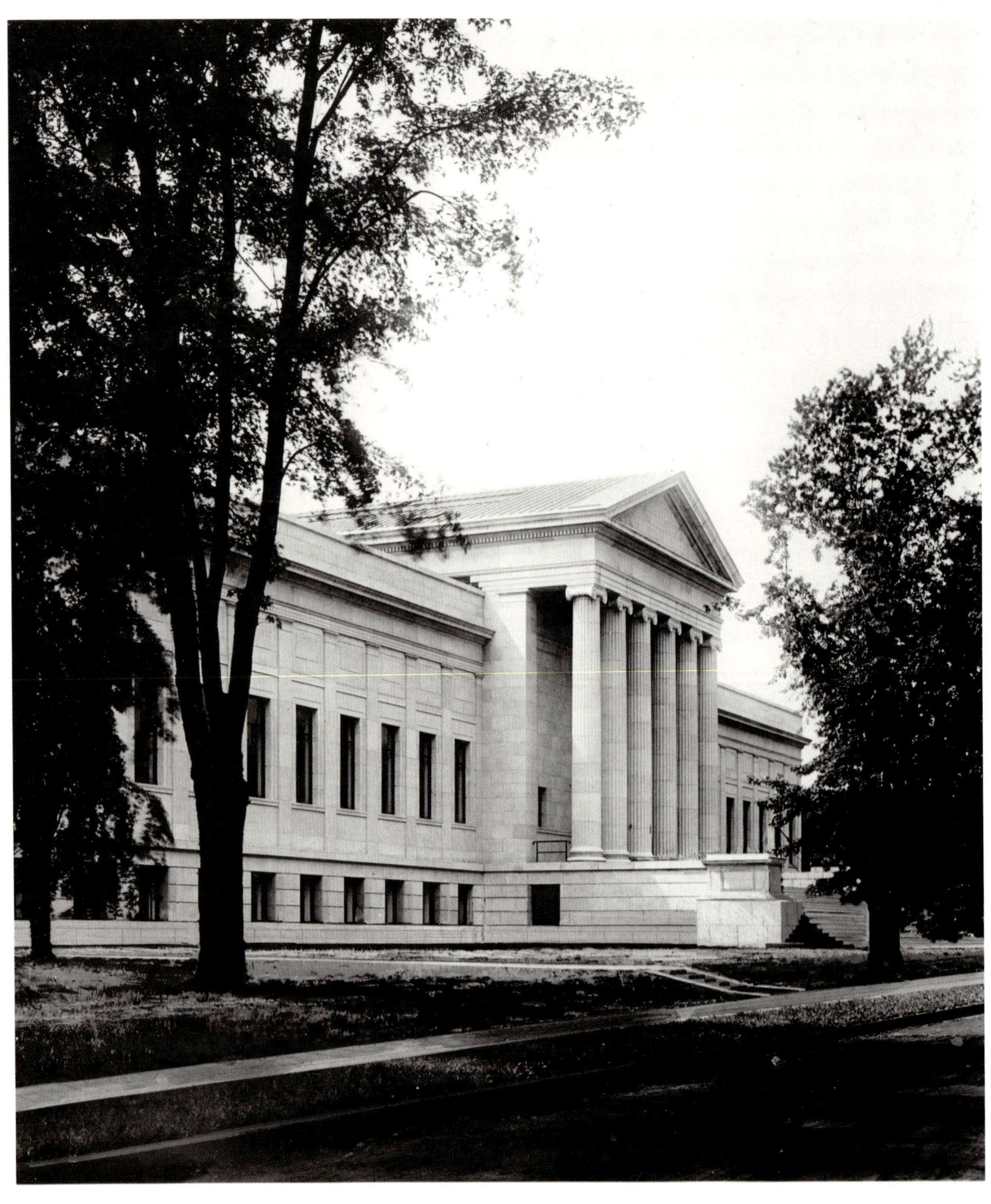

INTRODUCTION

AN ART MUSEUM FOR MINNEAPOLIS

In 1908 when The Minneapolis Institute of Arts was still only the dream of a few prominent trustees of the Minneapolis Society of Fine Arts, Robert Koehler presented the Society with a rational and novel direction for their proposed museum. Koehler was a recognized artist and, as head of the Minneapolis School of Art, he was the Society's highest-ranking professional staff member. From a position of experience in the art world and prominence in the community, he discussed the future collections of the new institution:

> European art galleries . . . have captured all of the works by the old masters that are worth having or at all obtainable, and when an American institution attempts to form a collection of old masters, it must be . . . content with inferior works, and make most of them appear as far more valuable than they really are, thus cultivating a false standard for such of our art lovers as are unable to visit the European collections.

> Being a firm believer in American art, and considering its best examples as more worthy of a permanent place in public galleries than many spurious and indifferent examples of past ages that have already found their way into some of our collections I would advocate the acquisition of the best modern and early American works obtainable; not only pictures and works of sculpture, but also the choicest examples of handicraft as well. ("Some Ideas on the Founding of an Art Museum," *Proceedings of the American Association of Museums*, vol. 2 [1908], pp. 127-28.)

Koehler's opinion was colored by his own professional loyalties, derived from his position as an active painter working in America at the turn of the century. He was sincere, however, in his belief that first-quality European works would never be available to a museum recently established in the New World. Born in Germany, Koehler was familiar with public collections in Europe, many of which were formed under royal patronage over the course of several centuries. To him, the exhibition of paintings by Michelangelo or Raphael, Dürer or Rembrandt represented the standard by which the greatness of museum collections would forever be measured. In Koehler's judgment such a level of quality was unattainable in a small, young city like Minneapolis, beginning its museum in the early twentieth century. There was nothing of importance left to buy that could propel the young institution to prominence; no way to insure a standard of excellence if the new museum were to concentrate on the European artistic tradition.

"Nothing left to buy." These are words that professionals in the art trade and museum field have echoed for centuries, each generation repeating the phrase with its own special sense of omniscient discovery. The litany of concern began as early as the Renaissance and has been voiced regularly ever since. In 1815 the French art critic Quatremère de Quincy even felt compelled to condemn the common belief that "there are no longer any masterpieces to fill the museums" because so many public collections had been created during his time. In our era the concern has heightened as the abstract fear of earlier centuries draws closer to becoming reality. Objects are entering public collections in increasing numbers. Countries are closing their doors to export. Well-supported institutions in England, Germany, and the United States are positioning themselves for the final purchase of those notable objects that we consider to represent the artistic heritage of the past.

While Koehler's advice foreshadowed a real concern of the late twentieth century, his warnings were perhaps premature in 1908. Important paintings from certain favored European schools, such as the Italian High Renaissance, would not always be considered the only standard on which to judge a representative museum collection. Furthermore, Koehler could not have anticipated the sale of notable European private collections in the economic upheavals after World War I. In many instances the buyers were Americans, motivated by a new desire for a material demonstration of their wealth and culture, and during this period an enormous number of works of art came to this country. Also, in the half century before the end of World War I, public museums had been established in almost every sizable city in the land. Soon the growing collections of private individuals would fill those institutions and America's public museums would rank among the most respected in the world.

At the time, however, Koehler's advice had a ring of practicality about it. The commitment of the Minneapolis Society of Fine Arts to its arts collection was modest, at best, and Koehler saw no indication that the situation would change very quickly. James J. Hill had given the Society a small group of paintings in 1886, the donation which had begun the region's public collecting activities. Gifts from other members of the community were added occasionally thereafter. Most were contemporary American and European paintings, however, not important Old Masters. While a public art museum for Minneapolis was everyone's dream at the turn of the century, it was difficult to imagine what would be available to exhibit there. T. B. Walker was the only major art collector in the community, but by 1908 he had indicated his unwillingness to participate in the Society's museum venture. Koehler, therefore, was presenting a reasonable and pragmatic program, one that still has the ring of common sense to many museum boards attempting to carry out their responsibility appropriately: focus on what you can do well and don't try to do everything. Given Koehler's advice and Minneapolis's early collecting history, it seems astonishing that the Society's trustees rejected his proposal and chose to pursue a far more ambitious goal: the development of a collection of masterpieces that repre-

sented the entire history of art.

The large civic art museums established in this country in the late nineteenth century had been founded as educational institutions whose purpose was twofold: to form collections that provided young artists the opportunity of studying genuine works of art, and to represent to the general public masterworks of our Western artistic heritage along with objects from cultures held in high esteem at the time. This dual purpose brought ancient and medieval art into American museum galleries, along with European paintings, period rooms and their decorative accessories, Old Master prints, and Chinese sculpture. Public museums in New York, Boston, Philadelphia, and Chicago were developing in this fashion, and if a museum were to be established in Minneapois the founders decided that it would have to aspire to these same goals.

The person who motivated the trustees to adopt this course was the museum's guiding spirit during its earliest years: Joseph Breck, the Institute's first director (1914-17). Breck came to Minneapolis from the Metropolitan Museum where he had been a colleague of William Valentiner, a well-known expert in Renaissance sculpture and Dutch painting. Breck was first employed as an advisor to the proposed Institute, but William Dunwoody's 1914 bequest of one million dollars for acquisitions encouraged him to make the relationship more permanent. In discussing the expenditure of this future endowment income Breck outlined a comprehensive plan for the museum:

> The Minneapolis Institute of Arts will be a public museum of painting, sculpture and decorative arts, past and present, of all countries. It seeks quality, not quantity; that is the only limitation of its scope.... It is the intention of the Institute to illustrate these by small but carefully chosen collections of material, which will include examples of Oriental art, of Egyptian and Classical art, and of the art of the early Christian, Gothic, Renaissance and later

periods, which lead up to that of our own time.

And his reason for bringing them together:

> Nothing . . . is more instructive, aids more to understand and appreciate the work of our own time, than to have the opportunity of tracing in one museum the history of art from the remote past to the present day, noting how one period of art is developed from another, each new period being the result of all that has gone before. ("The Minneapolis Institute of Arts: Its Purpose and Collections," *Bulletin of the Minneapolis Institute of Arts*, vol. 3 (October 1914): 120-21.)

Breck was supported in his philosophy by the board of trustees, many of whom were relatively young and newly appointed to their positions. They were determined to create a great institution and each was willing to assume a personal responsibility in forming its collections. Many of them provided money to develop acquisitions within the Institute, others began private art collections with the intention of bequeathing them to the museum. Breck's successor, Russell Plimpton (1921-56), cultivated and often directed these new art patrons. Mrs. Charles Martin bought tapestries; John Van Derlip, Old Master paintings; James F. Bell, English and American silver; Alfred Pillsbury, Chinese bronzes; Augustus Searle, Chinese jades and gold. By committing to the development of the young museum, these donors formed many of the collections for which the Institute is now famous.

After an energetic beginning, the museum grew more slowly during the years of the Depression and World War II, but in the postwar era a new group of trustees guided by a brilliant and energetic curator, Richard Davis (1956-59), began to revitalize and redirect the museum's collecting activity. They felt that the encyclopedic collecting of the past had not always procured "masterpieces" for the Institute. To upgrade the collections and increase its holdings in twentieth-century art, many objects were sold when Davis became director. Egyptian, medieval, and oriental objects were deaccessioned in great number, along with American paintings and European decorative arts. Although the sales were unfortunate in many ways, the museum acquired some of its most important works with Davis's advice: Poussin's *Death of Germanicus* and the thirteenth-century Limoges *Deposition*, to name only two. The collections were also greatly enriched in the field of early twentieth-century painting and sculpture by the addition of spectacular modernist works that are now among the most loved and respected objects in the collection.

Davis's personal interest in twentieth-century art strongly influenced his museum acquisitions, and subsequent directors also developed the collections in terms of their specific areas of interest. After the short and distinguished directorship of Carl Weinhardt (1961-63) the trustees chose Anthony Clark to head the Institute (1963-73). Clark's commitment to Italian baroque painting led the museum to many important purchases in a little recognized field. Under his leadership the museum's collections increased in size and developed in other unusual areas as well, particularly Italian decorative arts and French neoclassical painting. Clark also laid the foundation for a department of photography, and his successor Samuel Sachs (1973-85) built this department to its current distinction. Sachs made constructive use of the accessions philosophy Clark had employed: purchasing first-quality objects in somewhat overlooked fields. He increased the museum's holdings dramatically in ethnographic art, particularly African art; late nineteenth-century painting and sculpture, Old Master prints; textiles; Asian art; European decorative arts; and American nineteenth-century furniture. In this way, Sachs built upon the tradition of encyclopedic collecting, but he provided a more scholarly focus for acquisitions by developing curatorial departments in many fields.

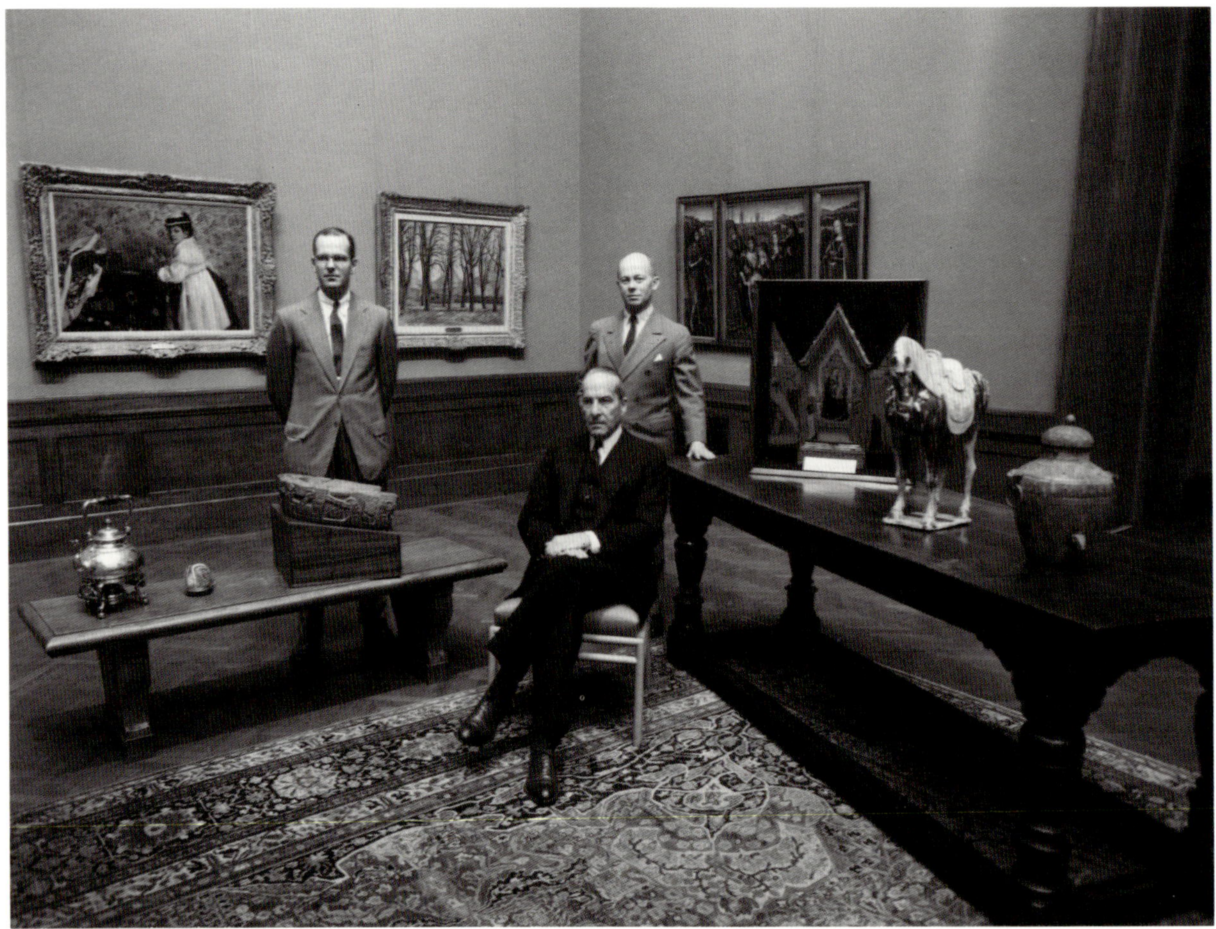

The Department of Prints had been established in 1916, but until the last years of Anthony Clark's administration there were no other separate curatorial departments. The accessions program of the museum was determined solely by the director, supported by one or two curatorial staff members. In the last fifteen years, however, departments have been established not only in paintings and decorative arts, but also in Asian art; African, Oceanic, and New World cultures; textiles; and photography. Recently staff positions for specialists in American paintings, American decorative arts, Old Master drawings, and early photography have been added to existing departments. This

expansion has enhanced the quality of exhibitions and other programs, and it has had a marked effect on acquisitions as well.

During this period of curatorial growth, each department has had to evolve a separate philosophy to structure the development of its collections. Given the many new departments and the specialized programs for collection expansion which have been established in the last few years, we have chosen 1986 to review the Institute's recent acquisitions in *The Art of Collecting: Acquisitions at The Minneapolis Institute of Arts 1980-85*. In this exhibition we hope to clarify the objective of each curator's recent purchases by presenting them in the context of the history of each department and the collecting philosophy that is determining departmental expansion. Museums rarely discuss their accessions program in detail with the public. However, by concentrating on collection development and elucidating each curator's rationale for growth, we hope to create a greater appreciation of the role of acquisitions in the evolution of the character of the Institute's permanent collection, the permanent collection that is Minnesota's visual link to cultural history.

THE ACQUISITION PROCESS

The procedure for purchasing art at The Minneapolis Institute of Arts is similar to that of other major museums in the country. The board of trustees, ultimately responsible for the expenditure of all funds, appoints a committee to review all recommendations for acquisitions and gifts of works of art. A standard procedure has recently been outlined by the American Association of Art Museum Directors:

> The Director must submit for the Board's approval all recommendations for acquisitions through purchase. No object may be considered for purchase without the Director's consent. While the final decision rests legally with the Board, it should approve no acquisition without full knowledge of the Director's opinion and, as required by museum policy, that of the curator concerned.

> This procedure is particularly important in the case of purchases, since they represent the expenditure of monies committed to public trust for which the Board is responsible. The one exception to this procedure may be purchases from Discretionary Funds made available to the Director and the Director's staff for this purpose, said acquisitions to be reported to the Board.

> A similar procedure should be followed for gifts offered to the collection. While circumstances may dictate some necessary deviations, it is strongly advised that gifts and bequests be of clear and unrestricted nature and that no work be accepted with a guarantee in perpetuity of an attribution or the circumstances of exhibition. (*Professional Practices in Art Museums*, American Association of Museum Directors, 1981, p. 11.)

These brief guidelines give no indication, however, of the complex and time-consuming preparations necessary to present potential acquisitions. The purchase of works of art for a museum involves four steps: developing a direction for collection growth; finding objects appropriate to that accessions program; securing the necessary funds to support the purchase; and obtaining approval of the director and accessions committee of the board. Throughout the process, however, the museum and its representatives also must rely heavily on imagination, tact, persistence and scholarship in securing the most significant available works for its collection.

In large institutions with separate curatorial departments, the search for acquisitions is carried on primarily by the curatorial staff in consultation with the director. Along with the organization of special exhibitions, the quest for objects is the most difficult and time-consuming activity of a curator's professional life. In the past art dealers regularly offered significant objects directly to museums, but in recent years almost all institutions, particularly those with smaller budgets, have had to compete aggressively in the marketplace, as fewer and fewer objects of museum quality are available at affordable prices. At present, The Minneapolis Institute of Arts receives $800,000 income from its endowment funds designated for acquisitions. The amount we have spent annually in the last two years ($1,500,000 from endowment income and gifts) places the Institute within the top fifteen civic art museums in the country, but significantly below the buying power of many private collectors, the richest American museums (Cleveland, Toledo, Kansas City, Fort Worth et al.), and the many foreign museums which receive government support.

Because of our modest purchasing power, our curators have had to be particularly ingenious and dedicated in enlisting the cooperation of dealers. Only when a dealer senses that a curator is a serious and knowledgeable buyer, and recognizes the scope and ambition of a museum's collection, is there a chance that important objects will be brought to an institution's attention when they come to market. To develop relationships with collectors and dealers, to examine works of art at first hand and to try to be in the right place at the right time on occasion, curators must be frequent travelers to international centers of market activity.

Once objects have been offered to the museum the internal process of researching the work and presenting it to the director begins. If the curator is confident of the aesthetic quality of the work, and its appropriateness to the collection, he or she undertakes extensive research in various areas. First, there is a close examination of the condition of the object, including a scientific analysis of its materials and fabrication. Next a bibliography is prepared for research. Visual comparisons to objects of similar type are evaluated. The curator then tries to discover as much as possible about the provenance, or history, of the work, and compares the price to that of similar works recently on the market. This can be a difficult process, for if the piece is rare, an appropriate comparison can be nearly impossible to find. Finally, curators consult outside scholars and colleagues, especially when an object is not within their specific area of expertise.

The object is then presented to the director, who employs a number of criteria in determining whether to recommend it to the board: the aesthetic impact of the piece, its importance to the collection as a whole, and the relative allocation of funds among the various departments. Each department maintains a list of desiderata, and the

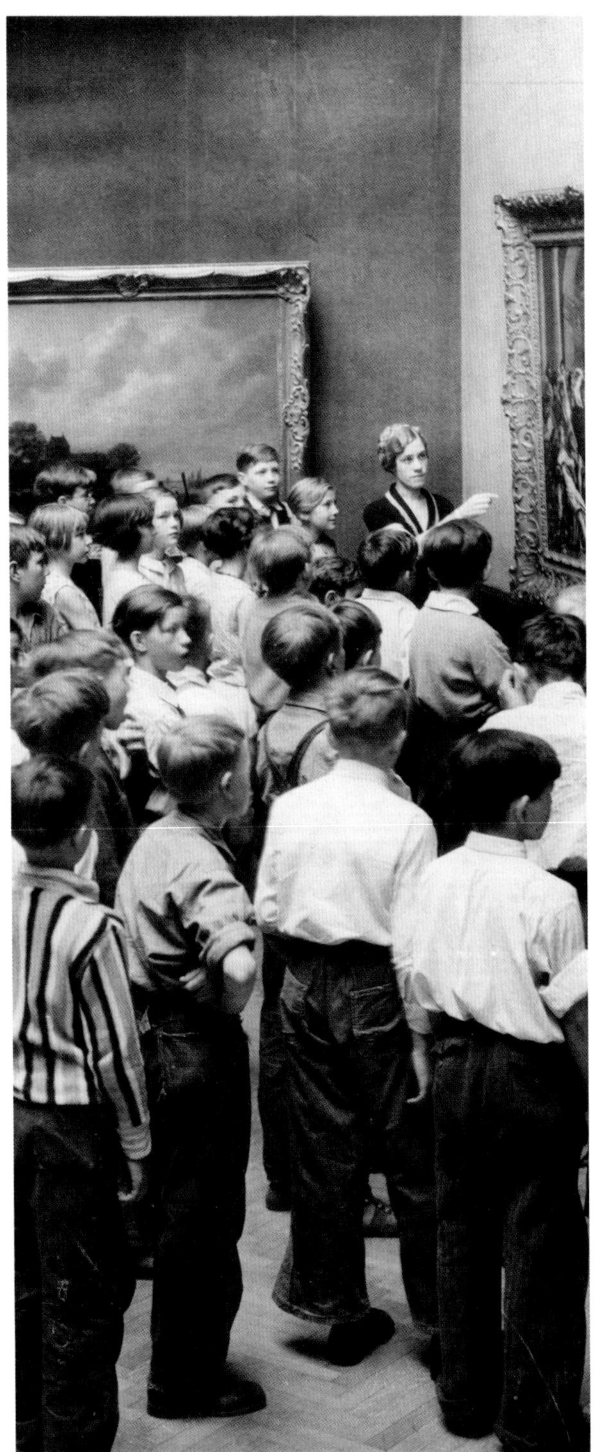

director will consider these expressed acquisition goals in making a judgment. If an object has been considered a priority for some time, it is more likely to be approved. The director will also be aware of the other purchases a department has made in recent months as well as the objects proposed by other departments at the same time which may present a challenge in funding. Two desirable works of art may appear simultaneously, and often the director has to make a choice. This choice is made easier if special sources of funding appear for one object and not the other. Funds from private individuals are often available only in specific fields, and certain acquisitions are more "fundable" than others. In the end, a limited percentage of objects proposed to a director is actually presented to the accessions committee.

In the following pages, the Institute's curators will present their department's accessions program through a discussion of its acquisitions over the last five years. It should be noted that the curators have been asked not to describe the circumstances surrounding individual purchases, the special maneuverings, the personal triumphs and disappointments associated with a particular acquisition. Such anecdotes can be fascinating, but they distract from the ultimate aim of each essay: to present each department's acquisitions program in terms of the history and nature of its existing collection.

It will be apparent that the director allows each department to interpret the collecting mission of the museum in different ways, responding to existing departmental collections, curatorial expertise, and the availability of money in the museum and objects in the marketplace. During the last five years, the Department of African, Oceanic and New World Cultures has focused on one collecting area, making almost all of its important acquisitions in the field of Oceanic art. The Paintings Department has concentrated on Dutch seventeenth-century works. On the other hand, the Decorative Arts and Sculpture Department and the Department of Asian Art have chosen to collect in a number of areas within their purview, attempting to fill a variety of perceived needs.

Differences appear in the curators' interpretations of the museological ideal expressed in the term "masterpiece" as well. It is used both for individual objects and groups of objects whose collective aesthetic and iconographic relationship can represent a "masterpiece" collection. There is a differing curatorial consciousness regarding the issue of quality as well. For the Photography Department, searching for quality in the field of contemporary art amidst the quantity of objects under consideration, the problem is recognizing the exceptional among a myriad of images available. In his essay, the photography curator is specific in listing his criteria for these judgments. Curators in other departments find it less difficult to discern desirable objects, but harder to find such works in the marketplace.

However a department is realizing the development of its collection, each is still committed to the museum's original mission of creating a representative and encyclopedic collection of works of art, a collection that represents the whole of human artistic achievement held in perpetuity for the people of this state. The Minneapolis Institute of Arts was founded as an educational institution whose mission was to develop a public art collection for Minnesota and maintain it for future generations. While preserving those existing collections, the Institute's staff will continue to enhance the artistic legacy of Minnesota by thoughtful and innovative acquisitions for the region's art museum.

Michael P. Conforti
Chairman, Curatorial Division
Bell Memorial Curator of
Decorative Arts and Sculpture

AFRICAN, OCEANIC, AND NEW WORLD CULTURES

When The Minneapolis Institute of Arts opened its doors in 1915, its express purpose was to exhibit "the art of all times and places." It is not surprising, however, to discover that "all places" in practice referred principally to Western Europe and European North America, with some attention given to the Near East, China, and Japan. The material culture of the rest of the world—Oceania, Africa, Latin America, and the indigenous peoples of North America—was entirely omitted from the Institute's collections. Nor was this situation unusual at the time, for ethnographic materials were almost never admitted to the privileged category of "art."

Objects such as African sculpture, pre-Columbian gold, and American Indian textiles had been known in Europe since the beginning of the Age of Discovery in the fifteenth century, collected with exotic natural specimens and kept in the private curio cabinets of wealthy merchants and intellectuals. Some, like the booty of the Spanish conquistadors, entered royal collections. A more systematic pattern of collecting began during the fresh wave of colonialist expansion in the second half of the nineteenth century, when newly imported curiosities were assembled in national museums specifically devoted to the artifacts from colonized regions; these collections formed the base for the great European ethnographic museums.

In the early period of museum development in this country, however, ethnographic art was principally collected by natural history or natural science museums and kept under the rubric of anthropology or archaeology, undifferentiated from such other examples of material culture as tools, weapons, and food containers. It was only in the 1930s and 1940s that American art museums like the Institute began to take an interest in objects from the third world. Minneapolis was in fact rather advanced in this regard; the museum sponsored an archaeological dig

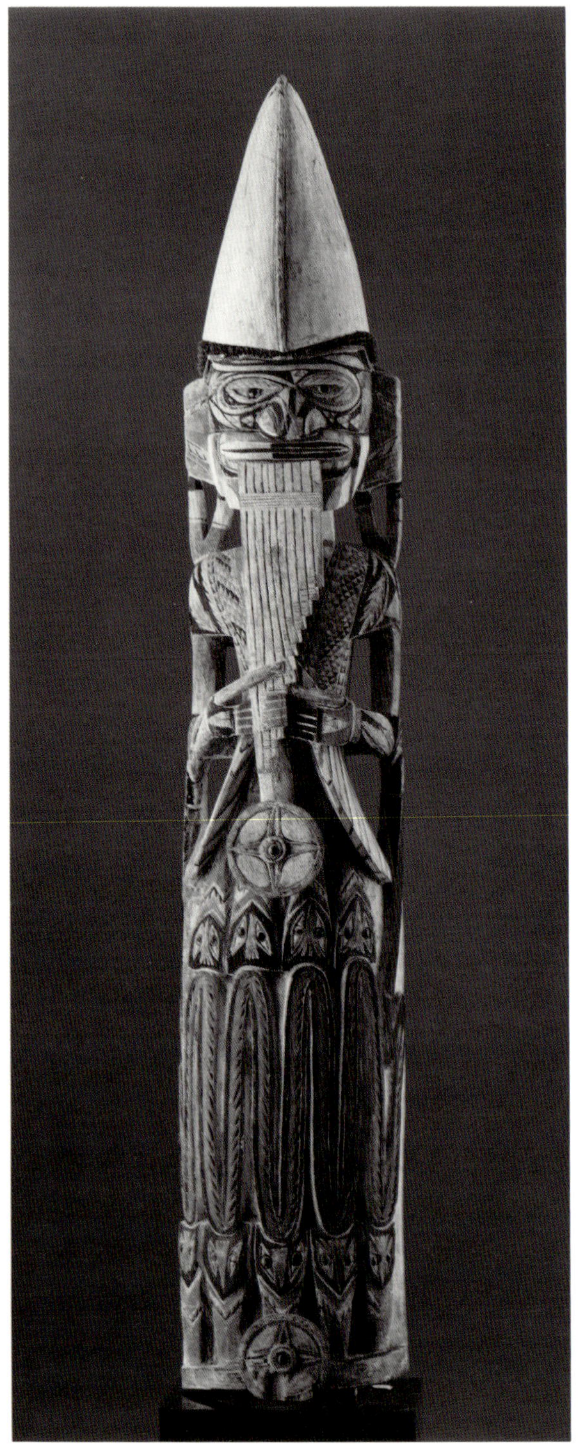

with the University of Minnesota at a prehistoric
Mimbres site in New Mexico in 1928. Although
the funds were insufficient to complete the work
there, the excavated pottery was displayed at the
Institute, and later transferred to the care of the
University. After this ambitious beginning the
museum made only sporadic acquisitions: a few
pre-Columbian objects were purchased in the late
1930s, and some Native American materials were
donated at about the same time. Not until the
years following World War II did the collection
as such begin to evolve.

In certain ways the war contributed to the
formation of collections at Minneapolis and other
museums. American military operations in the
Pacific aroused general interest in the cultures of
the Pacific islands, and thus, in 1946, the Metropolitan Museum organized the first large-scale
exhibition of art from the South Seas. In the
following year the Institute was given its first
Oceanic object, an Austral Islands ceremonial
paddle. More important, during the postwar
period several of the great German ethnographic
museums dispersed objects from their collections
in order to alleviate their dire financial condition, and Minneapolis was among the American
museums to benefit from this unprecedented
opportunity. The extraordinary bronze Benin
leopard and the Ejagham skin-covered headdress
were purchased from the Munich Museum für
Völkerkunde and the Linden Museum in Stuttgart,
respectively.

By the 1950s general interest in ethnographic
art had increased, largely a result of popular
awareness of the ways in which African sculpture
had influenced cubism, expressionism, and
other modern art movements. For artists and the
general public alike, it was the formal qualities
of this kind of sculpture that were most notable.
Schooled in the long Western tradition of classical
realism, they found the distorting of proportion
and expression powerful and moving, and they

saw in it an evocation of contemporary interest in
psychoanalysis and the unconscious. They sought
out a quality of primitivism, in the sense of raw-
ness and strength, in the artifacts of third-world
peoples, and grouped geographically and chrono-
logically disparate cultures together on the basis
of this presumed common factor.

While this attitude had the laudable effect of
increasing the museum's holdings, it also shaped
the new collections to a peculiar set of aesthetic
standards. Objects were acquired because they
were reminiscent of the works of one or more
contemporary artist, or because they seemed
to conform to contemporary ideas about form,
design, or expression. In 1952, when the Institute
was given its first African sculpture, a magnificent
Luba helmet mask, a *Bulletin* article provided no
information about the great artistic tradition of
the Luba people, instead dwelling on the French
provenance of the piece and speculating improb-
ably that it might have been seen by Picasso.

In Minneapolis and elsewhere this limited view
of "primitive" art changed somewhat during the
1960s and 1970s. Ethnographic art was exhibited
less often with reference to contemporary European objects and more frequently as an entity in
itself. An important influence was the opening in
1957 of the Museum of Primitive Art in New York
(which housed Nelson Rockefeller's collection,
begun twenty-five years earlier), with the explicit
goal of "integrating primitive art into what is
already known of the arts of man." Art museums
gradually realized that they had to respond as
public interest in such materials increased, in part
because of the changing social climate of the
1960s, and as objects accumulated, often through
unexpected gifts. Some museums decided against
forming collections, arguing that such materials
were better kept in ethnological museums.
The Philadelphia Museum of Art, for example,
deferred to the excellent collections of the
nearby University Museum. Others established

formal curatorial departments: Chicago in 1957, San Francisco in 1970, Detroit in 1976. The formation of these infant departments represented changes more radical than the simple addition of a new curatorial division to a museum, however. By including objects previously thought to be inappropriate, directors and trustees acknowledged a redefinition of the nature of an art museum. The new departments challenged the primacy of the traditionally prestigious fields of painting and sculpture, by implication, if not in reality. In the outside world, they broadened the public's conception of art, and raised in a direct way the issue of the meaning and function of art in any society.

In the past two decades the number of departments established, objects acquired, and exhibitions organized in museums across the country has increased steadily. The incorporation of the Museum of Primitive Art into the Metropolitan in the Michael C. Rockefeller Wing, which opened in 1983, was widely interpreted as an indication that ethnographic art had finally arrived.

With the expansion of the Institute's building in 1974, the Minneapolis collection had for the first time a permanent gallery space. In the same year ethnographic objects, until then under the care of the Decorative Arts Department, were transferred to the newly formed Department of Primitive Art, and Ellen Bradbury was appointed part-time curator. (The department's title was changed in 1978 to the unwieldy but more accurate Department of African, Oceanic, and New World Cultures.) By the mid-1970s the Institute had established its present pattern of regular, although infrequent, acquisitions in ethnographic art, and its present policy of a representative, rather than a comprehensive, collection.

In more recent years the department's approach to acquisitions and exhibitions has reflected the changing attitude of scholars and collectors toward the art of third-world peoples.

No longer confined merely to displaying the exotic, no longer operating on the mediating principle that "if Picasso liked it, it must be good," we are now seeking out not what is appealing or interesting by Western standards, but rather objects of aesthetic and historical significance in the context of their own culture. It is often forgotten that other cultures keep their own tradition of art history and art criticism. There are elaborate and well-defined hierarchies of artistic achievement; in their proper environment objects are evaluated and criticized, the hands and influence of certain artists noted, and a higher rank is accorded to certain classes of objects which are considered most significant in historical or religious terms, or most prestigious, or most beautiful. It is in the study of ethnoaesthetics that the most exciting research in the entire field of art history is being done, as Western scholars attempt to gain an understanding of the artistic values of other cultures. Museums are in a unique position to show the results of this work in a graphic way, and many of our recent purchases are just such rare, valued examples.

The African collection, although small, is reasonably well balanced and contains some highly unusual pieces. A Bamana female figure, acquired in 1982, can be confidently dated to the nineteenth century; its relative age and archaic style lead to significant conclusions about the evolution of later carving styles in the region. The 1978 purchase of a twelfth-century Djenne terra-cotta figure has been greatly augmented by the 1983 acquisition of a wooden equestrian figure from the same region and probably of a slightly earlier date. This is one of the oldest known wooden sculptures from Africa and a piece of astonishing rarity and importance. Nevertheless some of the great artistic traditions of Africa, notably those of the central region, remain unrepresented (Chokwe, Kuba, Bembe, to name a few) and for others we have only a single example though we

North American, Shoshoni, 19th century
Elk hide with representation of sun dance
Attributed to KATSIKODI
Elk hide and pigment
Gift of Bruce B. Dayton, 85.92

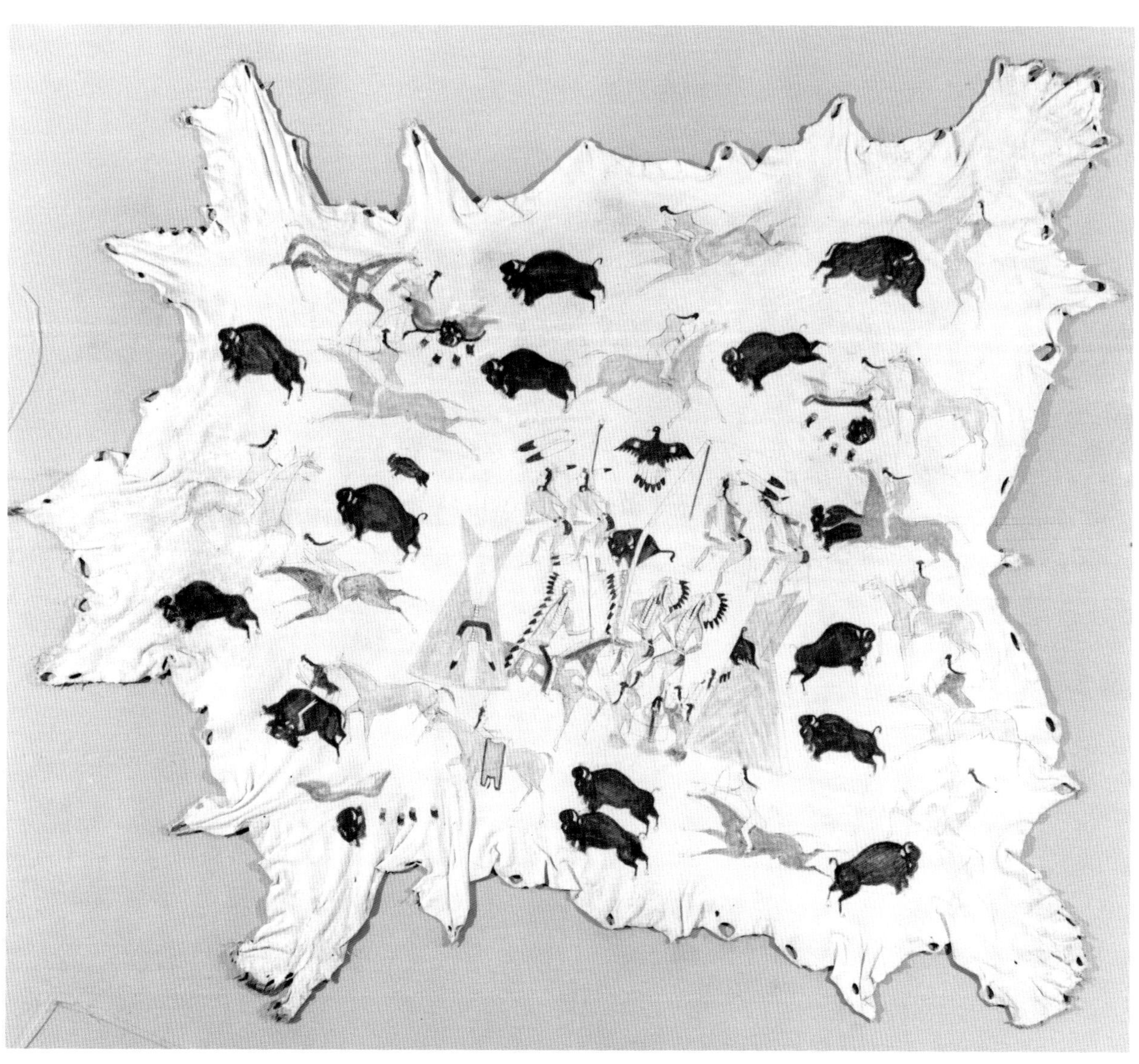

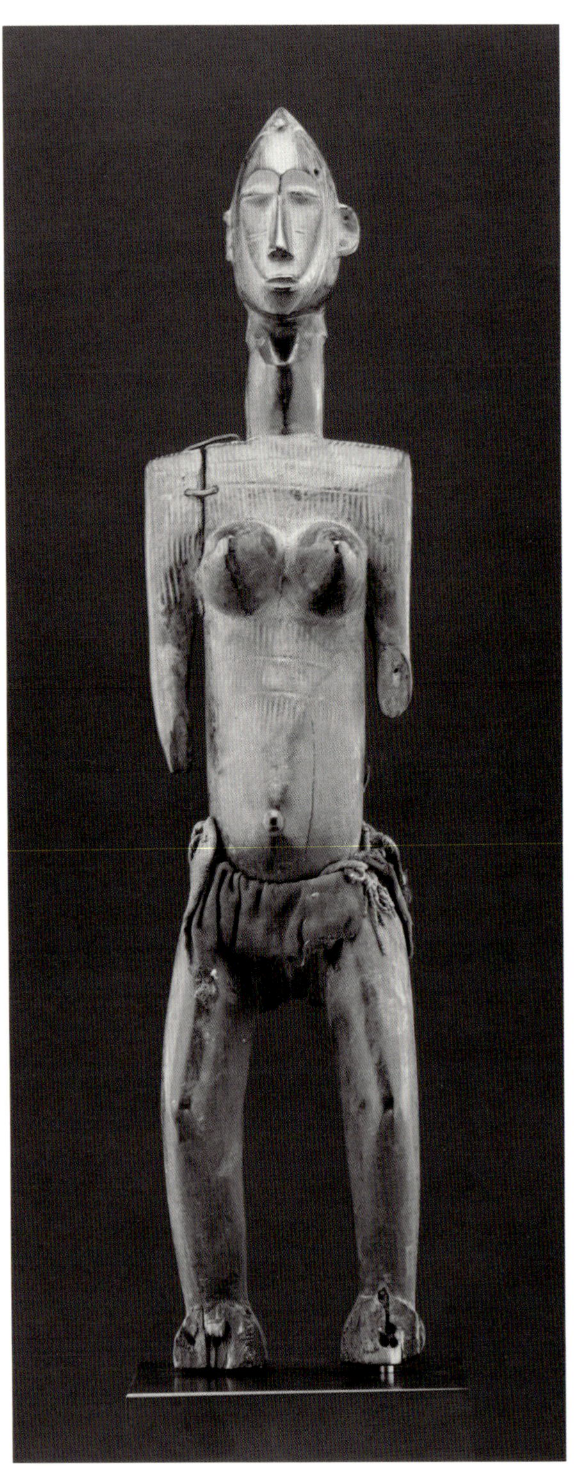

would like to be able to demonstrate the richness and complexity of regional art production.

Our North American holdings reveal the numerous lacunae to be expected in a collection never conceived of as comprehensive. The sparseness of our Native American Plains material is particularly glaring, given our geographic location, and thus a recent gift by Bruce Dayton of a Shoshoni painted elkhide depicting the Sun Dance is especially welcome. We hope to expand our collection of Southwest historic-period ceramics in order to complement our extensive metalwork. Eventually we will also build in other geographic areas: Eastern quill- and beadwork, California basketry. A beautiful Anvik Eskimo mask, purchased in 1981, has helped to represent the old and complex artistic traditions of the North.

The richest area of our pre-Columbian materials is ceramics, of which we have broad holdings from the Peruvian areas and from Mesoamerica. The generosity of Mr. and Mrs. Arthur Weiss, of Westfield, New Jersey, over four successive years has substantially increased the number of objects, permitting us not only to rotate the exhibitions, but also to undertake research projects not possible with a more limited sample. Like all collections with any interest in pre-Columbian art, we wish for more stone sculpture and more examples of metalwork, but recognizing the need for export limitations we are also, like many museums, extremely cautious in the market.

In the past our Pacific holdings have constituted the smallest and weakest group of all, and it is here that we have recently made our most spectacular purchases in terms of the quality, age, and scale of the objects. Learning of the dispersal of a private Swiss collection of Oceanic art, we were able to acquire two sculptures from New Ireland. The magnificent pan-pipe player given by the Regis Corporation and the delicate New Ireland bird frieze donated by Bruce Dayton transform our Melanesian collection, adding significantly to our ability to display and discuss the art of the region. While the lively forms of Polynesia and Micronesia are now almost entirely absent, we intend to build these areas gradually to a comparable level of quality.

The same concern for the history and context of art objects has guided our organization of exhibitions. We want to explore the connections between the art a given people produce and other cultural manifestations of their society; their social and economic organization, their religious practices, their traditions of literature, music, and dance. Beyond this, we hope to discover behind all of these aspects certain common ideas, assumptions or values that form the basis for an entire world view. Thus a 1982 exhibition of Navajo silver jewelry demonstrated that, far from being tourist trinkets, such objects are carefully thought-out, highly symbolic representations of Navajo ideas about order and harmony in the natural world and in social relations. A forthcoming exhibition on the art of New Ireland will explore the use of sculpture in ceremonies that express in microcosm all of New Ireland life and thought.

The pattern of acquisitions at The Minneapolis Institute of Arts is well within the normal limits of art museum collecting, emphasizing the old and rare over newer, less "classical" forms. Thus far the museum has been well served by this policy. It is very important at this point to elucidate the artistic history and context of remote societies, and this kind of collecting will continue to be vital as the field develops. Nevertheless, other collecting strategies remain to be explored. Most art museums, including The Minneapolis Institute of Arts, have not yet dealt adequately with the issue of whether they should be acquiring ethnographic works made after Euro-American cultures began exerting strong influence (through sources as diverse as missionaries and television). The usual view is that museums should confine their

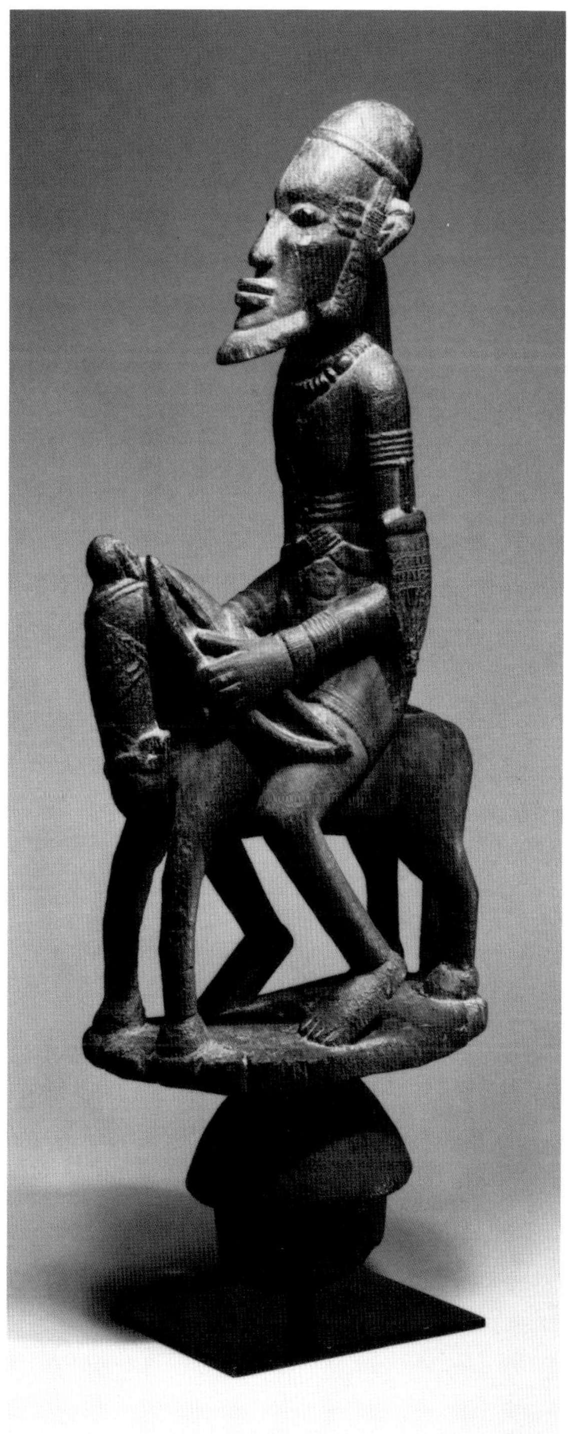

collecting to older, classic forms, the Old Masters of African, Oceanic, and Native American arts, because the more recent works are somehow corrupt and inferior.

Yet many of these classic pieces themselves show considerable external influence. The so-called Afro-Portuguese ivories, commissioned of African carvers by sixteenth-century Portuguese traders, were made to appeal to European taste; historic-period American Southwest pottery and textiles, much prized by museums and collectors, were made for a tourist market. Although we sometimes imagine that traditional societies existed in a pure and unchanging state before contact with Europeans, such a view reflects our self-image more accurately than it reflects reality. Most societies undergo steady change in a context of stability, and the results are reflected in art, as in other aspects of the culture. When the process of change in third-world countries was accelerated by colonialism and Westernization, art changed rapidly. New tools, new visual images, and new societal pressures produced alterations in traditional styles; colonial schools trained students in Western fine art techniques and traditions; and the growing importance of tourism in many areas spawned objects made for sale.

Recent and contemporary art from the third world poses particular difficulties for Western museums, and most museums have avoided buying in these fields, probably in part because the perceived inferior technical quality of tourist art has tarnished the legitimacy of the other types. In part it is also a problem of categorization. How is a Western museum to classify the work of an African painter in the distinctly foreign medium of oil, whose subject matter is based on the oral tradition of his village and whose style borrows from the contemporary European avant-garde? Only a handful of these assimilated artists are known outside their continent, yet their work documents in visual form the broad process of

social and economic change. Some specialized American museums are attempting more eclectic collecting, recognizing that changing traditional styles, western-influenced works, and even tourist pieces are valid expressions of cultural change. For the art museum these issues will remain problematic for some time, because they are linked to broader questions. As communication and trade bring distant parts of the world into proximity, however, it is less easy to dismiss even remote cultures as irrelevant.

It is precisely for this reason that objects like those now held in the Department of African, Oceanic, and New World Cultures have entered museum collections, and that such collections have expanded dramatically in the last twenty-five years. It is frankly astonishing to consider how much museums have grown in these areas over a short period of time, and how much of our understanding and knowledge of the subject have increased. In certain ways we still know very little of these objects from our own perspective. On the other hand, the kinds of basic knowledge that have been established for decades in other areas of art history—chronologies, chains of influence, iconographic studies, even names of artists—are now being achieved for Africa and, to a slightly lesser extent, for other geographic areas as well.

Yet the presence of these objects in museum collections cannot be explained simply by some notion of increasing global consciousness. Museums are often thought of as repositories of the past, as storehouses of cultural heritage. Museum collections are, finally, the things that seem worth preserving at a given time, but they are also subject to changing attitudes about the past, and therefore the categories change over time. Each generation extracts from the mass of historical data those aspects of the past that are relevant to the present, and in so doing defines both the past and the present. The founding trustees of Minne-

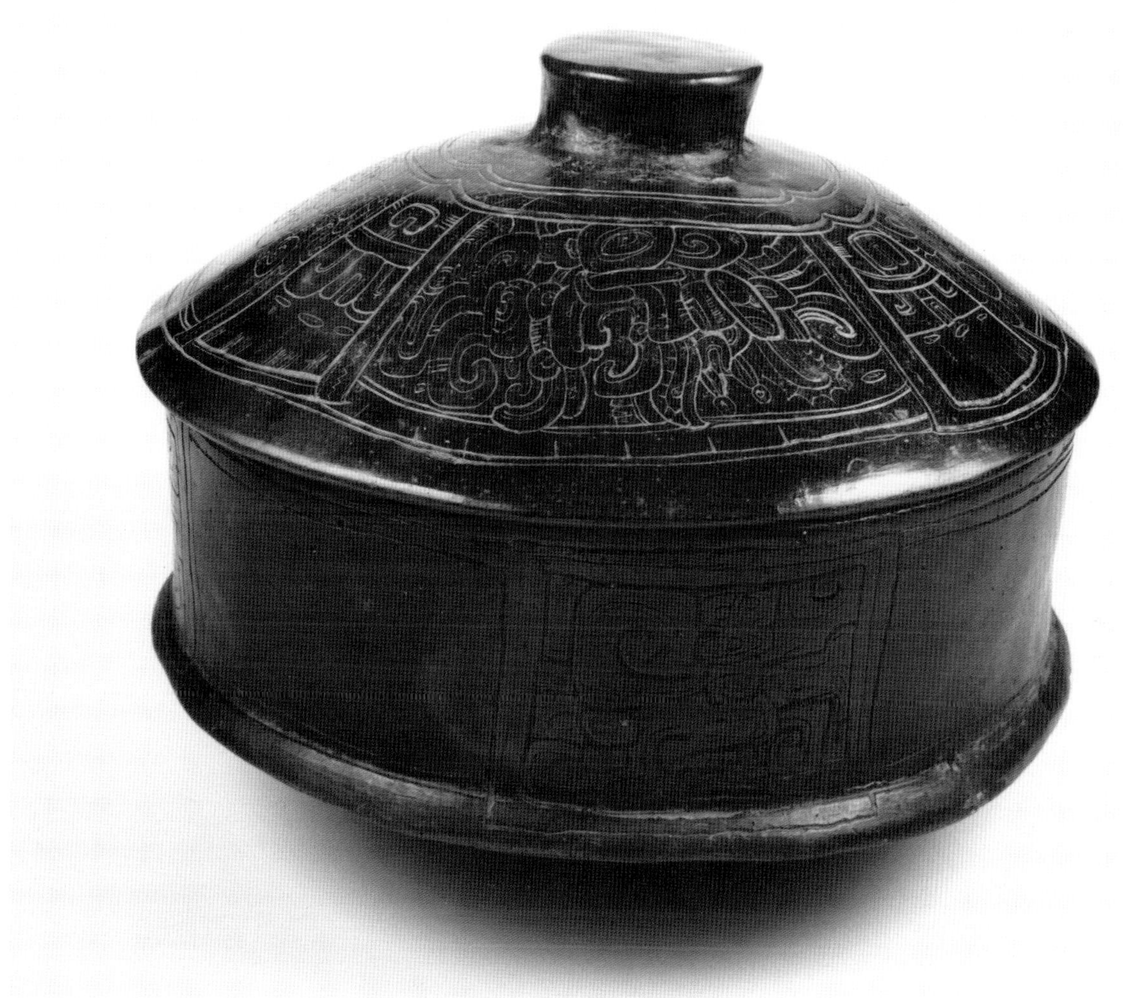

apolis, in formulating guidelines for collecting activities, ranked "medals and medallions" high on the list, yet for all practical purposes these objects have disappeared in favor of categories the trustees probably never dreamed of: photography, for example, or ethnographic art. The presence of permanent collections in the area of African, Oceanic and New World cultures is perhaps the best possible means of demonstrating that although museums preserve the past, they also change to reflect the ideas and conditions of the present. The way we collect ethnographic art will undoubtedly evolve in different directions in response to the conditions of the future.

Louise Lincoln
Associate Curator
African, Oceanic, and New World Cultures

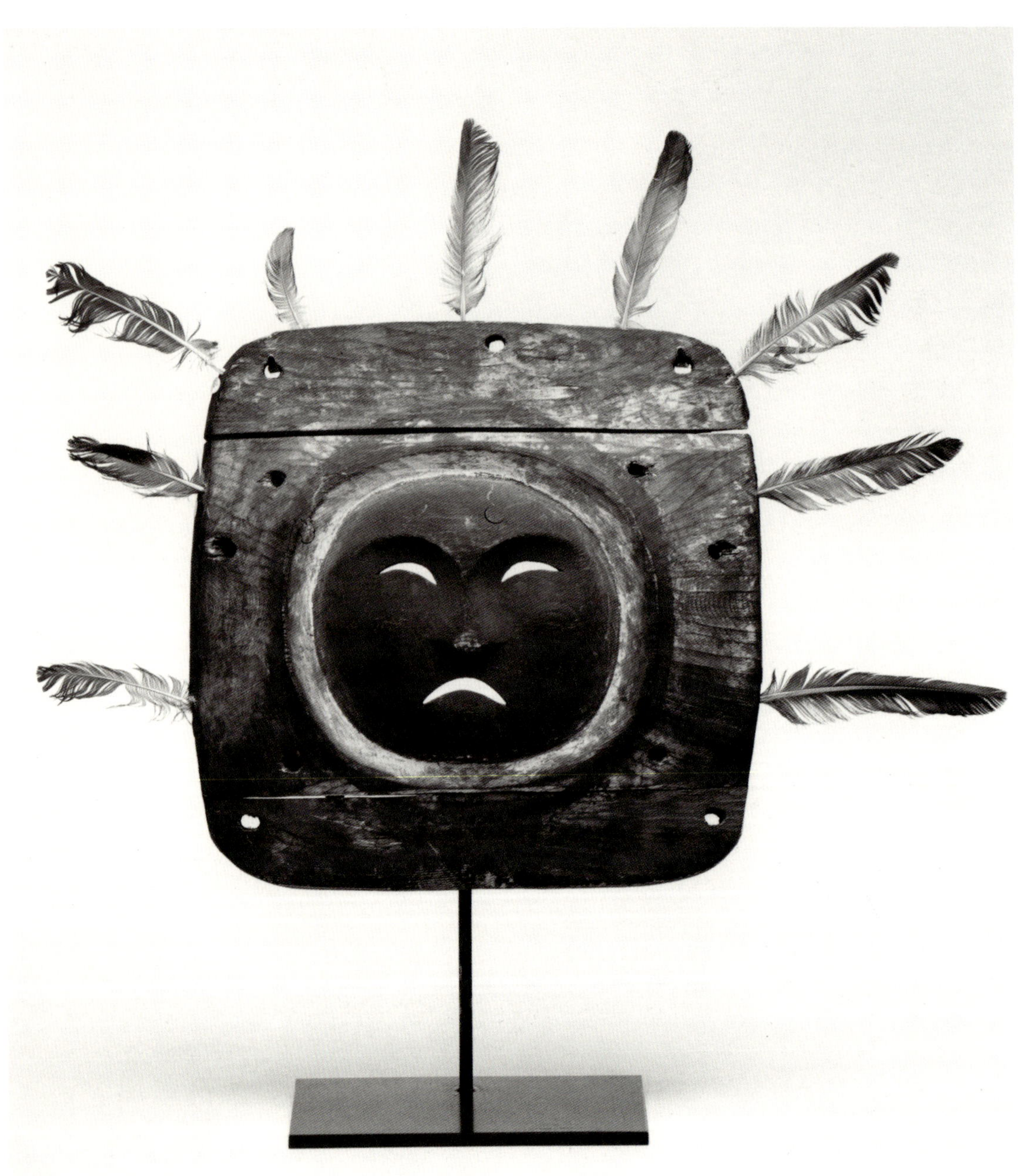

Inuit, Anvik, 19th–20th century
Mask
Wood and feathers
The John R. Van Derlip Fund, 81.14

Papua New Guinea, Papuan Gulf,
Epegau village, Wapo area, 20th century
Ancestral tablet (gope)
Wood and pigment
Gift of Evelyn A. J. Hall and John A.
Friede, 83.160.5

African, Mali, Mali Empire, 10th–13th
century
Equestrian figure
Wood
Gift of Aimee Mott Butler Charitable
Trust, Anne S. Dayton, Mr. and Mrs.
Donald C. Dayton, Mr. and Mrs. William
N. Driscoll, Clarence G. Frame and Mr.
and Mrs. Clinton Morrison, 83.168

African, Mali, Bamana, 19th century
Female figure
Wood and cloth
Gift of Mr. and Mrs. Benton Case, Jr.,
and the Christina N. and Swan J.
Turnblad Memorial Fund, 82.26

African, Cameroon, Bamum, 20th
century
Beaded cap
Wool and raffia
The John R. Van Derlip Fund, 81.39

Papua New Guinea, New Ireland, 19th
century
Standing figure with pan pipes
Wood and pigment
Gift of Myron Kunin, 85.93

Papua New Guinea, Papuan Gulf,
Epegau village, Wapo area, 20th century
Ancestral tablet (gope)
Wood and pigment
Gift of Evelyn A. J. Hall and John A.
Friede, 83.160.5

North American, Shoshoni, 19th century
*Elk hide with representation of sun
dance*
Attributed to KATSIKODI
Elk hide and pigment
Gift of Bruce B. Dayton, 85.92

North American, Tsimshian or Tlingit,
about 1860
Shaman's charm
Ivory with gold patination
Gift of Avery Z. Eliscu, 82.12

Inuit, Anvik, 19th–20th century
Mask
Wood and feathers
The John R. Van Derlip Fund, 81.14

Mexican, Jalisco, 200 B.C. – A.D. 300
Basket-headed figure
Earthenware
The Ethel Morrison Van Derlip Fund,
82.99

Mexican, Jalisco, 200 B.C. – A.D. 300
Seated male figure
Red slip on buff earthenware
Gift of Lucille and Arthur Weiss,
81.125.10

Mexican, Colima, 200 B.C. – A.D. 300
Modelled vulture
Burnished buff clay with red head
Gift of Lucille and Arthur Weiss,
82.136.19

Guatemalan, Mayan, 7th–10th century
Covered pot with incised design
Beige clay with burnished brown slip
Gift of funds from Ben Heller, 80.8ab

Mexican, Chihuahua, Casas Grandes,
1160–1260
Seated figure
Polychrome ceramic
The John R. Van Derlip Fund, 83.90.3

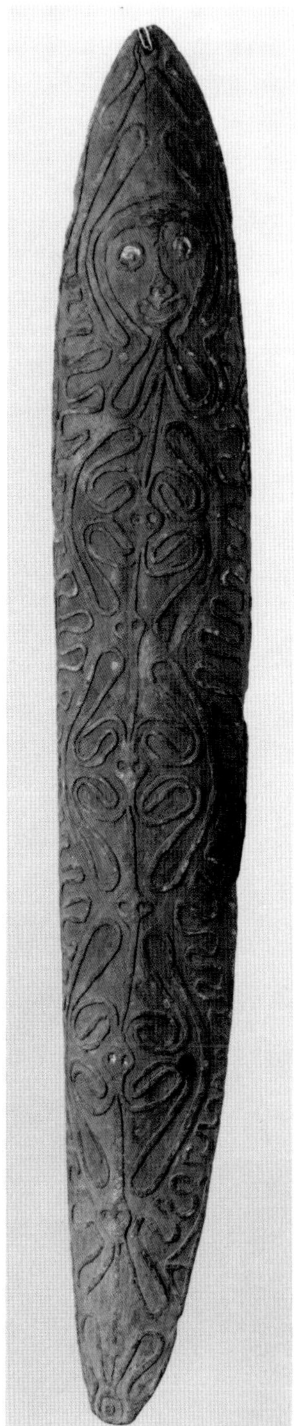

Department of

A S I A N   A R T

With the exception of the Cleveland Museum of Art and the Nelson-Atkins Gallery in Kansas City, where museum directors Sherman E. Lee and Laurence Sickman systematically built collections through endowment-funded purchases, the majority of specialized public collections of Asian art in this country were initially formed by philanthropic private collectors rather than curators. Minneapolis conforms to this pattern and has benefitted greatly from generous gifts of serious and knowledgeable collectors. Augustus L. Searle, Alfred F. Pillsbury, Richard P. Gale, and an anonymous St. Paul friend have each donated specialized collections of international reputation: ancient Chinese bronzes, ancient and post-Sung jade, Chinese gold and silver, Chinese monochrome ceramics, Ukiyo-e paintings, Japanese prints, and more esoteric objects such as carved rhinoceros horn and snuff bottles. In addition, two specialized collections were purchased over the years which also have international importance: Ch'ing dynasty textiles and the Mitchell collection of Shijo school *surimono* prints.

Despite this level of collecting activity, however, the Institute did not establish a curatorial department until 1977, and there was thus no purchase policy before that time. Accordingly, the collections, important as they were, were molded by the personal taste of the private benefactors, and for all the wonderful peaks they provided there were, and to a degree still are, some regrettable valleys. For instance, the museum is extremely weak in most types of classical Indian sculpture, miniature painting, and decorative arts. Chinese painting is likewise thin, especially the Buddhist and landscape traditions, the latter one of China's major contributions to world art. We are nearly unrepresented in calligraphy, a major art form of China. On the Japanese side, our holdings in ink paintings of the Muromachi period, the decorative tradition of the Rimpa school, and the literati works of the Nanga masters are all in need

of enrichment. Chinese furniture, Japanese ceramics and lacquerware in general, as well as Korean painting and Himalayan art, are areas that remain to be developed systematically.

Unlike European art, Asian art in our country still lacks a cultural context. The extraordinary record of Asian material culture, aesthetic priorities, and highly accomplished art forms is not understood to the same degree as we understand our own classical heritage. Because of this it is necessary to gather significant numbers of Asian art objects in order to provide a meaningful context by which the magnificent scope of Oriental art can be studied and appreciated and outstanding works recognized as such. Collecting art is not random accumulation. While seeking beautiful and important objects our goal is to be historical and comprehensive as well. When all three aims are accomplished the significance of any collection, Asian or otherwise, will far exceed the sum of its parts.

Happily, however, a number of masterpieces both purchased and donated can be pointed to in areas of strength as well as in areas of weakness. Certain ancient Chinese bronzes, jades, ceramics, and stone sculpture, as well as some of our Ukiyo-e paintings, Japanese screens, prints, and wood sculpture are of world-class stature. Remarkable progress has been made in recent years in strengthening areas of weakness. Since the department was founded eight years ago, around 2,500 Asian works have been added, nearly doubling in number the original holdings. The vast majority of these new works are in the area of Japanese prints (about 1,800), and include exceptional groups of Hiroshige and Shijo school material, all added through donations or money donated for purchase. Equally important areas in which the museum was totally unrepresented, such as Chinese carved lacquer; Ming and Ch'ing blue and white porcelain; Indian miniature paintings; Japanese Buddhist painting; prehistoric

Chinese, late Chou dynasty, late 6th–5th
century B.C.
Ting (ritual food vessel)
Bronze
Gift of an anonymous St. Paul friend,
81.113.5

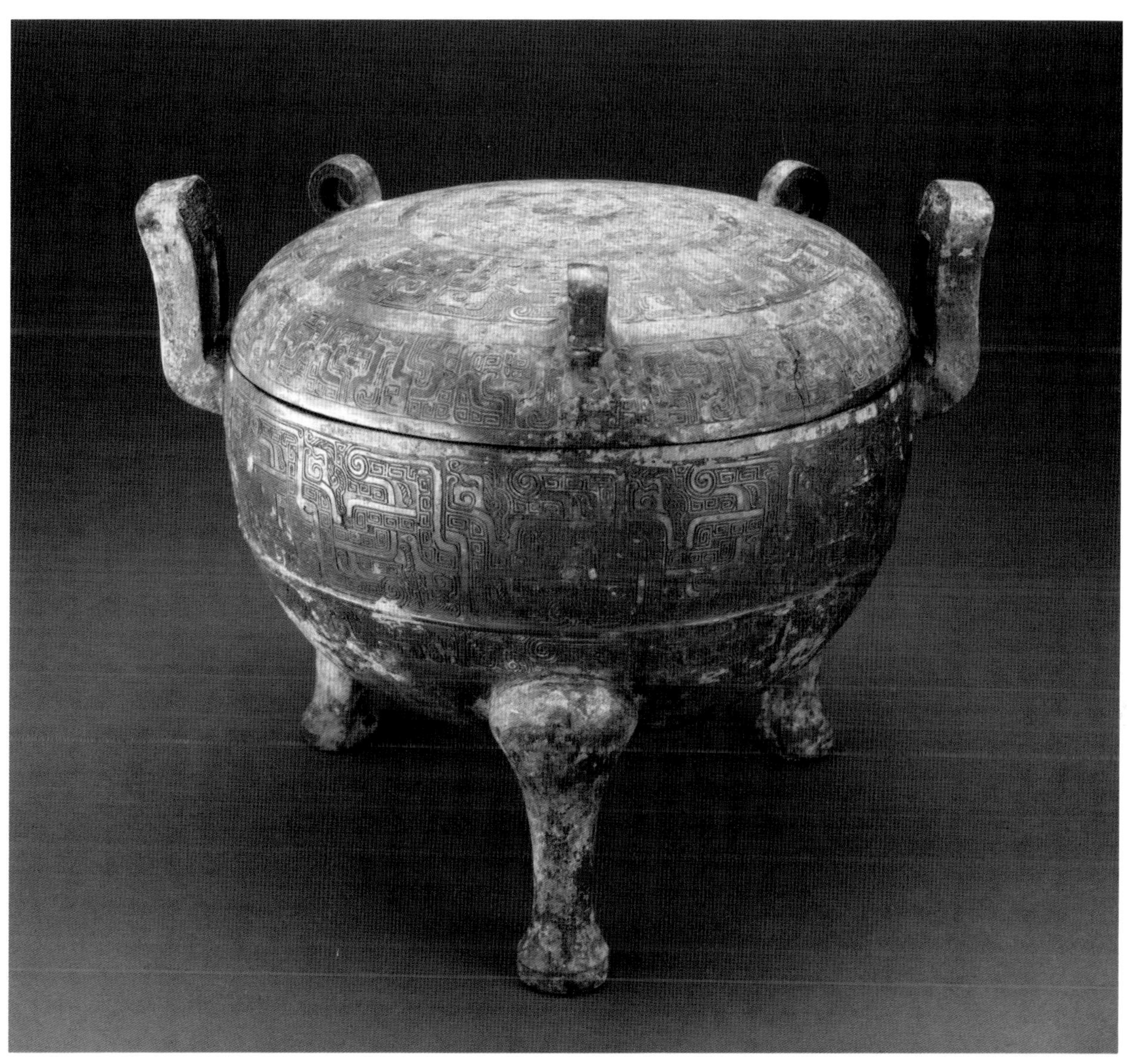

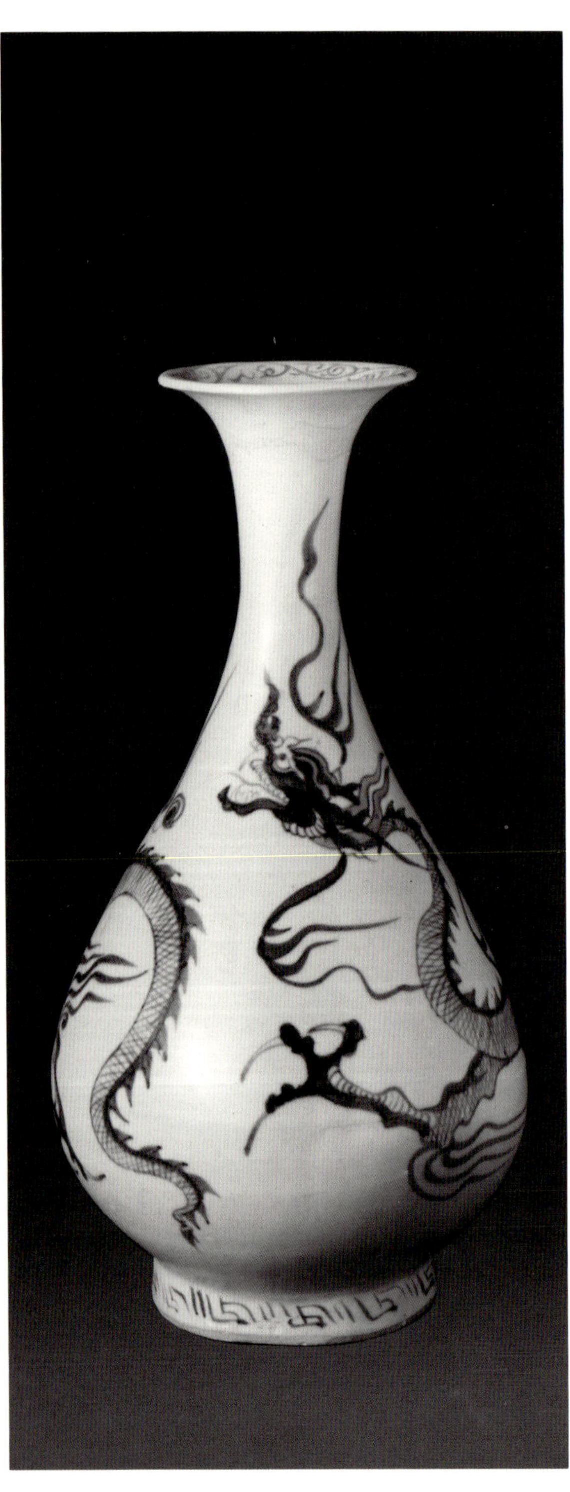

Japanese ceramics; Shijo school prints; Korean ceramics; and Japanese textiles, have been built up to the point that small but representative displays can now be made to the public. The chief motivation in developing these minor areas has been to create public awareness and provide a context into which a masterpiece might someday be placed. In these areas our acquisitions have come about through private donations of museum-quality works.

We have taken the opposite approach, however, in purchases made with endowment funds. When such purchases are made, each object has to stand as a sole but important representative of an entire tradition, style, or artist's work. Examples demonstrating this policy include the beautiful, late twelfth-century Amida Nyorai; our extremely rare complete set of twelve Juniten paintings; the Tiger and Dragon screens by Doan; the superb late Momoyama Tagesode screens; and the stunning pair of large Nio guardian figures from the Nambokucho period. The list of major purchases would also include the set of sixteen *fusuma* paintings attributed to Kano Sanraku from the Soga palace and the monumental eighteenth-century imperial portrait of Prince Duo-lo, although both were realized through private contributions. The areas in which this policy of major purchases through combined endowment and private funding can be focused in the future include T'ang dynasty stone sculpture; Sung dynasty wood sculpture; Japanese esoteric and portrait sculpture; Yüan and Ming blue and white porcelain, Rimpa school painting; Kushan and Gupta sculpture; Sung, Yüan, and Ming dynasty landscape painting; and Far Eastern Buddhist painting.

The collecting policy described above underscores our intention to develop our collection in two ways: to add major works whenever possible in what Asian aesthetic philosophy defines as the important areas (i.e., sculpture, monochrome

Chinese, Yüan dynasty, 14th century
Vase
Porcelain with underglaze blue decor
Gift of Mr. Allan Rhoades, 84.116.5

Japanese, Kofun period, 250–522
Haniwa figure of a horse
Earthenware
The John R. Van Derlip Fund and an
anonymous St. Paul friend, 83.130

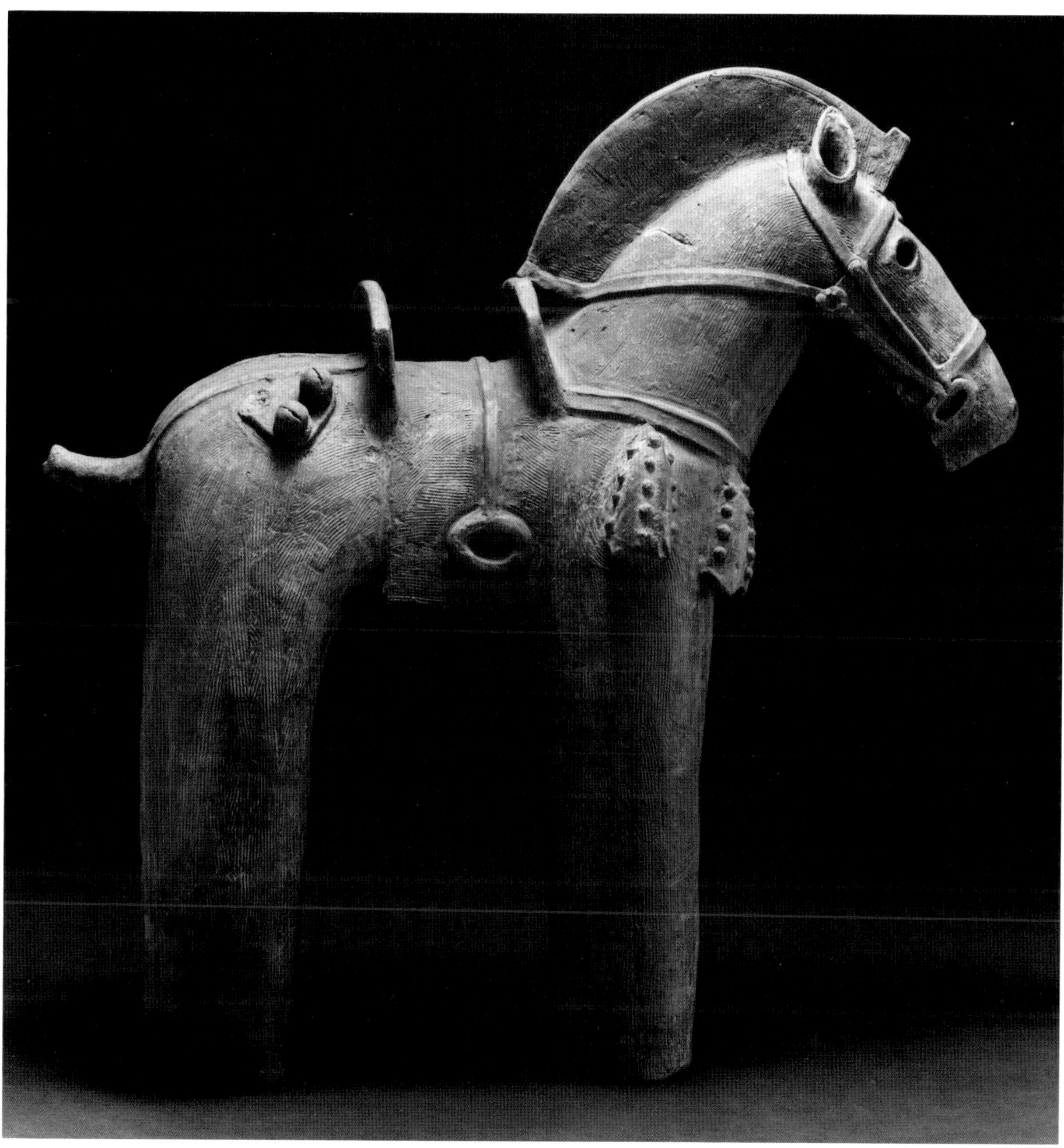

ceramics, paintings, calligraphy) and to acquire numbers of good objects in the minor areas (i.e., prints and what we generally term the decorative arts—most later ceramics, glass, ivory, furniture, lacquer, cloisonné, textiles, wood). This policy is based on the fact that scholars and public alike typically visit the department to see both the masterpieces of any medium, such as the Sesson screens or the owl ritual vessel, and to examine material where there is significant depth in specific fields, such as Shijo school *surimono* prints, Chinese jades, or ancient bronzes.

The department's collecting has been dependent upon the enthusiasm and generosity of some very dedicated private patrons. This support has benefitted the museum greatly, both in donations of Asian works of art and in matching funds for purchase. This outside support, however, is often based on personal interest and, in this respect, the record shows that the majority of private funding has been directed towards the purchase of Japanese art. In the short term this has been extremely helpful, for in the last few years we have built a significant collection of Japanese screens, quadrupled our print collec-

tion, and provided an excellent group of works by Shibata Zeshin, all necessary to the museum. In the long run, however, a more balanced pattern of giving that considers all Asian art forms and traditions should evolve, and it should be linked to a large and reliable purchase endowment.

At present the purchasing power of the museum is not strong enough for the department to fill in systematically where private donations and interests taper off. Ironically, however, within certain areas of Asian art significant objects can still be purchased within the museum's budget. The relative "affordability" of Asian art, however, will decline rapidly as the availability of good objects, even in minor areas, decreases and Asian economies continue to prosper. In terms of availability and prices, the market will ultimately determine which collections can realistically be developed by a museum and which cannot.

We must recognize that certain areas of Asian art will never be fully represented in Minneapolis. T'ang and Sung sculpture, Sung and Yüan landscape painting, and classic Indian sculpture are virtually unavailable on the market today. Most important objects are already in public collec-

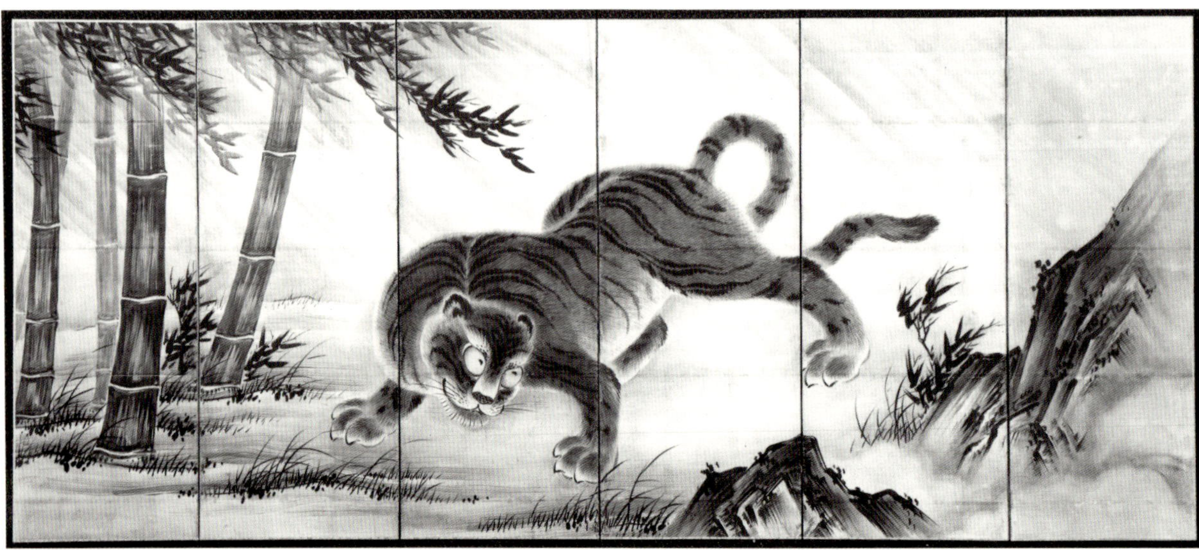

YAMADA YORIKIYO
Japanese, 1520?–1571
Muromachi period
Tiger and dragon folding screens
Ink on paper
Gift of Mr. and Mrs. Charles H. Bell, the
James Ford Bell Foundation, Aimee Mott
Butler Charitable Trust, the Centennial
Gala Committee, and Carl A. Weyer-
haeuser Charitable Trusts, 83.75.1, 2

tions or protected by the country of origin. This does not mean that good works within these fields will never be found or added, but rather that it is already too late to achieve significant depth in these areas. Due largely to the interest of Japanese collectors and the high prices they are willing to sustain, the costs of certain East Asian art forms, including tea ceremony ceramics, calligraphy, Noh robes, early ink paintings, and high caliber Chinese ceramics, are often prohibitive.

Export laws further constrict the pool of available Asian works. Indian laws are extremely restrictive regarding the export of important art objects, especially sculpture, and therefore little Indian sculpture of exceptional significance can be added to our collections. Korean laws are likewise strict, and the official Chinese policy since 1949 has been to sell nothing of museum quality abroad. The Japanese have a well-structured cultural protection system that does allow some significant art to leave the country, but it is becoming increasingly difficult and expensive to procure a license to export museum-quality material. Accordingly, collectors of Asian art are now left to trade primarily within the

Tokyo, Hong Kong, New York, and London markets through dealers, private collectors, and at auction. Within this realm, certain fields such as Chinese ceramics, Japanese prints, Chinese and Japanese decorative arts, some later categories of Chinese and Japanese painting, and Indian miniature painting should enjoy a relatively stable market for at least another decade. It is precisely in these areas where we have made our greatest progress and where most of the museum's future accessions, both purchased and donated, will likely occur.

It is often assumed that curatorial taste is the major factor in shaping department collections. Personal taste should have little to do with the development of a museum collection, in fact. A curator's eye, expertise, enthusiasm, and ability to develop patronage typically have more impact on establishing and realizing a successful accessions program than does personal preference. In the interest of balanced collecting, personal and scholarly interests are better expressed in research and object interpretation than in buying. In keeping the department's needs above the individual curator's likes or dislikes, I have

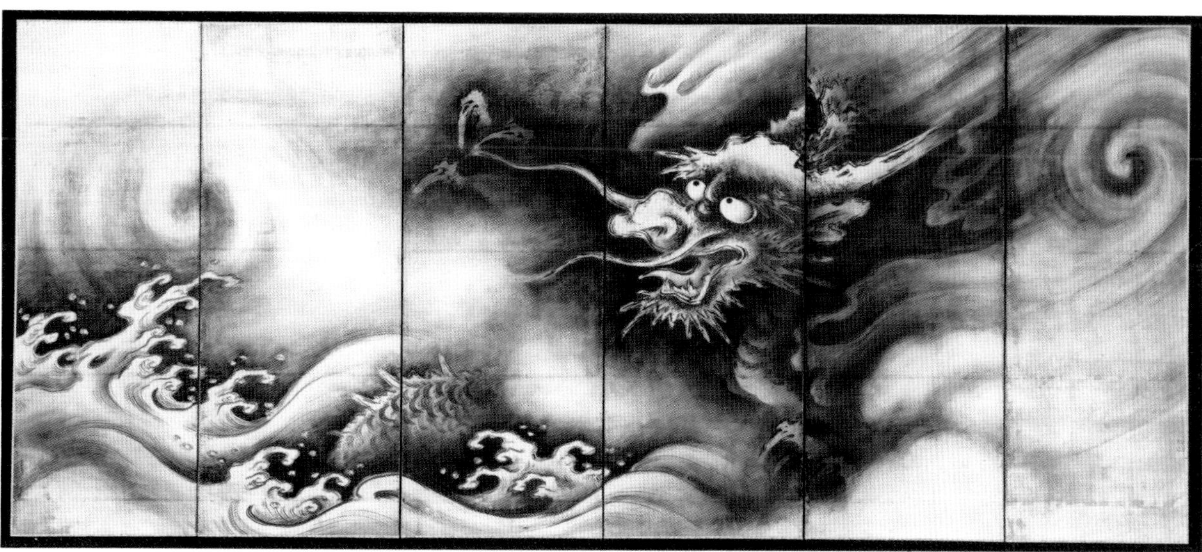

added several works necessary to our collection, such as carved lacquer and blue and white porcelain, that are not to my personal taste. Since works are discovered randomly in the market, a sound general knowledge of the traditional art forms, the ability to judge their visual quality, and a clear sense of program are the most important curatorial attributes. These factors, when coupled with the specialized expertise of a curator, can best benefit a museum's accession program through buying at auction. In the field of Chinese painting, with the purchase of the Duo-lo portrait, *River Landscape*, and the Mien-yi album, we have already shown modest success. In certain market areas, especially Chinese ceramics and later Chinese painting, Himalayan art, Chinese archaeological material, Islamic manuscripts, Japanese prints, and Chinese textiles and furniture, the auction houses now provide the greatest supply and potential for savings. It is here at auction that curatorial expertise and judgment, rather than taste, could have its greatest impact on purchasing over the ensuing years.

An enormous amount of time and energy is required to survey the market systematically, maintain the extremely important collector and dealer relationships, and generate purchase funds. Even when these pursuits are well coordinated, a curator needs luck in timing to move a work successfully through the accession process. It is partially for this reason that private patronage has been so successful in the past and remains the department's most viable avenue for focused collection development in the future.

Though not easily attained, an ideal situation for museum purchasing might combine curatorial collaboration with the energy and flexibility of a discerning collector whose long-range goal is donation to the museum. The obvious benefits are cost savings to the museum and tax benefits to the donor, but such a joint effort also saves curatorial time and offers a marketplace advantage, for private collectors can act more quickly than a museum organization. Enlightened collectors can often provide much of the curatorial footwork necessary to collection building, and develop specialized expertise beyond that of museum personnel. The Institute has been successful in attracting noted collections of Asian art as well as single objects over the years, and the department's close relationship with private patrons and collectors will continue to be an important aspect of accessioning policy.

American interest in and understanding of Asian art and culture has grown rapidly in recent years with the opening of China and the increased prominence of Japan in the global economy. These trends will continue well into the twenty-first century. The Minneapolis Institute of Arts is already an important primary source for Asian art and material culture. The department is well situated—considering its present strengths, commitment to balanced collection growth, excellent private support, and market realities—to strengthen itself in several important fields and create a significant context of Asian art. Twentieth-century Japanese prints, later Chinese and Japanese paintings, Chinese and South East Asian ceramics, Indian miniature paintings, lacquer, and ceramics, and Islamic decorative arts will undoubtedly be areas of continued growth. Due to the difficulty in adding great numbers of "masterpieces" to the collection in the major areas, it is useful to keep Sherman Lee's words in mind: "There are greater possible areas for varieties of style and flavor to be found in the periphery of the circle than in the vortex." It is in the periphery that most of the significant action will take place in our collecting future.

Robert D. Jacobsen
Curator of Asian Art

Japanese, Nambokucho period, late 14th century
Pair of temple guardian statues (Nio)
Cypress wood with traces of gesso and lacquer
Gift of the Regis Corporation, 83.76.1, 2

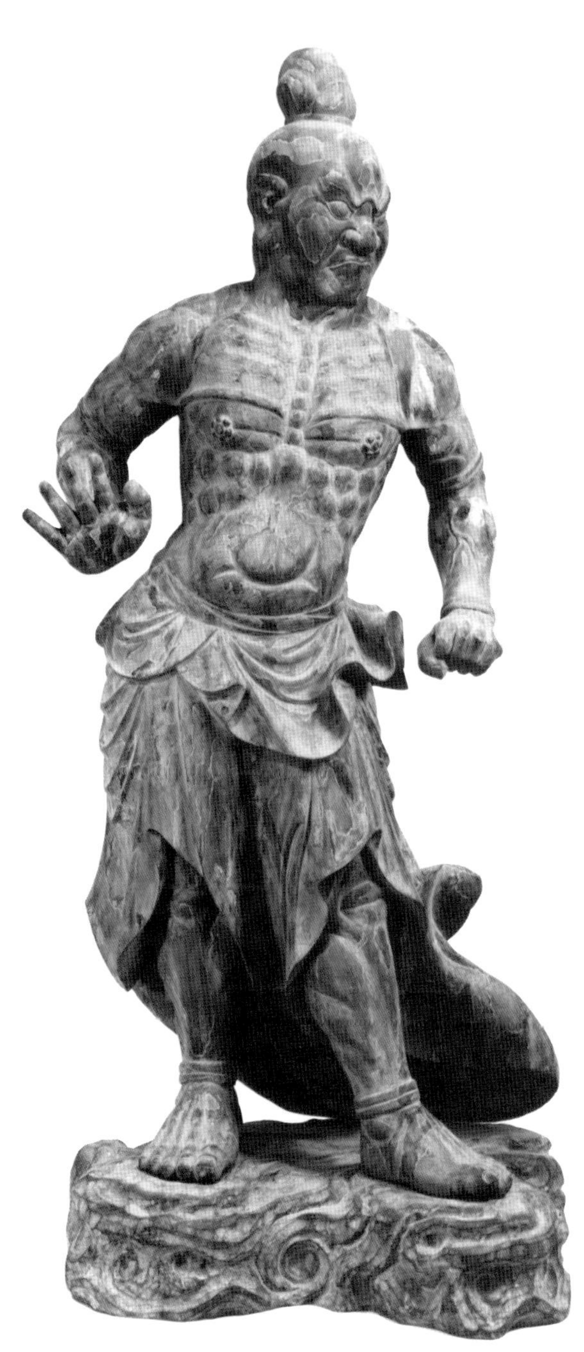

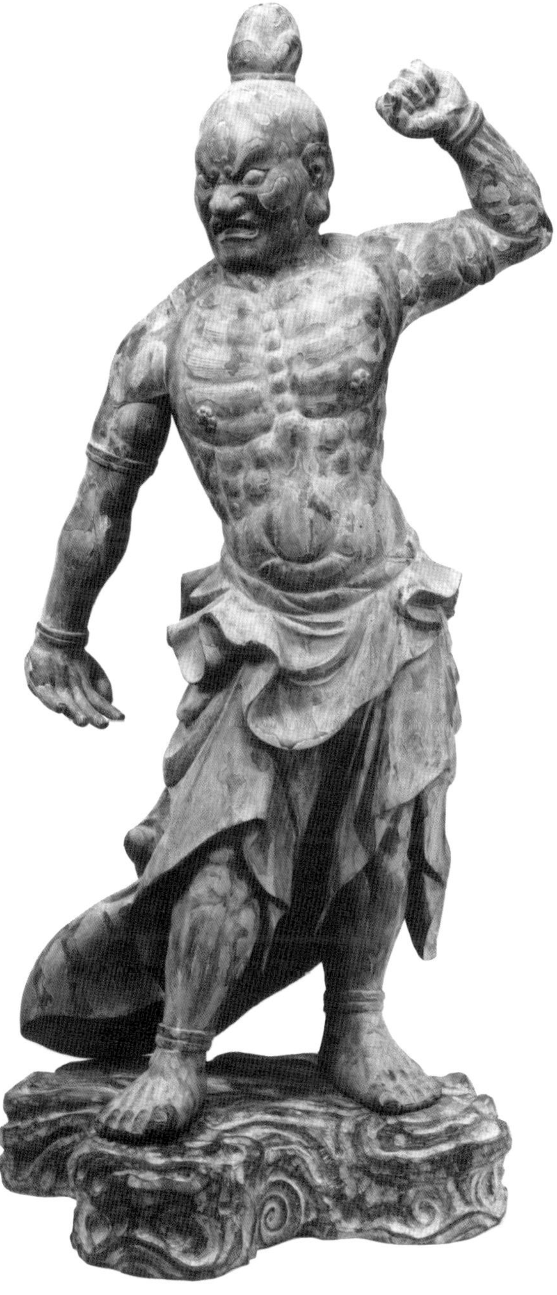

Department of

A S I A N   A R T

Chinese, late Chou dynasty, late 6th–5th
century B.C.
Ting (ritual food vessel)
Bronze
Gift of an anonymous St. Paul friend,
81.113.5

Chinese, Han dynasty, 1st–2nd century
Tomb tile
Earthenware
Gift of James and Laura Miles, 83.29

Chinese, early T'ang dynasty, 8th century
Flask
Stoneware with slip glaze
Gift of Mr. and Mrs. Gene Quintana,
85.100

Chinese, Northern Sung dynasty,
10th–11th century
Tea bowl
Henan ware
Porcelaneous stoneware with tortoise
shell glaze
Gift of Mr. and Mrs. Gene Quintana,
84.115.3

Chinese, Sung dynasty, 11th century
Bowl
Yao-chou celadon
Gift of the Regis Corporation, 85.32

Chinese, Sung Dynasty, 11th–12th
century
Bowl
Chun ware
Porcelaneous stoneware with blue glaze
Gift of Mr. Allan Rhoades, 80.60

Chinese, Sung dynasty, 11th–12th
century
Ewer
Chun ware
Porcelaneous stoneware with blue glaze
Gift of Mr. and Mrs. Gene Quintana,
84.115.1

Chinese, Sung Dynasty, 12th century
Bowl
Yao-chou celadon
Gift of anonymous St. Paul friends and
the Ethel Morrison Van Derlip Fund,
85.34

Chinese, Northern Sung dynasty, 12th
century
Bowl
Chun ware
Porcelaneous stoneware with blue glaze
Gift of Mr. Allan Rhoades, 80.60

Chinese, Yüan dynasty, 14th century
River Landscape
Ink on silk
Gift of an anonymous St. Paul friend,
84.82

Chinese, Yüan dynasty, 14th century
Vase
Porcelain with underglaze blue decor
Gift of Mr. Allan Rhoades, 84.116.5

Chinese, Ming dynasty, 16th century
Pair of point neck vases
Porcelain with underglaze blue decor of
flowers
Gift of Mr. and Mrs. Gene Quintana,
83.113.7, 8

Chinese, Ming dynasty, 16th century
Table
Cinnabar lacquer
Gift of Mr. and Mrs. James B. Serrin,
80.89

Chinese, Ming dynasty, Chia-Ching
period, 1522–66
Bowl
Porcelain with underglaze blue decor
Gift of Mr. Allan Rhoades, 83.112.1

Chinese, Ming dynasty, Chia-Ching
period, 1522–66
Bowl
Porcelain with underglaze blue decor
Gift of Mr. Allan Rhoades, 83.138

CHENG CHIA-SUI
Chinese, 1565–1643
Ming dynasty, about 1630
Album of landscape paintings
Ink on paper
Gift of an anonymous St. Paul friend and
the Ethel Morrison Van Derlip Fund,
82.8.1–10

Chinese, Ch'ing dynasty, K'ang-hsi
period, 1662–1722
Pair of bowls
Porcelain with underglaze blue decor
Gift of Mr. Allan Rhoades, 84.116.3, 4

MIAN YI
Chinese, 18th century
Ch'ing dynasty
Album of flower paintings
Ink and color on paper
Gift of an anonymous St. Paul friend and
the Ethel Morrison Van Derlip Fund,
85.12

Chinese, Ch'ing dynasty, Yung-cheng
period, 1723–35
Bowl
Porcelain with underglaze blue decor
Gift of Mr. and Mrs. Gene Quintana,
83.113.3

Chinese, Ch'ing dynasty, Yung-cheng
period, 1723–35
Bowl
Porcelain with underglaze blue decor
Gift of Mr. and Mrs. Gene Quintana,
83.113.4

Chinese, Ch'ing dynasty, Yung-cheng
period, 1723–35
Moon flask
Porcelain with blue and white
underglaze
Gift of Mr. Allan Rhoades, 84.116.2

Chinese, Ch'ing dynasty, Yung-cheng
period, 1723–35
Pair of shallow bowls
Tou-ts'ai ware
Porcelain with overglaze enamels
Gift of Dr. and Mrs. James B. Serrin,
83.134.1, 2

Chinese, Ch'ing dynasty, Ch'ien-lung
period, 1736–95
Drum-shaped box with lid
Cloisonné
Gift of Mrs. John Roller, 85.101

Chinese, Ch'ing dynasty, Ch'ien-lung
period, 1736–95
Hexafoil box
Polychrome lacquer
Gift of funds from an anonymous St.
Paul friend and the Ethel Morrison Van
Derlip Fund, 85.33

Chinese, Ch'ing dynasty, Ch'ien-lung
period, 1736–95
Imperial Portrait of Prince Duo-lo,
about 1775
Ink, colors, and gold on silk
Gift of funds from an anonymous St.
Paul friend and David Bradford, Bruce
Dayton, and Myron Kunin, 83.30

Chinese, Ch'ing dynasty, Chien-lung
period, 1736–95
Landscape in the Sung Manner, 1741
Ink and colors on silk
Gift of Mr. David Dudley, 85.102

Japanese, Kamakura period, about 1325
Taima mandala
Colors and gold on silk
Gift of Mary Griggs Burke in memory of
Jackson Burke, 85.9

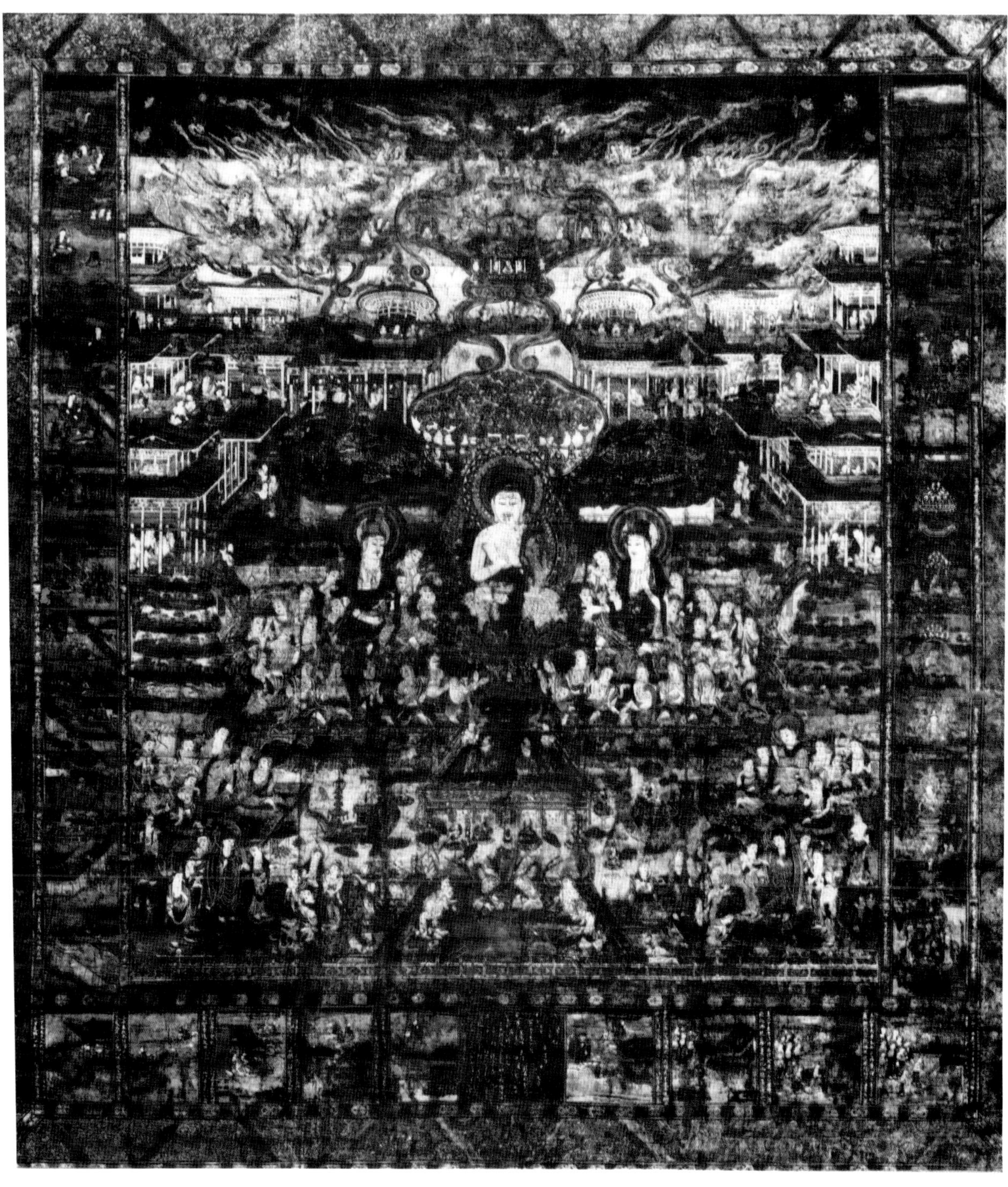

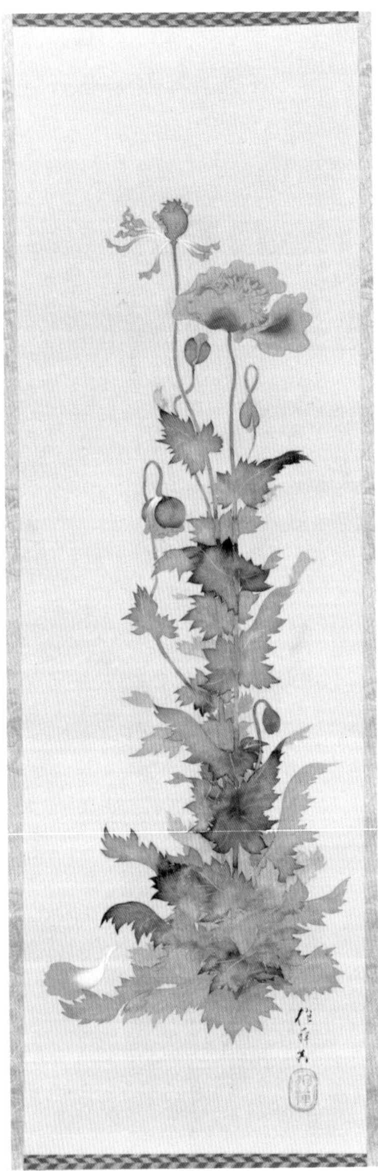

WUCIUS WONG
Chinese, 1936–
Mountain Thoughts I–IV, 1981
Ink and colors on paper
Gift of a Minneapolis friend, 83.114.1–4

Egyptian, Mamluk dynasty, 14th century
Door panel
Wood with ivory inlay
The Katherine Kittredge McMillan
Memorial Fund, 83.79

Indian, Moghul dynasty, about 1600
Majnun in the Wilderness, from a
Khansa of Nizami
Ink and colors on paper
The Katherine Kittredge McMillan
Memorial Fund, 85.80

Indian, Deccan Region, about 1670
Portrait of Nawab General Firoz Khan
Gouache on paper
The Ethel Morrison Van Derlip Fund,
80.41

Indian, Moghul dynasty, 18th century
Frontispiece to an album
Ink, colors, and gold on paper
Gift of an anonymous donor, 84.44a

Indian, Moghul dynasty, 18th century
Tray
Bidri ware
Bronze inlaid with silver
The Katherine Kittredge McMillan
Memorial Fund, 82.10.3

Indian, Moghul dynasty, about 1700
Ewer
Bidri ware
Bronze with brass and gold inlay
The Katherine Kittredge McMillan
Memorial Fund, 82.10.1

Indian, Kishangarh School, about 1760
Portrait of a Nobleman
Pencil and ink on paper
Gift of Mr. and Mrs. Charles Cleveland
and Helen Winton Jones, 84.118.7

Indian, Jaipur School, about 1800
An Aesthetic at Court
Inks, colors, and gold on paper
Gift of Mr. and Mrs. Charles Cleveland
and Helen Winton Jones, 84.118.2

Japanese, about 2000 B.C.
Jomon vessel
Terra-cotta
The Ethel Morrison Van Derlip Fund,
82.9.1

Japanese, Kofun period, 250–522
Haniwa figure of a horse
Earthenware
The John R. Van Derlip Fund and an
anonymous St. Paul friend, 83.130

Japanese, Kamakura period, about 1325
Taima mandala
Colors and gold on silk
Gift of Mary Griggs Burke in memory of
Jackson Burke, 85.9

Japanese, Nambokucho period, late 14th
century
Pair of temple guardian statues (Nio)
Cypress wood with traces of gesso and
lacquer
Gift of the Regis Corporation,
83.76.1, 2

YAMADA YORIKIYO
Japanese, 1520?–1571
Muromachi period
Tiger and dragon folding screens
Ink on paper
Gift of Mr. and Mrs. Charles H. Bell, the
James Ford Bell Foundation, Aimee Mott
Butler Charitable Trust, the Centennial
Gala Committee, and Carl A. Weyer-
haeuser Charitable Trusts, 83.75.1, 2

TOSA MITSUYOSHI
Japanese, 1539–1613
Momoyama period
Butterfly Dance
Ink, colors, gold, and silver on paper
Gift of Mr. and Mrs. Louis Zelle, Mr. and
Mrs. Charles Cleveland, and the L.Z.
Turnblad Fund, 80.40

Japanese, Momoyama period, about 1610
Tagasode folding screens
Ink, colors, gold, and silver on paper
The William Hood Dunwoody Fund,
84.81.1, 2

Attributed to SUMIYOSHI JOKEI
Japanese, 1599–1670
Edo period, early 17th century
The Story of Grasshoppers
Ink and color on paper
Anonymous gift, 84.1

Japanese, Edo period, 18th century
Kesa (priest's robe)
Silk brocade
Gift of Dr. and Mrs. Arnold Kremen,
83.135

HOITSU SAKAI
Japanese, 1761–1820
Edo period, after 1798
Poppies
Ink, colors, and gold on silk
Gift of an anonymous St. Paul friend and
the Ethel Morrison Van Derlip Fund,
84.119

TOSA MITSUYOSHI
Japanese, 1539–1613
Momoyama period
Butterfly Dance
Ink, colors, gold, and silver on paper
Gift of Mr. and Mrs. Louis Zelle, Mr. and
Mrs. Charles Cleveland, and the L.Z.
Turnblad Fund, 80.40

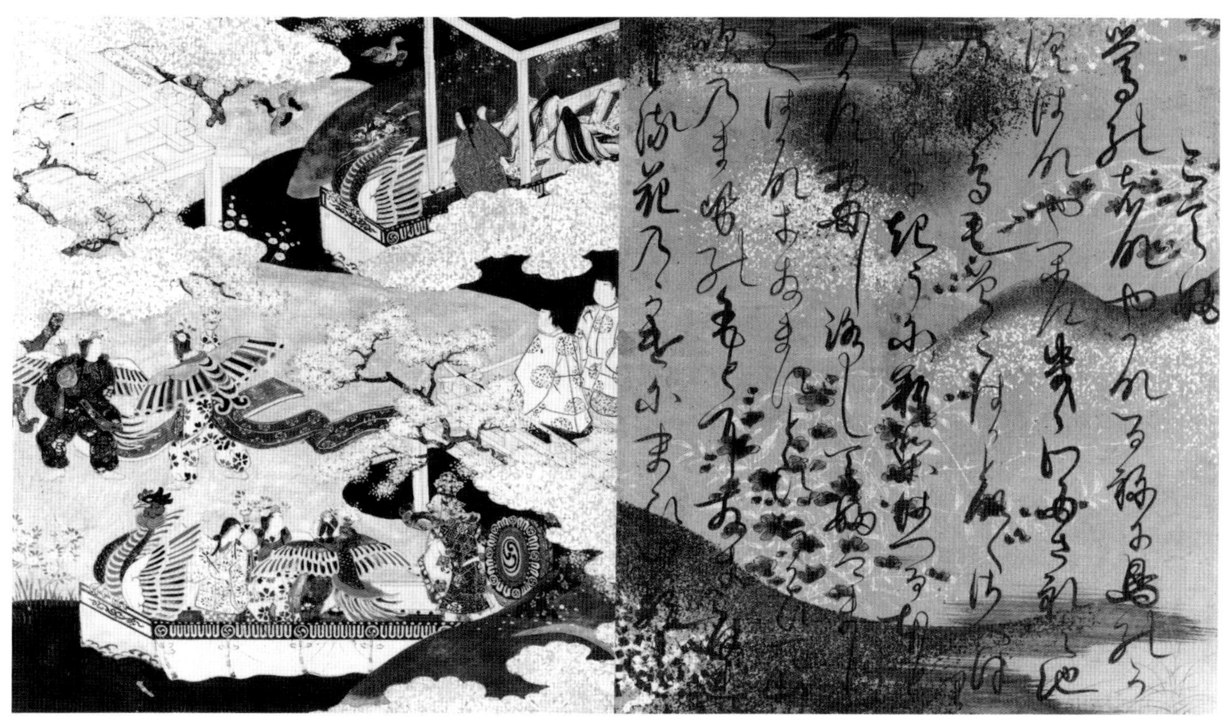

HOITSU SAKAI
Japanese, 1761–1820
Edo period, after 1798
Poppies
Ink, colors, and gold on silk
Gift of an anonymous St. Paul friend and
the Ethel Morrison Van Derlip Fund,
84.119

Japanese, 19th century
Group of Katagami
Mulberry-paper stencils
Gift of funds from Mrs. Charles
Cleveland, 83.3.1–30

Japanese, about 1810
Karaori (Outer Noh Robe)
Silk, Karaori brocade
The Ethel Morrison Van Derlip Fund,
81.90

Japanese, 20th century
Short jacket
Silk, warp and weft ikat
Gift of Mrs. Woodbury E. Andrews,
84.47.1

Japanese, Meiji period, about 1900
Man's kimono
Silk
The Bertha Evans Brown Estate for
Oriental Art, 85.103

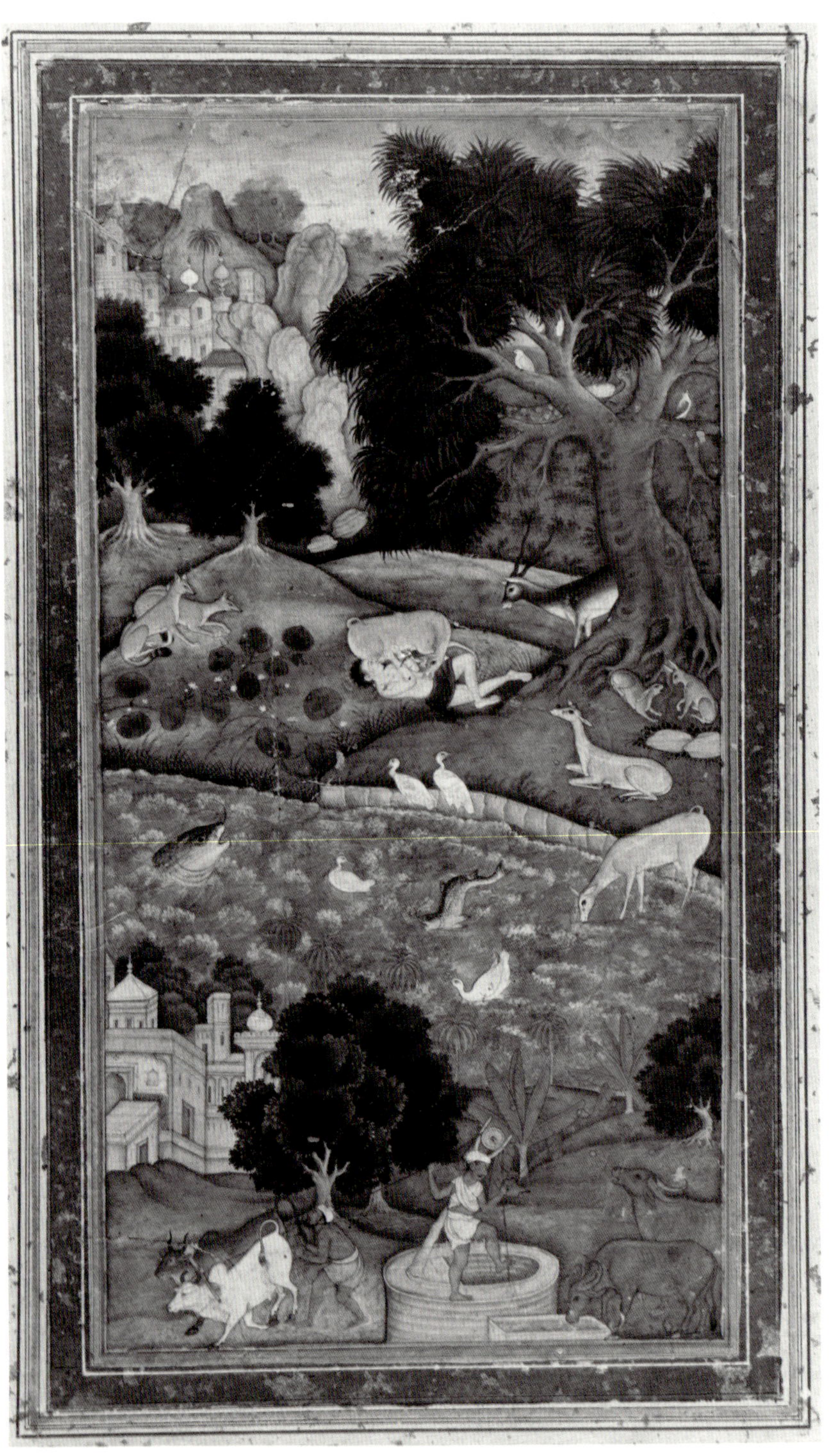

Indian, Moghul dynasty, about 1600
Majnun in the Wilderness, from a
Khansa of Nizami
Ink and colors on paper
The Katherine Kittredge McMillan
Memorial Fund, 85.80

CHENG CHIA-SUI
Chinese, 1565–1643
Ming dynasty, about 1630
*Landscape in the style of Ni Isan, from an
album of landscape paintings*
Ink on paper
Gift from an anonymous St. Paul friend and
the Ethel Morrison Van Derlip Fund, 82.8.2

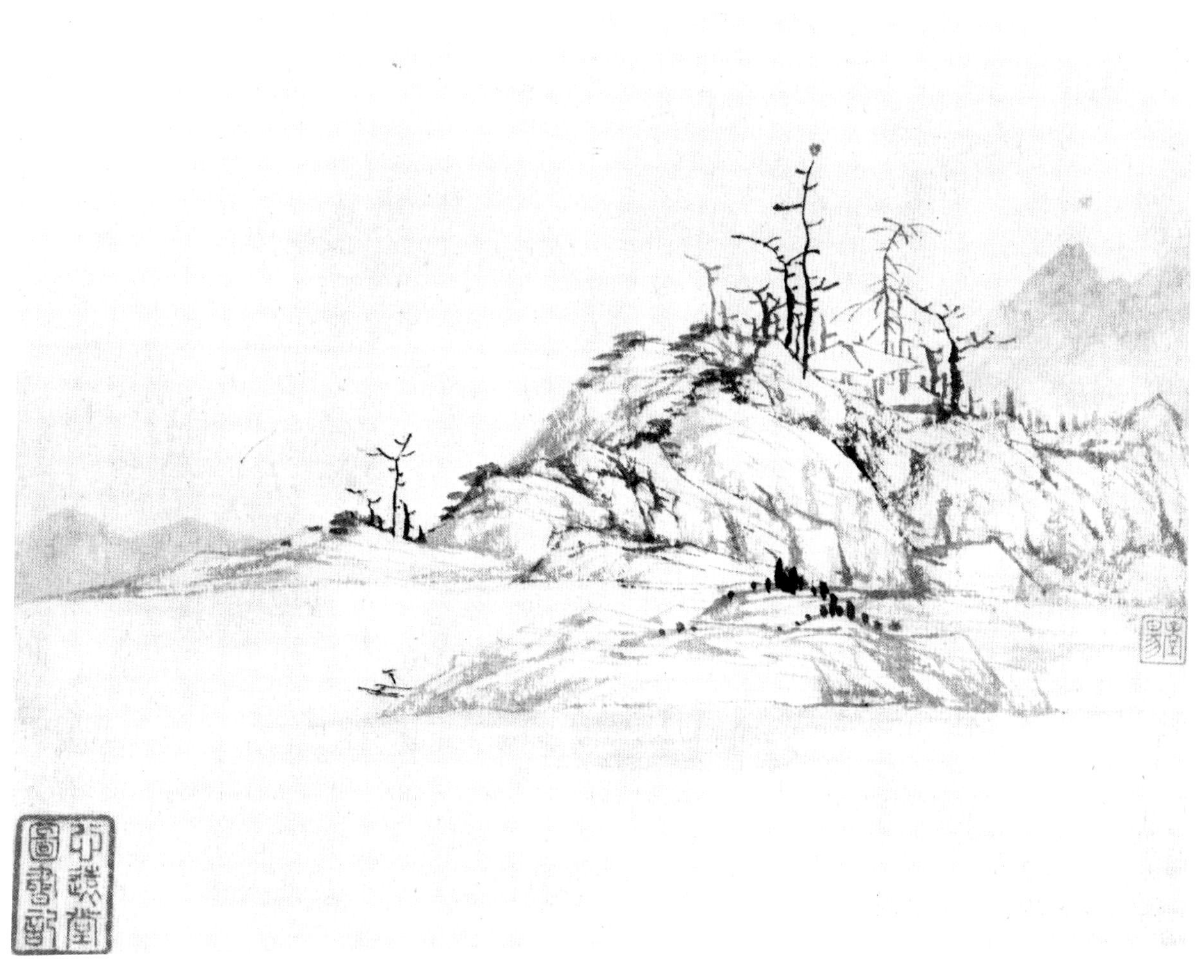

35

DECORATIVE ARTS AND SCULPTURE

The Institute's Department of Decorative Arts and Sculpture was not officially formed until 1969, when Anthony Clark appointed Merribell Parsons as its first curator. By creating a separate department that at the time included ancient and medieval art, ethnographic art, textiles, sculpture from the Renaissance to the present as well as the traditional decorative arts of furniture, glass, silver, and ceramics, Clark was employing a long-standing American museum practice that began at the Metropolitan Museum in the early twentieth century: placing three-dimensional objects that did not yet have a specific curatorial identity under the administrative jurisdiction of a decorative arts curator. Depending on the size of the museum, its budget and collection strengths, departments of decorative arts in America have in some instances encompassed oriental and ethnographic art; they frequently include ancient art and textiles, and they very often care for the medieval art and western sculpture collections. Many American departments are further blessed with installations of domestic interior paneling that are exhibited with accompanying furniture to create historicizing environments called period rooms.

The Minneapolis Institute of Arts was one of the first American museums to concentrate on the display of period settings in its galleries. In fact, when one considers the history of our decorative arts collection before the 1960s, one is continually reminded of the museum's early commitment to the display of architectural elements to evoke the style and mood of past cultures. For almost fifty years they were the catalyst for the growth of the Institute's decorative arts collections. In 1913, even before Joseph Breck was officially hired as the museum's first director— and two years before the Institute opened—the Institute's trustees commissioned Breck to purchase works in Europe for a "series of period rooms." Such romantic displays were common in

the largest American museums in the early twentieth century. At the time, however, the phrase implied any architectural fragment—gothic, Renaissance, or later—that could be utilized to create a historicizing environment. These settings, established for all fields of later western art, were intended to augment the encyclopedic direction for the collection that Breck and the trustees planned for Minneapolis. In 1919, when the trustees were preparing a long-term program for acquisitions development, an individual category for period rooms was placed third in the seven-section list of collections at the Institute, following "paintings" and "Egyptian, Near Eastern and Far Eastern Objects."

When Russell Plimpton became director in 1921, the collecting of decorative arts in Minneapolis was still understood in terms of the enhancement of these period settings that Breck had begun to buy a few years before. It was appropriate, therefore, for Plimpton to follow Breck's acquisition of gothic and Renaissance elements by purchasing architectural backdrops for seventeenth- and eighteenth-century decorative arts. In carrying out this task Minneapolis followed the lead of the Metropolitan and Philadelphia museums and acquired entire rooms for installation. The interiors these museums purchased occasionally had been altered, but they created appropriately atmospheric, if not always pure, historical settings for the numerous objects made at the time. Over the years eight such rooms were installed in Minneapolis. Happily, most of them were altered in only minor ways and two of them, the reception rooms from the Stuart House in Charleston, South Carolina, were installed in the Institute in their original form. Plimpton encouraged gifts of furniture and decorative objects from the families who had donated the period rooms to the Institute. Eventually they became beautifully appointed and evocative memorials to the highest level of the prevailing

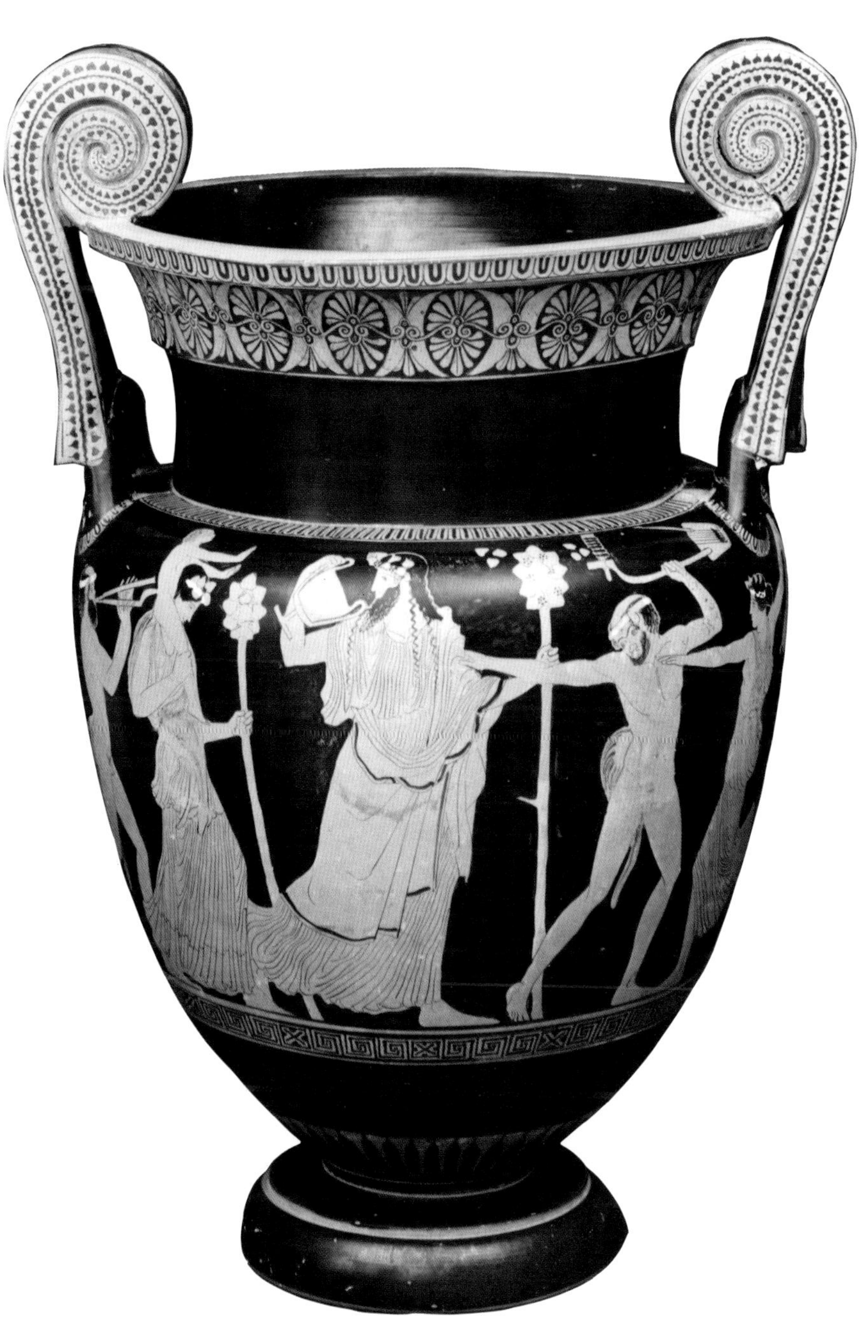

Athenian red-figured volute krater
The Methyse Painter
Greek, 455–450 B.C.
Slip-glazed earthenware
Gift of Mr. and Mrs. Donald C. Dayton,
83.80

taste for the historical interior.

The purchase of decorative arts as furnishings for period rooms led to the acquisition of objects that formed attractive ensembles, but were only occasionally distinguished when considered individually. Few museums in America bought important individual decorative arts objects before the 1950s, however. The significant early collections now in museums usually reflect the collecting activity of private individuals, carried out in some instances with curatorial advice. Understanding this tradition of private giving, it is not surprising that when the Minneapolis collections began to develop their notable strengths in the 1950s and 1960s, it was as a result of gifts from individuals. Our important collection of American and English silver formed by James Ford Bell, and enhanced by many other local collectors, is the Institute's largest and most distinguished holding in the decorative arts field. The outstanding private collections from which it stems were often formed on the advice of Plimpton, who encouraged members of the community to collect in one of his own favorite fields. Other important collections were given in the 1950s and 1960s as well. One of the most notable is the group of French faience objects which Richard Davis asked Mrs. John Rutherfurd to donate. Mrs. Vernon Wright collected American glass and here, too, through an early bequest, Minneapolis received one of its most important decorative arts holdings.

If Minneapolis did not always purchase outstanding examples of decorative arts before the 1960s it did maintain a many-faceted, encyclopedic direction for acquisitions that supported its educational goal of teaching the history of art. When Anthony Clark became director in 1963, however, he interpreted this course differently. He consciously sought to expand the scope and raise the quality and importance of our decorative arts collections by concentrating in one field where there was little American private or museum interest at the time—Italian seventeenth- and eighteenth-century furniture and silver—and by buying the best that was available to him. It was one of the most brilliant acquisition directions in the history of the museum. The objects he assembled, though few in number, are each rarely paralleled outside of Italy. When Clark established the Decorative Arts Department in 1969, he encouraged Merribell Parsons to follow a similar philosophy and purchase the best in the less popular fields of sculpture of the last two hundred years. A distinguished collection of nineteenth-century European terra-cotta, bronze, and marble sculpture was formed during her tenure, giving Minneapolis a well-deserved reputation for excellence in this field. Significant purchases in silver were also made by Miss Parsons's colleague, David McFadden, further contributing to the notable strengths of the department in this area.

The decorative arts department which Clark formed initially included art from ancient civilizations, medieval art, and ethnographic art, as well as textiles. Separate departments of textiles and African, Oceanic and New World cultures were established in the late 1970s, and in the future other departments, a department of ancient art, for example, may be spawned as separate entities. Although as a group the areas that comprise the nontraditional decorative arts within the early Decorative Arts Department—ancient and medieval art, textiles and tapestries—had received the least attention from the 1940s until 1980, they represented one of the most important areas of acquisition at the Institute before that time. Classical sculpture, smaller Egyptian objects, late-medieval architectural fragments were bought in great quantity in the teens and twenties. Despite the deaccessioning of the 1950s, which weakened our Egyptian and medieval holdings significantly, the collection of Greek and Roman art remains small but distinguished. The tapestries bought by Mrs. Charles

Attributed to THE MASTER OF THE
PASSION DIPTYCH
French, 14th century
Diptych with Scenes of the Life of Christ
Ivory
Gift of Mr. and Mrs. John E. Andrus III,
Atherton and Winifred W. Bean, and an
anonymous donor, 83.72

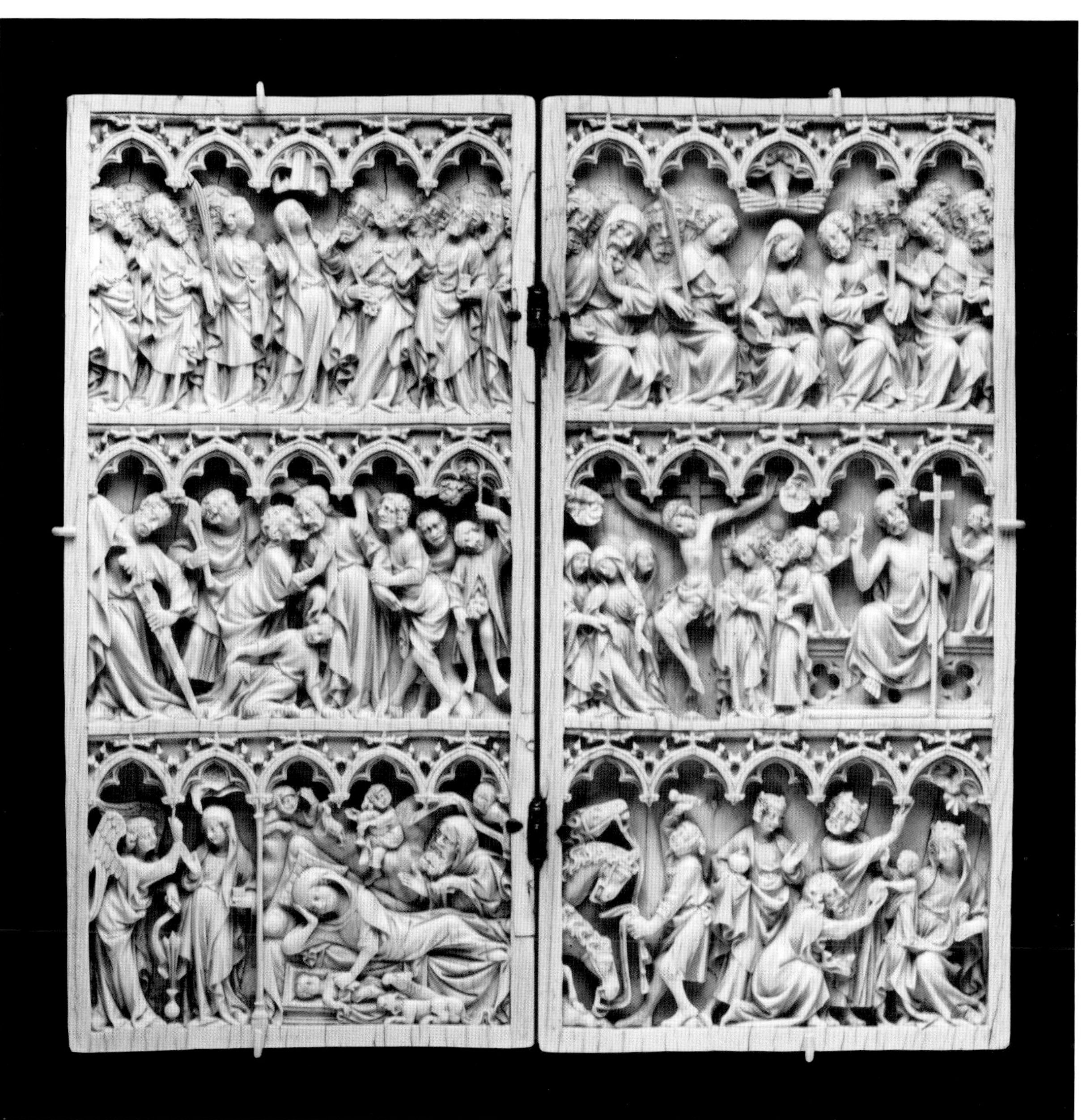

Martin during the first years of the museum's
history form one of the outstanding collections
in the country.

The Institute's Decorative Arts Department is
still large and amorphous. It is a department of
enormous breadth and exposure, with more
objects on view than any other in the museum,
a department whose scope is difficult for the
public to understand because of its wide and
somewhat incompatible collection responsi-

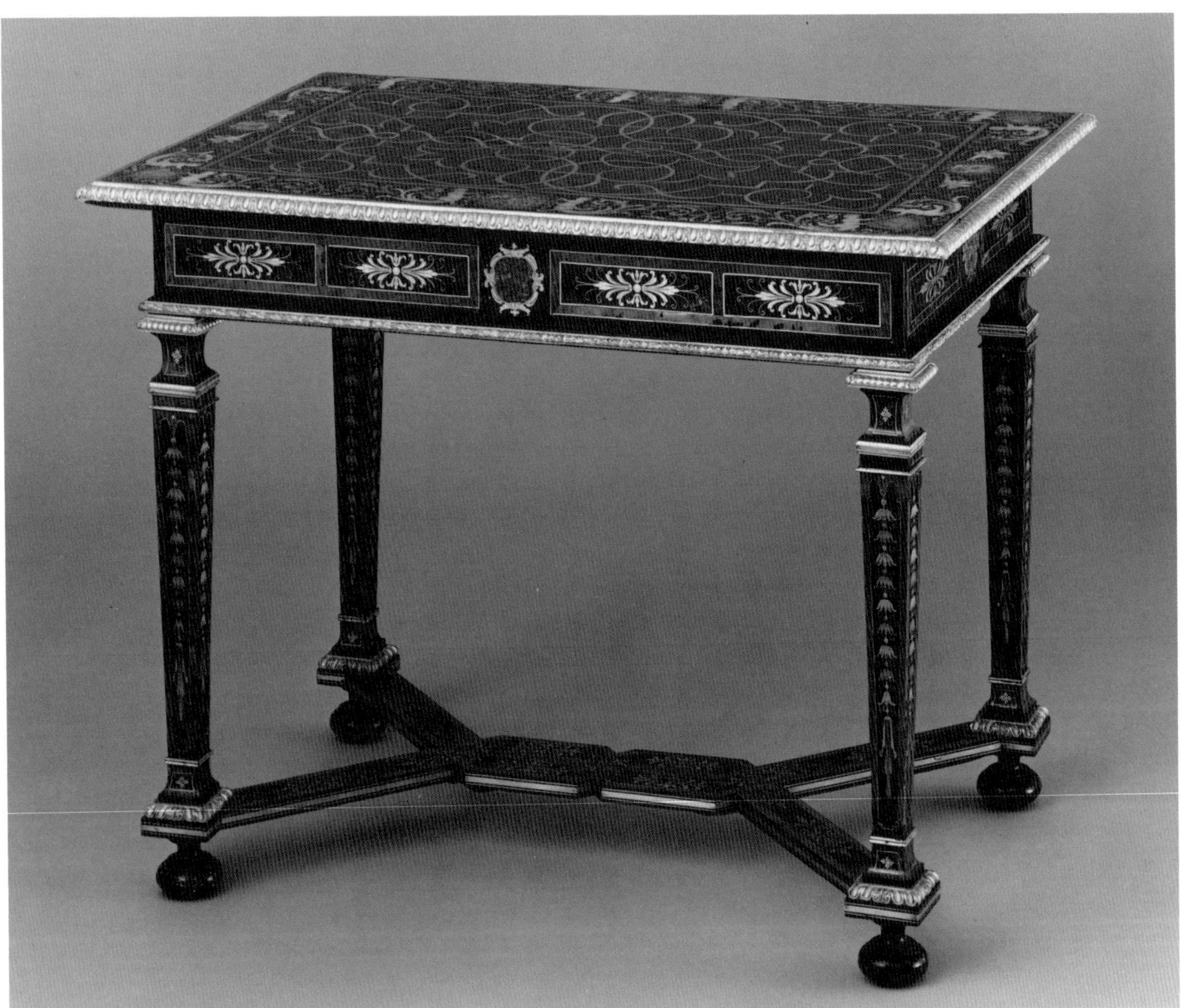

bilities. Given its nature, the present curators, who were appointed in 1980, might have chosen to concentrate on one or two fields in establishing their accessions philosophy, focusing the department's energies on specific areas of growth. This would not have been an unintelligent move, for it would have concentrated resources and community attention on a few well-defined fields of collecting. These fields could have been drawn from the present curators' primary areas of expertise, European sculpture and American decorative arts, or they could have represented Anthony Clark's tradition of collecting well in unfashionable fields by moving this philosophy into the more uncharted areas of museum collecting in the 1980s. In so doing, the community could have been presented with a sense of accomplishment when a new gallery was inaugurated for a new collection, a collection that easily communicated a sense of direction, purpose and achievement. Furthermore, there are problems in making intelligent purchases when a department chooses more than a few areas in which to collect. When curators buy in fields where they have modest expertise and the museum little collection strength, greater time is necessary to develop the relationships with dealers and collectors that will eventually result in important objects being offered for purchase or gift. Also, time must be spent with specialized experts in a field to confirm the desirability of an acquisition.

In spite of these difficulties the department has chosen to maintain an encyclopedic direction in its collecting philosophy, modified by an understanding of the Institute's success in the past few decades in making purchases in less popular fields. There are two reasons for our following this course. The first is the museum's mission to represent the artistic achievement of all cultures, in all media, for the education and edification of the people of the region. We believe, as did our founders, that there is no more important catalyst in directing the growth of the department's collections. Second, the situation in the art market has changed enormously since the 1960s. While there are still less fashionable fields of collecting, as there were in Anthony Clark's time, quality objects in almost any area involve more significant financial commitments than in the 1960s. There are only attractive opportunities, not real bargains, in the 1980s. Also, while curators and dealers too frequently use the phrase "the last opportunity" in encouraging a client or a museum board to purchase an object, there is no question that in many important areas of museum collecting, this fear has become a fact. We feel strongly that "the last opportunity" to strengthen the weak areas of our collection should not come and go without serious consideration on our part. The education of future generations will suffer if we fail in this regard.

Our intention to enhance the representative nature of the museum has not been carried out haphazardly, however. We have bought in areas where quality objects are rare, and consequently expensive, and where objects are more available, relatively less fashionable, and consequently less expensive. Our collectors' interests, market availability and existing endowment funds have been the significant factors in directing our course. We have, for example, not ignored the established strengths of the museum such as American and English silver, but we have added objects from periods where the silver collection is weak. For example, from the nineteenth century we bought a beautiful covered tureen, made about 1830 by the American firm of Gale and Moseley; an English gilt-silver christening set of 1864 with a provenance to the English royal family; an Aesthetic Movement tea service by Gorham and Company of Providence, Rhode Island, of about 1883, as well as a unique Gorham coffee pot on a stand, about 1890. We extended our collection of silver tea services to the twentieth century when we purchased a set designed in 1983 by the Viennese architect Hans Hollein. We are fortunate, too, that gifts continue to be received from the community in the field of silver. Most outstanding are the four saltcellars by Paul de Lamerie, about 1728-29, and the magnificent Tiffany commemorative tray presented by the citizens of Minneapolis to James J. Hill in 1885. Adding to other strengths, we were given a very unusual Strasbourg tureen of about 1750, realistically modeled in the form of a cabbage, that complements our faience collection. My colleague, Francis Puig, arranged for the purchase of an entire collection of midwestern glass, one of the most important ever formed, which has enhanced our American glass collection along with a number of other choice nineteenth-century pieces representing Eastern American glass houses.

I probably spend more time investigating the sculpture market than any other field, as it is my area of specialization, but our sculpture purchases have not been a significant part of our

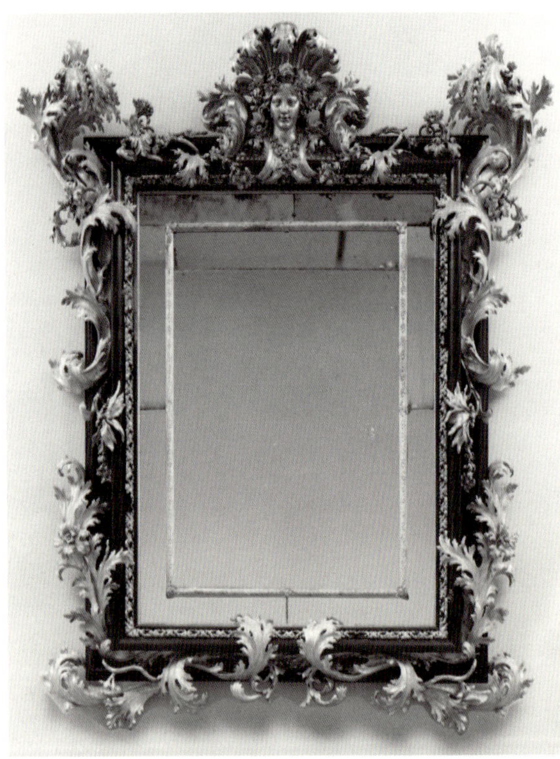

collecting activity. Knowing that the pursuit of objects in one's own primary area of expertise occasionally induces a nearsightedness resulting in a pedantic collection, I have been particularly harsh when considering objects in this field. Where our sculpture collection is weak, i.e., sculpture before 1800, the market has produced only one object of appropriate quality that timing and available money would allow, the extraordinary late seventeenth-century French *Corpus*, which is a splendidly expressive addition to our small collection of works in ivory.

It is a curious result of the Institute's history and the community's collecting patterns that the fields usually strongest and most important to a decorative arts collection—American, English and French furniture, European glass and ceramics—were never established in Minneapolis with a significant commitment. Consequently, in the last five years our department has put much of its resources into developing these collections. To our ceramics holdings, we have added objects as diverse as a rare, early Meissen pokal, about 1712, made of red Böttger stoneware, and a fanciful and brightly glazed majolica game pie dish made in 1877 at the Minton factory in England. We have complemented our American glass collection with the purchase of several European pieces, such as the English goblet enameled with a land-scape within a rococo border by the Newcastle firm of Wiliam Beilby. A seventeenth-century Netherlandish glass executed in a delicate *latticino* technique is an exciting addition to our modest collection of earlier European glass. We have increased the collection of American decorative arts significantly by purchasing three important pieces of case furniture made before 1800: a kas by Roeloeff Demarest, 1740-60, repre-senting the early eighteenth-century Dutch influence in New York; a Massachusetts chest-on-stand, 1730-40, veneered in burl walnut; and a late eighteenth-century Connecticut cherry-wood linen press of unprecedented form. We have also acquired a documented wing chair by Moses Grant, about 1800, and a pair of chairs by the Rhode Island maker Stephen Badlam, all of which have been placed in one of our newly renovated period rooms.

In nineteenth-century American furniture, we have taken advantage of a favorable market situa-tion to acquire important and elegant objects such as a dolphin sofa attributed to Charles-Honoré Lannuier, made in New York around 1820; the graceful, carved rococo-revival etagère attrib-uted to the New York furniture maker Joseph Meeks; and the chair and stool, about 1880, imaginatively fashioned from horn and uphol-stered in ocelot skin, by the San Antonio crafts-man Wenzel Friedrich. We have made an effort to begin a collection of Arts and Crafts and other turn-of-the-century objects in Minneapolis as well. Starting with the gift of a room and its accompanying suite of furniture by the Minneapolis designer John Bradstreet, we have acquired chairs by Frank Lloyd Wright, the Greene and Greene firm, and ceramics made by Shirama-yadani at Rookwood and George Ohr at Biloxi.

No acquisitions have done more to change the nature of our department's collections during the short five-year period under discussion than the French objects given by the Groves Foundation. While French furniture is traditionally the most respected category of decorative arts, the high prices it commands in the market would have

kept Minneapolis from ever forming a collection were it not for the commitment of Mr. and Mrs. Franklin Groves to establish French decorative arts collections at the Institute. Over twenty pieces of furniture and objets d'art by well-known eighteenth-century craftsmen such as Sené and Foullet were bought at auction by Mr. and Mrs. Groves and given to the museum. A chair by Jacob Frères of about 1795 and four important suites of Sèvres porcelain, as well as a rare bust of Louis XV made at the Chantilly factory in the 1740s were purchased by the museum from an endowment established by the Groves Foundation in 1981.

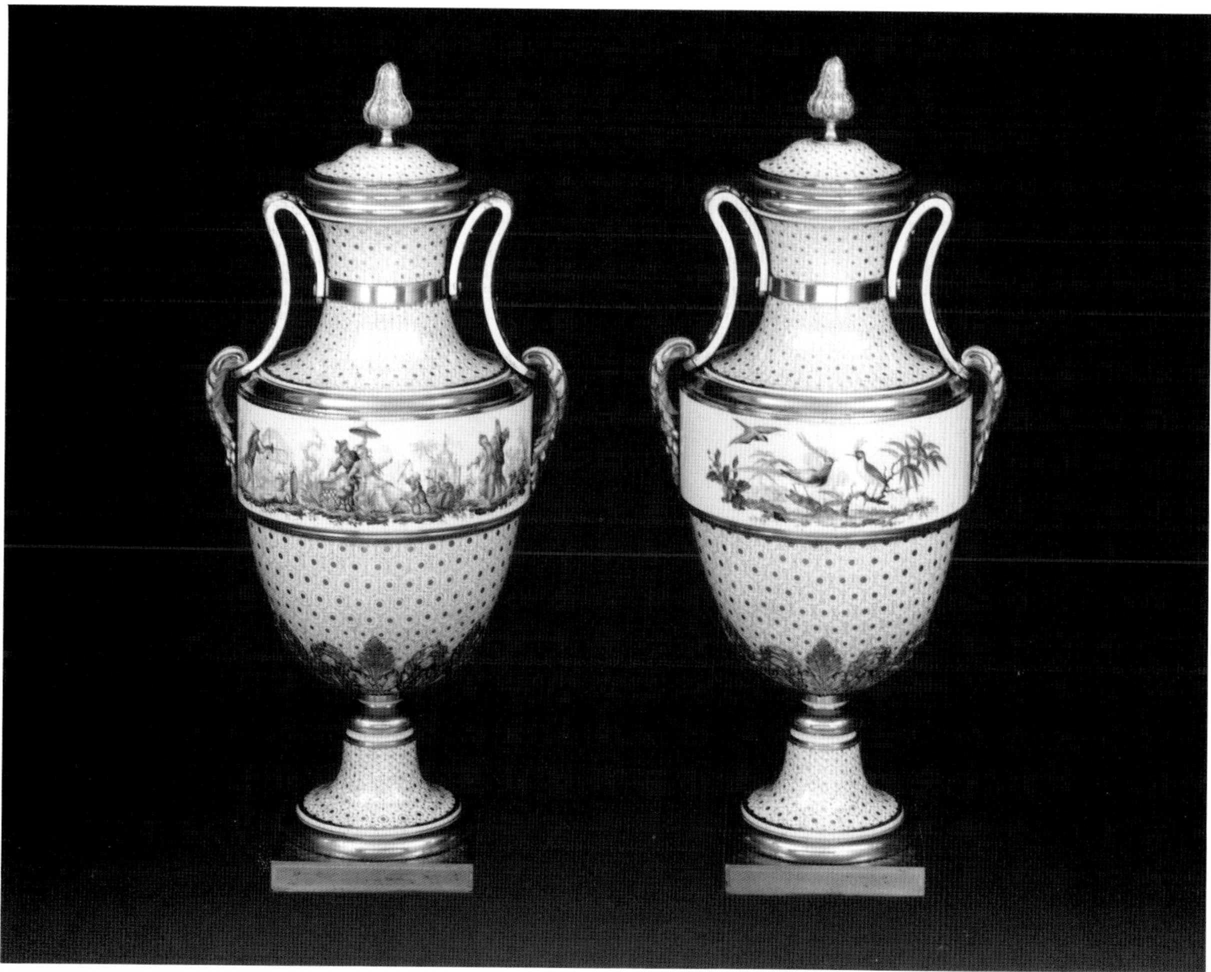

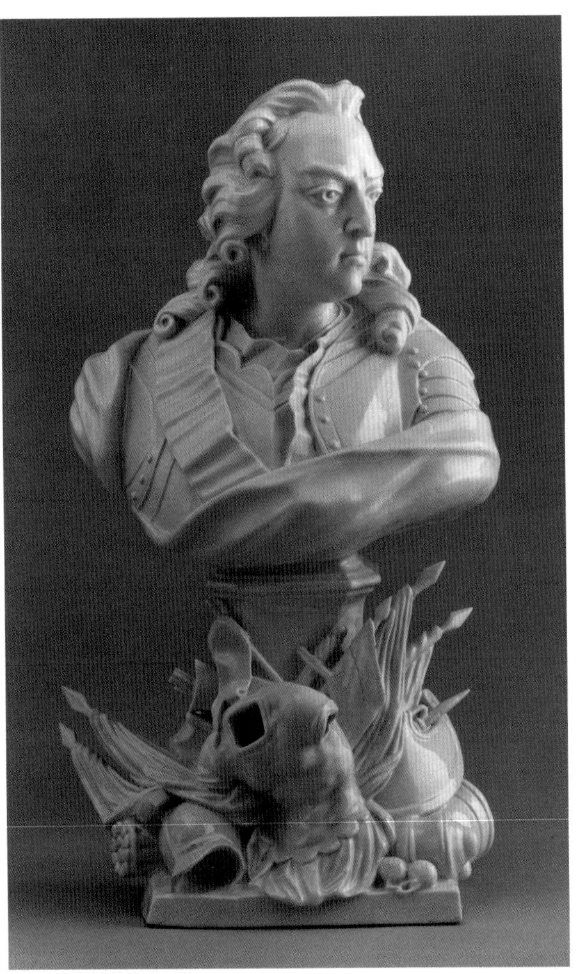

The complete salon from the Hôtel de Pomponne in Paris, about 1720, one of the last important Louis XV rooms that will ever be available, was also a gift of the foundation. We plan to install it in an expanded suite of decorative arts galleries that will eventually give French decorative arts a prominent place in Minneapolis.

Gifts from the Groves Foundation have also enhanced the English furniture collection. The foundation has presented a beautiful pair of Chippendale armchairs carved with gothic fretwork, about 1745, and a pair of gilt chairs and a window seat designed by John Linnell. We would eventually like to add outstanding pieces of nineteenth-century English furniture to the collection and we hope to establish a sufficient commitment from private supporters for this task.

We have been successful in finding endowment and private support for five spectacular Continental European objects. We acquired a Portuguese side chair from a well-known suite made in the mid-eighteenth century and two important German pieces: an extraordinary late seventeenth-century tortoise shell and pewter marquetry table by the German cabinetmaker Hans Daniel Sommer, and a beautiful South German horn and gold picqué box containing six crystal and gold perfume bottles, probably made in Augsburg around 1740. We have added to Anthony Clark's Italian decorative arts acquisitions with two outstanding purchases. The first is a large and elaborately carved Italian giltwood mirror that hung for more than a century above the central hall fireplace at Mentmore, the Buckinghamshire house built by Baron Meyer de Rothschild in 1853; the second is a pair of chairs designed in the 1830s for Racconigi, one of the royal palaces of the House of Savoy, by the greatest Italian designer of the nineteenth century, Pelagio Palagi.

Our collecting of twentieth-century art has taken various directions. Not only have we expanded our silver collection with the acquisition of a tea service by Hans Hollein, but we have bought two important sculptures as well, the twenty-four foot high *Hammering Man* by Jonathan Borofsky and *Ahab* by Alexander Calder, each of which has given a new life and dimension to our Sculpture Court. We also chose to transform a 1979 grant from the National Endowment for the Arts for the purchase of contemporary sculpture into a fund for the acquisition of ceramic sculpture. In a six-month period, we bought works by Stephen de Staebler, Ken Price, Peter Voulkos, Viola Frey, and many other well-known artists, forming a unique collection of contemporary ceramic sculpture in Minneapolis.

Perhaps the most important accessions activity of the department in the last five years has taken place in ancient and medieval art, areas where the existing collections are modest, the historical and educational significance considerable, and the opportunities for making important additions steadily decreasing. In the medieval field the department is proud of the addition of a pair of Viking brooches as well as the extraordinary early fifteenth-century North Italian reliquary head of St. Theobold. We were most fortunate, however, in being able to buy a mid-fourteenth-century French ivory diptych depicting scenes from the life of the Virgin, one of the finest ivories of its type anywhere.

In the field of antiquities we added the first important red-figure Greek vase to enter the collection, a volute krater attributed to the Methyse painter. Our only regret is that no Egyptian objects were purchased by the museum during this period. Although a beautiful head of Sekmet was given in 1983, and we have arranged

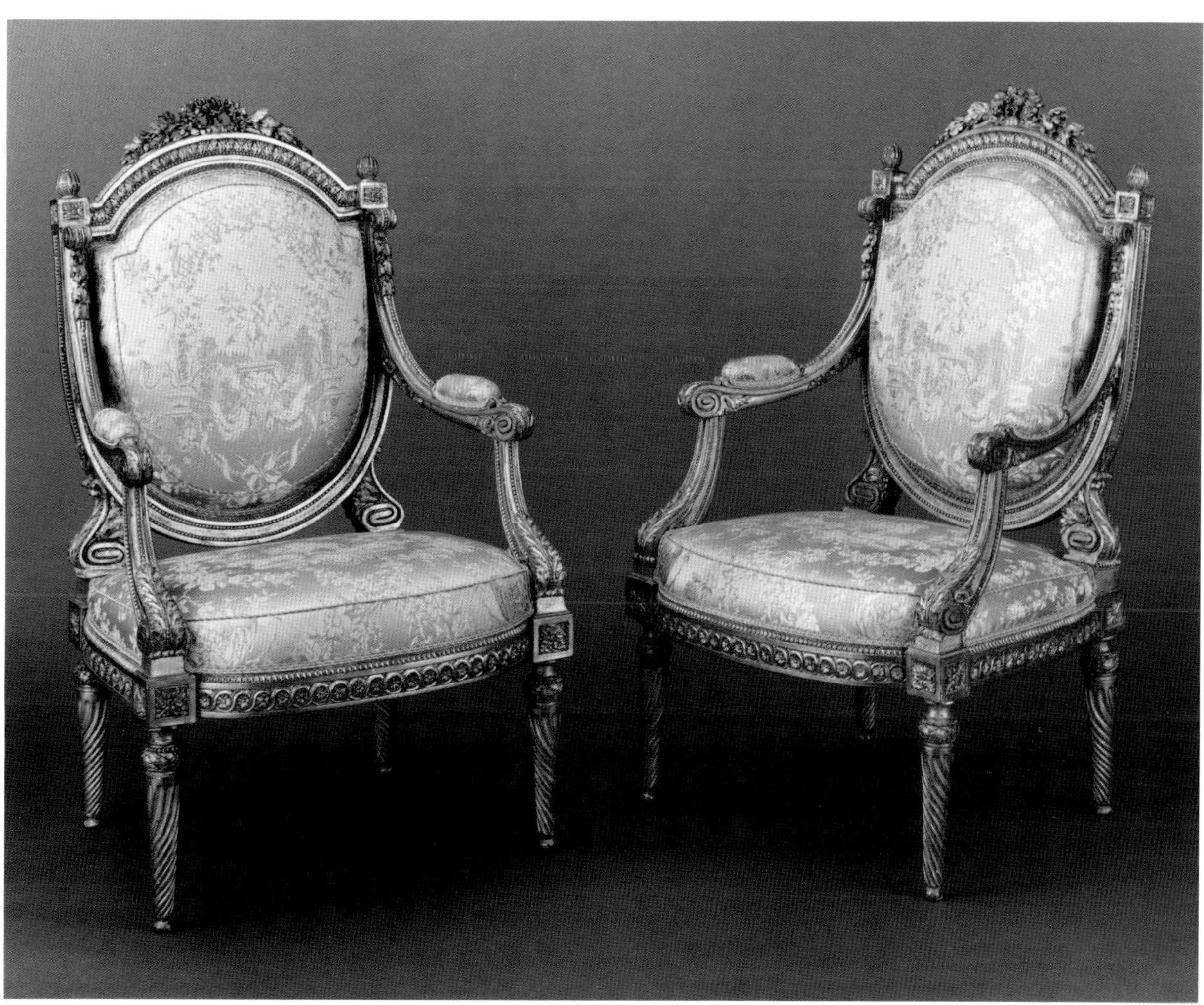

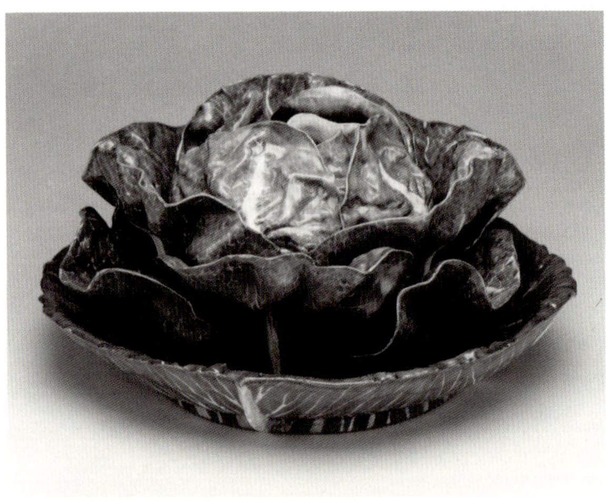

for the loan and conservation of two mummies brought to Minneapolis in the late nineteenth century, our repeated attempts to add significant Egyptian sculpture to the collection have not been successful.

In discussing the various collecting activities of the department, I am occasionally asked where my own taste in sculpture and decorative arts really lies. I believe that curators should have a variety of preferences in selecting objects, each relating to the nature of the collecting activity with which they are presented. What one buys for oneself, what one recommends to a collector with specific interests, what one recommends to a new museum with no collection or a large, older museum with existing collections must all vary in response to the nature of the task at hand. In buying for a museum, the taste of the curatorial professional has to adjust to the history and mission of the institution, its present collection, the money available from endowment or private collectors, and the mood of the art market at the moment.

Everyone has preferences, however, and my own are admittedly often catalyzed by market opportunities to acquire quality objects that represent the highest achievement of a culture, era,

or medium that is currently overlooked. For example, I tend to buy American early nineteenth-century furniture and objects for myself (still inexpensive and available). For the museum, the principle is the same. Much as Italian eighteenth-century decorative arts represented an overlooked area to Anthony Clark, exceptional continental decorative arts are still relatively available to our collection. I am particularly proud of our purchases in continental decorative arts outside France: the Sommer table, the Augsburg box, the Mentmore mirror, the Portuguese chair, the furniture from Racconigi. While not as inexpensive as Clark's Italian decorative arts acquisitions, they still represent the highest level of craftsmanship and design from their respective countries and they still are available and affordable with our modest accessions income.

I must admit, however, that if my taste were not modified by our existing collections, the art historical mission of the museum, local collector interest and limitations of gallery space, I would take my preference for purchasing the best from less recognized cultures to the area of objects from colonial regions other than early America, e.g., the finest Indian or Batavian export furniture, South American or Irish furniture, or Chinese furniture for the export market. I might have bought Scandinavian or Russian objects as well. I would have acquired more mid-twentieth-century decorative arts, as well as other objects currently underpriced, e.g., seventeenth-century oak furniture, or more nineteenth-century objects from countries other than the United States. Possibly, in time, we might encourage local private collectors to consider the value and beauty of these somewhat uncharted avenues of collecting.

While it is difficult for the Institute's decorative arts collection to move easily into these less recognized fields, for reasons stated above, our department will still remain committed to its current philosophy of developing all the collections

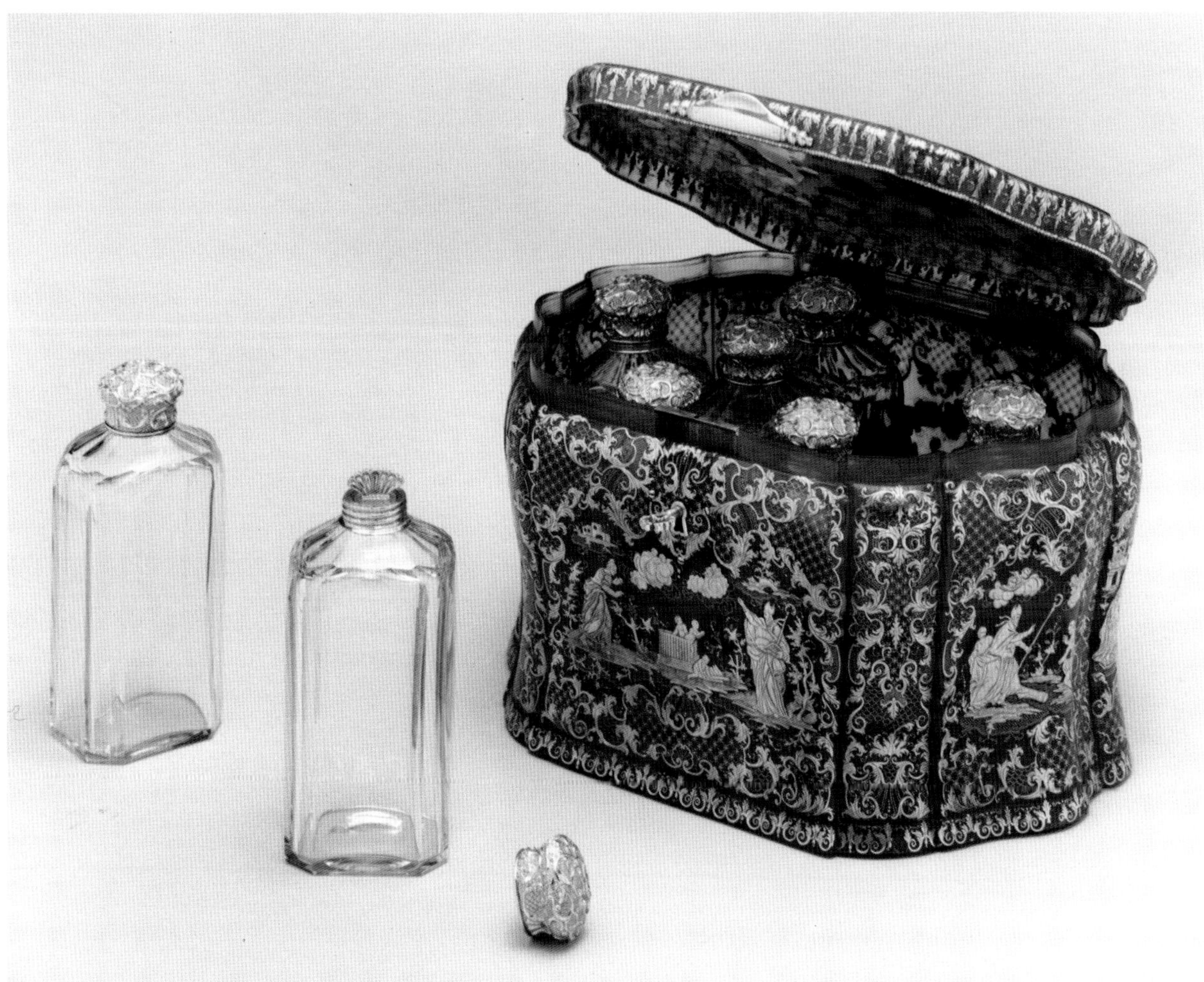

under its care. If the growth of the decorative arts
collection continues in an intelligent, historically
responsible, and aesthetically exciting way, the
Institute's mission to present the finest objects in
the history of art for the inspiration and education
of its public will be ever enhanced.

Michael P. Conforti
Chairman, Curatorial Division
Bell Memorial Curator of
Decorative Arts and Sculpture

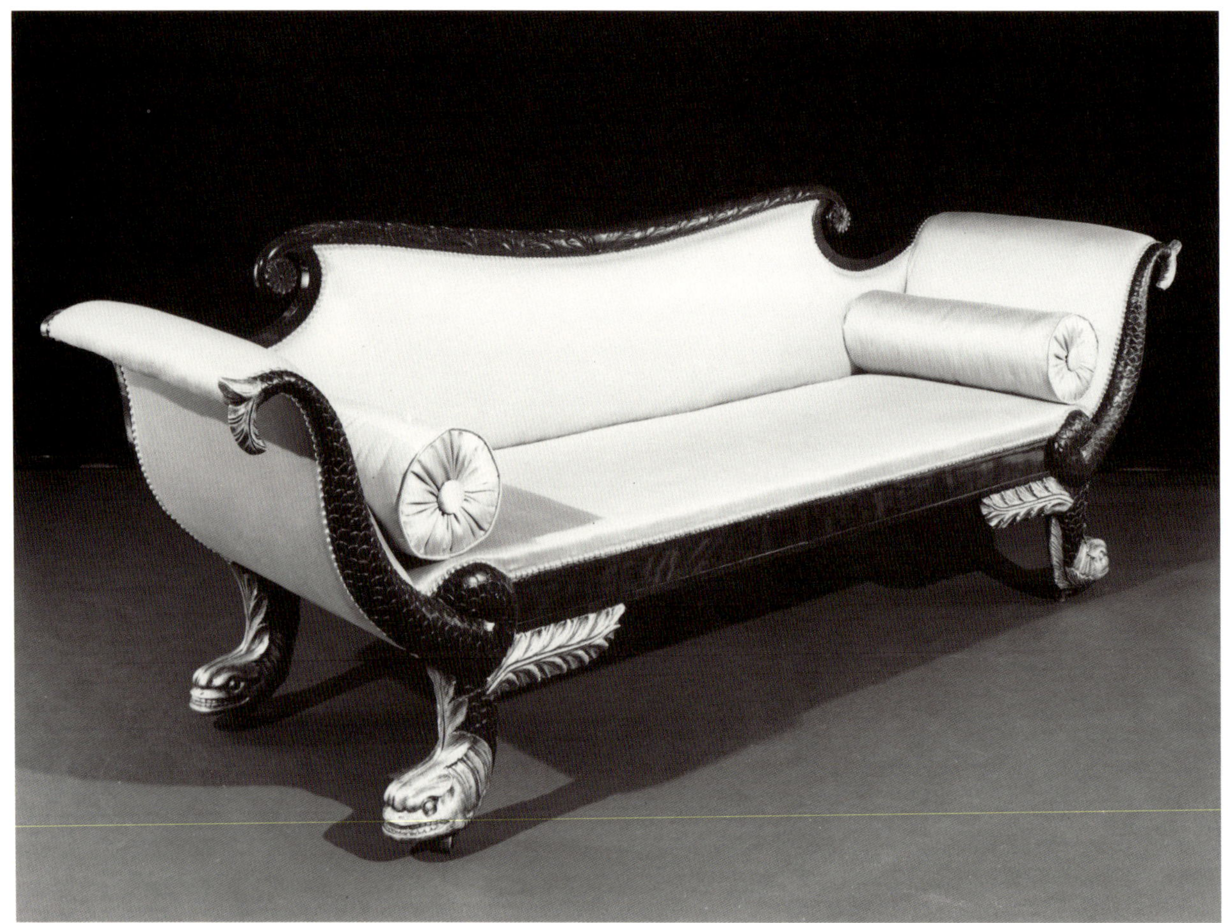

Sofa
Possibly from the shop of Charles
Honoré Lannuier, 1779–1819
American, New York, 1815–25
Mahogany, pine, maple, and ash
The William Hood Dunwoody Fund and
gifts from Harry McC. Drake,
Mr. and Mrs. Charles Bell, the James
Ford Bell Foundation, Mrs. John Roller,
and Mrs. Peter Anson, 82.75

Armchair
Pelagio Palagi, 1775–1860
Italian, 1835
Satinwood
The John R. Van Derlip Fund

SCULPTURE

Italian, 14th–15th century
Reliquary Head of St. Theobald
Silver and silver gilt
Gift of Bruce B. Dayton, 83.73

Italian, 16th century
Group of bronzes
Gift of Mr. and Mrs. Theodore W.
Bennett, 82.115.1–17

French, about 1680
Corpus
Ivory
Anonymous gift of funds and the Ethel
Morrison Van Derlip Fund, 82.24

ERNST BARLACH
German, 1890–1938
Der Geistkämpfer, about 1953–54
Reduced copy of 1928 version
Bronze
Anonymous gift, 83.82

ANTOINE-LOUIS BARYE
French, 1795/6–1875
Panther Devouring a Rabbit
Bronze
Gift of James J. Hill III, Maude Hill
Schroll and an anonymous St. Paul
friend, 81.108.3

LEONARD BASKIN
American, 1922–
Seated Bird Man, 1963
Bronze
Gift of the Maslon Foundation, 82.27

GIOVANNI BOLOGNA
Italian, Florentine, 1524–1608
La Fiorenza, 1562–64
Bronze
Gift of Mr. and Mrs. Theodore W.
Bennett and the John R. Van Derlip
Fund, 80.26

JONATHAN BOROFSKY
American, 1942–
Hammering Man, 1981
Wood and metal
Gift of funds from the Regis
Corporation, the Aimee Mott Butler
Foundation and the Christina N. and
Swan J. Turnblad Fund. 84.120

ANTOINE BOURDELLE
French, 1861–1929
Door knocker in form of Medusa, 1925
Bronze
Gift of Atherton and Winifred W. Bean,
83.31

ALEXANDER CALDER
American, 1898–1976
Ahab, 1953
Painted metal
Gift of Bruce B. Dayton and Mr. and
Mrs. Gerald A. Erickson, by exchange,
83.77

ALBERT ERNEST CARRIER-BELLEUSE
French, 1824–1887
Love and Friendship, about 1857
Bronze
Gift of Mrs. Helen A. Sturm, 84.23

AIME JULES DALOU
French, 1838–1902
Bust of a Child
Bronze
Gift of Mr. and Mrs. Alan Struthers,
83.116

VIOLA FREY
American, 1933–
Double Grandmother, 1978–79
Glazed white clay
Gift of the Regis Corporation with
matching funds from the National
Endowment for the Arts, 81.29.1, 2ab
and .3

VINCENZO GEMITO
Italian, 1852–1929
Portrait of Alexander the Great, 1923
Silver and gilt
The John R. Van Derlip Fund, 81.4

PAUL MANSHIP
American, 1885–1966
Flight of Night
Bronze
Gift of Atherton and Winifred W. Bean,
82.15

MARINO MARINI
Italian, 1901–80
Horseman, 1950
Bronze
A gift from the children of John and
Elizabeth Bates Cowles, 83.83

Attributed to THE MASTER OF THE
PASSION DIPTYCH
French, 14th century
Diptych with Scenes of the Life of Christ
Ivory
Gift of Mr. and Mrs. John E. Andrus III,
Atherton and Winifred W. Bean, and an
anonymous donor, 83.72

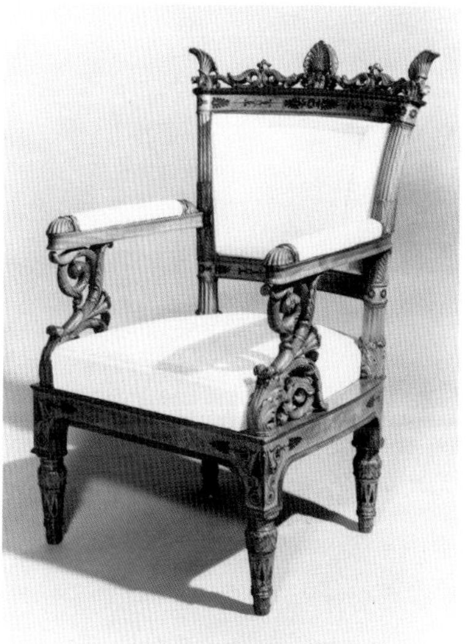

METALWORK

Pair of oval brooches, with Borré-style
ornamentation
Denmark, late 9th–early 10th century
Bronze, silver, and gold
The John R. Van Derlip Fund, 81.55.1, 2

Chocolate pot
Gabriel Sleath, 1674–1729
English, London, 1711
Silver with wood handle
Gift of Mrs. Margarette H. Crosby,
84.24.2

Six Salts
Paul de Lamerie, 1688–1751
English, 1728–29
Silver and silver gilt
Gift of Mrs. John S. Pillsbury, Sr.,
82.119.1–6

Circular bowl with cover
Philip Syng, 1703–1789
American, Philadelphia, 1740–50
Silver
Gift of Mr. and Mrs. Charles H. Bell,
81.36ab

Cake basket
John Lanford and John Sebille
English, 1764
Silver
Gift of Mrs. Margarette H. Crosby,
84.24.2

Teapot with stand and tea caddy
Thomas Daniell, active 1771–1793
English, 1791
Silver
The Thomas L. Daniels Memorial Fund,
81.56.1–3

Pair of candlesticks
French, probably Paris, about 1780
Gilded bronze
Gift of the Groves Foundation,
80.3.1, 2a–c

Epergne
James Young
English, London, 1790–1791
Silver
Gift of Charles H. Bell, J. Ford Bell and
Samuel H. Bell, 81.16.1–18

Coffee service
Attributed to John Angell
English, 1823
Silver
Gift of Mary Sue Zelle Reid and Mr. and
Mrs. Louis N. Zelle, 84.121.1–4

Lidded tureen
William Gale, 1799–1867, and Joseph
Moseley, partnership active 1828–33
American, New York, 1830
Silver
The James S. Bell Memorial Fund and
the Christina N. and Swan J. Turnblad
Memorial Fund, 80.57

Tea service
Martin Hall and Company
English, London 1857–58
Silver
Gift of Mrs. Roger Shepard, 80.38.1–7

Christening set
George Adams
English, London, 1864
Silver gilt
Gift of the Decorative Arts Council,
81.3.1–5

Tea and coffee service
Gorham Company
American, Providence, Rhode Island,
1883
Silver
Gift of the Decorative Arts Council,
84.87.1–8

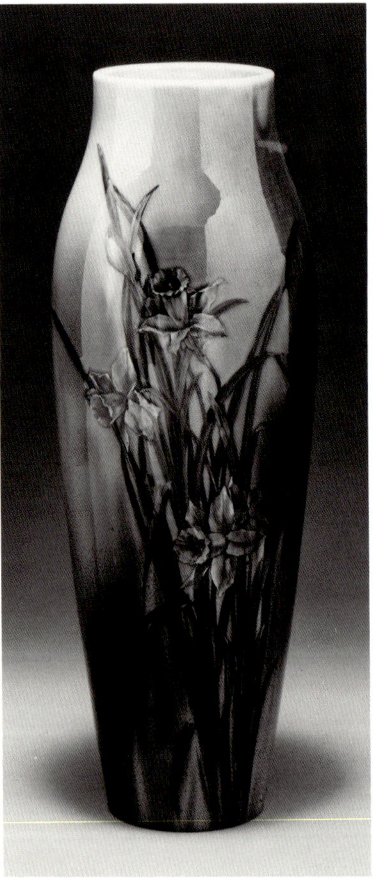

Presentation tray
Tiffany and Company
American, New York, about 1884
Silver
Gift of Mr. and Mrs. G. Richard Slade,
81.5

Coffee pot and tray
Gorham Company
American, Providence, Rhode Island,
1891
Silver
Gift of the Decorative Arts Council,
85.106.1, 2

American Beauty vase
Roycroft Copper Shops
American, East Aurora, New York, about
1912
Hammered copper
The Ethel Morrison Van Derlip Fund,
85.1

Coffee and tea service
Hans Hollein, 1934–
Austrian, 1983
Silver, blue metacrylate handles
Gift of Mr. and Mrs. Sheldon Sturgis and
Mr. Duncan Dayton, 84.86.1–5

CERAMICS

Athenian red-figured volute krater
The Methyse Painter
Greek, 455–450 B.C.
Slip-glazed earthenware
Gift of Mr. and Mrs. Donald C. Dayton,
83.80

Cup, saucer, and cream jug
Chinese exportware, 17th century
Hard-paste porcelain
Gift of Louise F. Drews in memory of
her parents, Mr. and Mrs. Carson
Jamieson, 82.110.1–3

Dish
Attributed to John Simpson
English, 18th century
Lead-glazed earthenware
The Ethel Morrison Van Derlip Fund,
82.79

Goblet
Made by Johann Friedrich Böttger after a
design by Johann Jacob Irminger
German, about 1710–13
Stoneware with silver gilt mounts
Gift of Bruce B. Dayton, 85.37ab

*Three plates showing the Nativity,
Crucifixion, and Resurrection of Christ*
Chinese exportware, 1735–50
Hard-paste porcelain
Gift of Thomas A. Jamieson, 82.45.1–3

Bust of Louis XV
French, Chantilly, about 1750
Soft-paste porcelain
Gift of the Groves Foundation and the
John R. Van Derlip Fund, 83.140

Pair of Vases
French, Vincennes, about 1753
Soft-paste porcelain and gilded bronze
The Groves Fund and gift of the Groves
Foundation, 82.42.1, 2

Cabbage Tureen
French, Strasbourg, before 1754
Porcelain
Gift of Mrs. Christian H. Aall in memory
of her grandparents, Mr. and Mrs. M. J.
Scanlon, 84.85abc

Vase
KATARO SHIRAYAMADANI
Rookwood factory
American, Cincinnati, Ohio, 1890
Earthenware with underglaze daffodil
design
The David Draper Dayton Fund, 84.90

Tea and coffee service
Gorham Company
American, Providence, Rhode Island,
1883
Silver
Gift of the Decorative Arts Council,
84.87.1–8

Vase
Derby Porcelain Factory
English, about 1756
Porcelain, painted and gilded
Gift of the Decorative Arts Council in
memory of Walter Briggs, 84.89

Partial dessert service
English, Staffordshire, 1776–1800
Creamware with printed designs
Gift of Mr. and Mrs. Charles H. Bell,
83.119.1–33

Pair of vases
Sèvres Factory
French, about 1780
Hard-paste porcelain with gilded bronze
mounts
The Groves Fund, 80.36.1, 2ab

*Tea service for twelve with scenes from
the Fables of La Fontaine*
Sèvres Factory
Painted by Christophe-Ferdinand Caron,
1774–1831
French, about 1780
Hard-paste porcelain with gilding
The Groves Fund, 81.101.1–28

Soup tureen with platter
Spode Pottery and Porcelain Factory
English, about 1790–1800
Creamware with enamel decoration
Gift of the Decorative Arts Council,
85.83abc

Pitcher
Factory of William Ellis Tucker; maker
probably Andrew Craig Walker
American, 1826–32
Soft-paste porcelain with enamel and
gilded decoration
The Christina N. and Swan J. Turnblad
Memorial Fund, 81.57

Game pie dish
Minton factory
English, 1877
Lead-glazed earthenware
The David Draper Dayton Fund, 82.78

Vase
KATARO SHIRAYAMADANI
Rookwood factory
American, Cincinnati, Ohio, 1890
Earthenware with underglaze daffodil
design
The David Draper Dayton Fund, 84.90

Vase with two handles
George Ohr, 1857–1918
American, Biloxi, Mississippi, about
1900
Glazed earthenware
Gift of Virginia and Bruce Dayton,
82.112

Bowl
George Ohr, 1857–1918
American, about 1900
Glazed earthenware
Gift of Virginia and Bruce Dayton,
82.111

Vessel
Richard De Vore, 1933–
American, 1979
Stoneware
Gift of Anne Dayton with matching
funds from the National Endowment for
the Arts, 81.27

Untitled
Thom Bohnert, 1948–
American, 1980
Ceramic and metal
Gift from Mr. and Mrs. W. John Driscoll
with matching funds from the National
Endowment for the Arts, 81.25

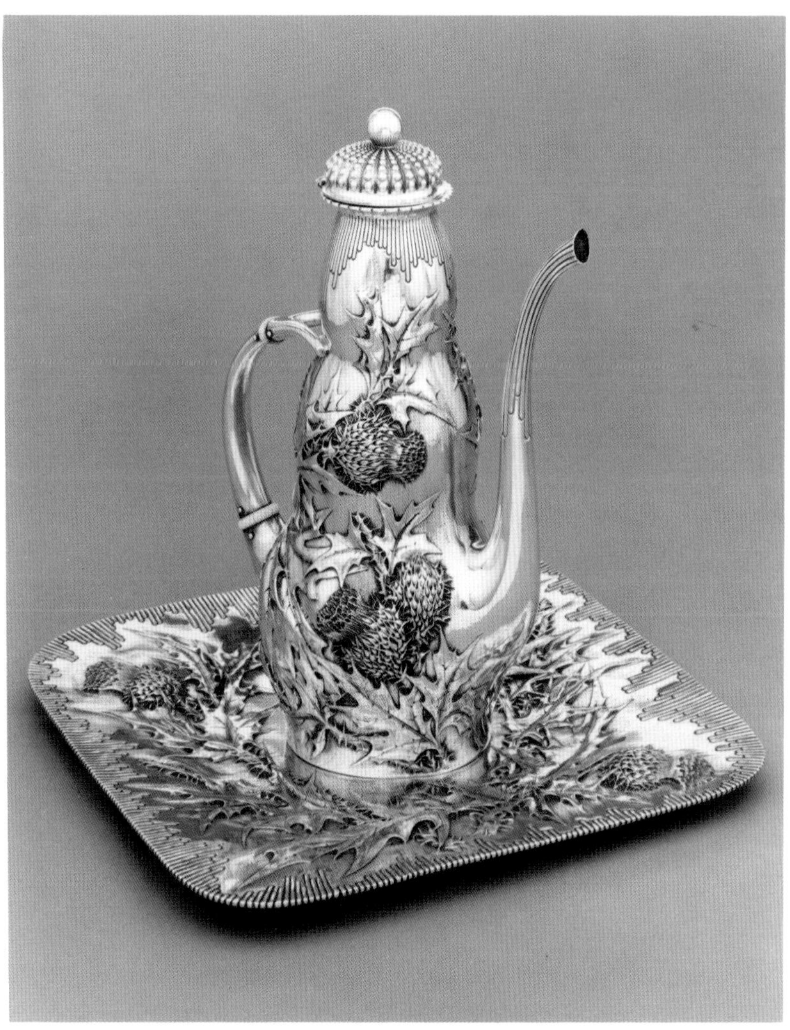

Painted Rocks Canyon
Wayne Higby, 1943–
American, 1981
Glazed raku-fired clay
Gift of Peter and Sandy Butler with
matching funds from the National
Endowment for the Arts, 81.30.1–5ab

Rose
Kenneth Price, 1935–
American, 1981
Porcelain with acrylic and glaze
Gift of Bruce B. Dayton with matching
funds from the National Endowment for
the Arts, 81.31

*Collection of Staffordshire and
European ceramics*
Gift of Mrs. Christian H. Aall in memory
of her grandparents, Mr. and Mrs. M.J.
Scanlon, 84.85.1–15

GLASS

Goblet
Northern European, second half of the
15th century
Colorless lead glass with *latticino*
decoration
Gift of Bruce B. Dayton, 85.15

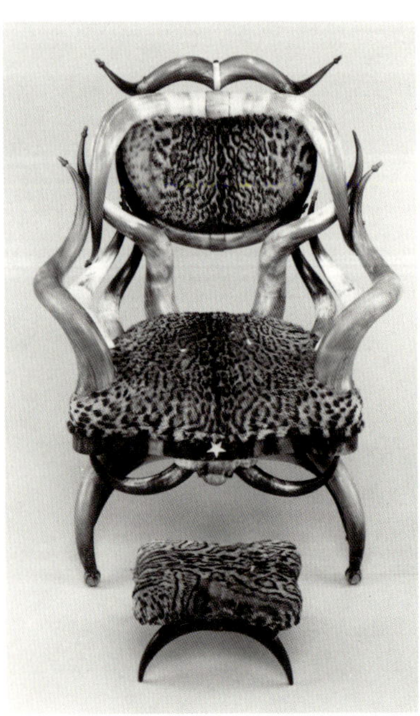

Goblet
Decoration attributed to shop of William
Beilby, 1740–1819 and Mary Beilby,
1749–97
English, Newcastle-on-Tyne, 18th
century
Lead glass with enamel decoration
Gift of the Decorative Arts Council, 85.38

Twelve wine glasses
English, Bristol, 1780–1800
Free-blown green lead glass
Gift of Raleigh L. Morgan, 81.60.1–12

Water, from series of the Four Elements
English, 19th century
Leaded stained glass
The Christina N. and Swan J. Turnblad
Memorial Fund, 81.92

Collection of bottles and dishes
American, Ohio, 19th century
Glass
Gift of three trustees, 84.122.1–159

Hurricane light with smoke bell
American, 1800–20
Free-blown amethyst glass, metal
Gift of Fred R. Salisbury II, 85.16

Bowl
American, New England, 1815–35
Colorless lead glass with applied blue
rim
The David Draper Dayton Fund, 82.76

Two decanters
American, Pittsburgh, 1820–30
Free-blown and engraved lead glass
Gift of the Decorative Arts Council,
83.4.1, 2

Tumblers
American, Pittsburgh, 1830–70
Cobalt blue and amber glass, made with
the use of an 18-rib dip mold
Gift of Mr. and Mrs. Charles DeLaittre,
82.114.1, 2

Pitcher
American, Pittsburgh, 1850–60
Pillar-molded colorless lead glass made
with the use of an eight-rib dip mold
Gift of funds of the Decorative Arts
Council, 82.80

Cruet
American, Pittsburgh, 1850–60
Colbalt blue glass made with the use of
a 16-rib dip mold
Gift of Fred R. Salisbury II, 84.33

WOODWORK

*Principal salon from the Hôtel de
Pomponne*
French, about 1720
Painted and gilded wood, marble, and
iron
Gift of the Groves Foundation, 83.147

MISCELLANEOUS

Toilet Box
South German, possibly Augsburg, about
1740
Horn, gold and glass
Gift of Mrs. Theodora H. Lang and Mrs.
DeWalt H. Ankeny, 85.81

Liquor chest
Spanish or Bohemian, 1780–1800
Oak with iron fittings, glass
Gift of the Decorative Arts Council,
81.59.1–17

Game box
Chinese, 1790–1810
Japanned box containing ivory, mother-
of-pearl, and cowrie shell game counters
Gift of Mr. and Mrs. Wayne H.
MacFarlane, 84.88

FURNITURE

Kas or Zeeuws cupboard
Dutch, 1648
Oak, inlaid with various woods
Gift of K. Waterman in honor of George
Keyes, 83.143

Center table
Johann Daniel Sommer, 1643–after 1685
German, Künselsau, about 1680
Marquetry of tortoiseshell, brass, pewter,
hardstone, ebony, horn, and
mother-of-pearl
Gift of funds from Mr. and Mrs. Atherton
Bean and the John R. Van Derlip Fund,
80.55

Commode
Pierre-Antoine Foullet, master in 1765
French, 18th century
Kingwood marquetry with gilded bronze
mounts
Gift of the Groves Foundation, 82.1

Set of eight fauteuils
Jean-Baptiste Lebas, master in 1756
French, 18th century
Gilded wood with upholstered arm rests,
backs, and seats
Gift of the Groves Foundation,
83.118.1–8

Platform rocker with stool
Wenzel Friedrich (b. Czechoslovakia),
1827–1902
American, San Antonio, Texas, about
1880–90
Horn, ocelot upholstery, ivory
The Fiduciary Fund, 84.4ab

Side chair
Frank Lloyd Wright, 1867–1959
American, from the Francis Little House,
Peoria, Illinois, about 1903
Oak
Gift of Mr. and Mrs. Sheldon Sturgis,
85.82

Mirror
Italian, probably Roman, about 1700
Ebonized and parcel-gilded wood
The John R. Van Derlip Fund, 84.30

Highboy
American, probably Boston, 1730–40
Maple, burl walnut veneer, and white
pine secondary wood
The Driscoll and Julia Bigelow Funds,
84.52

Clock
Attributed to Charles Cressent,
1685–1769
French, Paris, about 1735
Gilded bronze and boulle marquetry
Gift of the Groves Foundation, 80.1a–d

Kas
Roeloeff Demarest
American, New York, Hudson Valley
about 1740–60
Sweet gum and poplar
The Putnam Dana McMillan Fund,
81.3

Bureau bookcase
English, about 1745
Mahogany and secondary woods
Gift of the Groves Foundation,
81.103.1ab

Side chair
Portuguese, about 1750
Rosewood
The Ethel Morrison Van Derlip Fund,
84.51

Bureau de dame
Jean Gaspard Feilt, master about 1750
French, about 1750
Kingwood with marquetry and gilded
bronze mounts
Gift of the Groves Foundation, 80.35

Two armchairs
English, about 1755
Mahogany
Gift of the Groves Foundation,
83.99.1, 2

Pair of encoignures (corner chests)
J. Stumpff, 1732–1806
French, Paris, 1760
Kingwood with gilded bronze mounts,
marble tops
Gift of the Groves Foundation,
80.2.1, 2ab

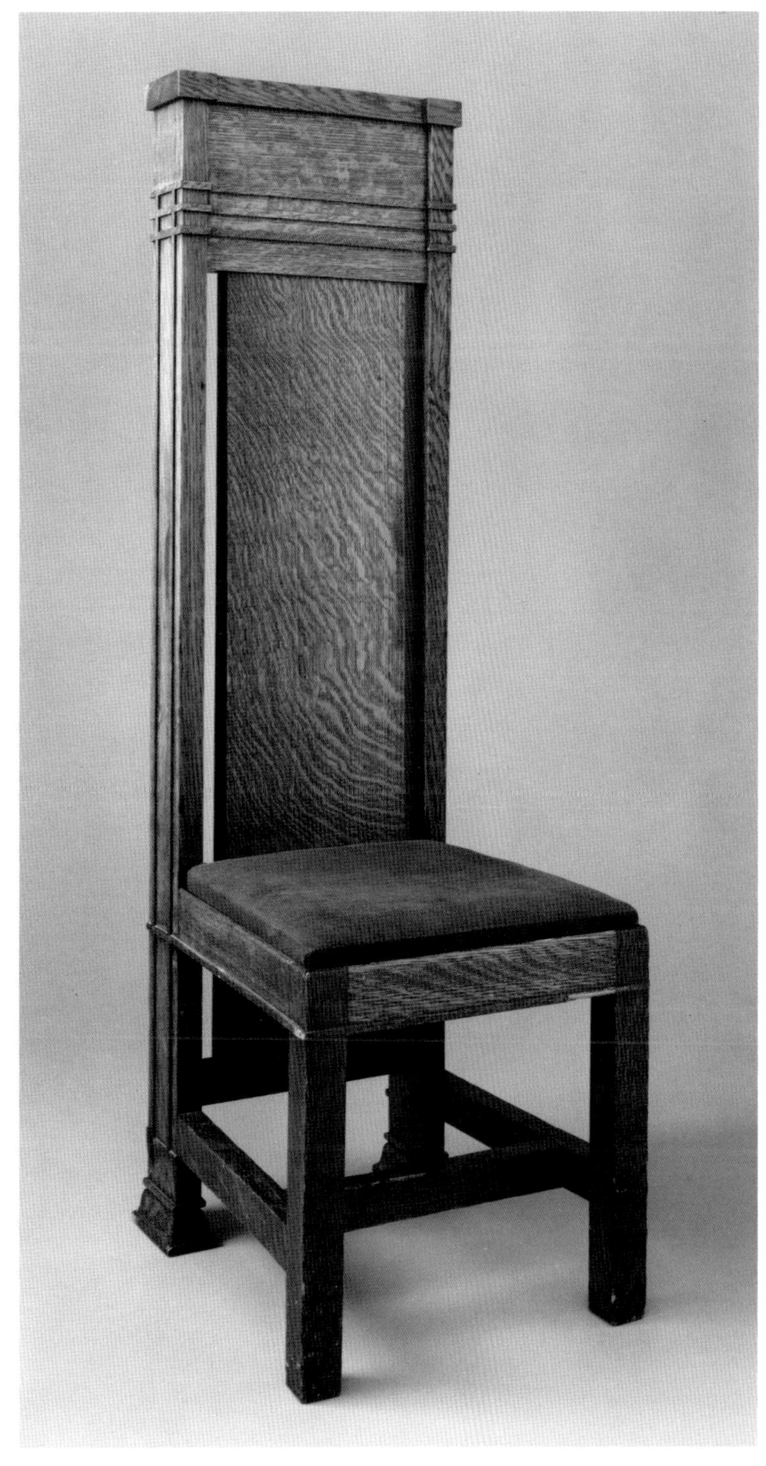

Pair of side chairs
Possibly by William Gordon, active
1754–79, and John Taitt,
active 1768–99
English, London, about 1772
Gilded beech
Gift of the Groves Foundation,
81.103.2.1, 2

Pair of chairs
Henri Jacob, 1753–1824
French, Paris, about 1780
Gilded wood
Gift of the Groves Foundation,
83.145.1, 2

Linen press
Attributed to Samuel Loomis, 1748–1814
American, Connecticut, 1775–90
Cherry; white pine, and tulip poplar
secondary woods
Gift of Carroll Simmons and the William
Hood Dunwoody Fund, 85.84

Set of four fauteuils
Jean-Baptiste-Claude Sené, master in
1769–1803
French, about 1785
Gilded wood
Gift of the Groves Foundation,
83.146.1–4

Clock
Attributed to Pierre-Philippe Thomire,
1751–1843
French, Paris, about 1790
Marble, bronze, and gilded bronze
Gift of the Groves Foundation, 82.25

Card table
American, Boston, about 1790–1800
Mahogany, satinwood veneers; pine,
maple and secondary woods
Gift of funds of Mr. and Mrs. Wayne H.
MacFarlane, 84.3.2

Fauteuil
George Jacob, 1739–1814
French, Paris, about 1796
Mahogany
The Groves Fund, 81.102

Pair of side chairs
Attributed to Stephen Badlam,
1751–1815
American, about 1800
Mahogany
Gift of Mr. and Mrs. Wayne H.
MacFarlane, 83.78.1, 2

Secretary desk and bookcase
Jacob Sanderson, active 1779–1810
American, Salem, Massachusetts, about
1800
Mahogany; white pine secondary wood
Gift of Mrs. Allyn K. Ford, 83.144

Side chair
American, Rhode Island, about 1800
Mahogany; red oak and birch secondary
woods
Gift of funds from Mr. and Mrs. Wayne
H. MacFarlane, 85.17

Side chair
American, Rhode Island, about 1800
Mahogany; pine and maple secondary
woods
Gift of funds of Mr. and Mrs. Wayne H.
MacFarlane, 84.3.1

Easy chair
Moses Grant
American, Boston, 1808
Mahogany, white pine secondary wood
The MacFarlane Memorial Period Room
Fund, 83.100

Sofa
Possibly from the shop of Charles
Honoré Lannuier, 1779–1819
American, New York, 1815–25
Mahogany, pine, maple, and ash
The William Hood Dunwoody Fund and
gifts from Harry McC. Drake,
Mr. and Mrs. Charles Bell, the James
Ford Bell Foundation, Mrs. John Roller,
and Mrs. Peter Anson, 82.75

Chest of drawers
American, Philadelphia, about 1825
Bird's-eye and tiger maple, pine and
tulip secondary woods
The Christina N. and Swan J. Turnblad
Memorial Fund, 80.56.1

Pair of side chairs
American, probably Philadelphia, about
1825
Bird's-eye and tiger maple
The Christina N. and Swan J. Turnblad
Memorial Fund, 80.56.2.1, 2

Two armchairs
Pelagio Palagi, 1775–1860
Italian, 1835
Satinwood
The John R. Van Derlip Fund

Slipper chair
John Henry Belter, 1804–63
American, New York, 1850–60
Laminated rosewood
Gift of Carroll B. Simmons, 84.21

Arm chair and pair of side chairs
American, probably Albany, New York,
1850–60
Rosewood and secondary wood
Gift of Mr. and Mrs. Merrill H. Gibbs,
82.6.1–3

Etagère
Attributed to the firm of J. and J. W.
Meeks
American, New York, 1855–60
Rosewood
Gift of a friend of the Decorative Arts
Council, the Decorative Arts Council,
and the William Hood Dunwoody Fund,
82.41

Platform rocker with stool
Wenzel Friedrich (b. Czechoslovakia),
1827–1902
American, San Antonio, Texas, about
1880–90
Horn, ocelot upholstery, ivory
The Fiduciary Fund, 84.4ab

Easy chair
Frank Lloyd Wright, 1867–1959
American, from the Francis Little House,
Peoria, Illinois, about 1903
Oak
Gift of Ruth L. and Walter Swardenski,
85.39

Side chair
Frank Lloyd Wright, 1867–1959
American, from the Francis Little House,
Peoria, Illinois, about 1903
Oak
Gift of Mr. and Mrs. Sheldon Sturgis,
85.82

A group of furniture and decorative arts
John Bradstreet, 1845–1914
American, from the Prindle House,
Duluth, Minnesota, about 1905
Cypress wood
Gift of Wheaton Wood, 82.43.1–57

Side chair
Charles Greene, 1868–1957, and Henry
Greene 1870–1957
American, from the Robert Blacker
House, Pasadena, California, 1907
Honduras mahogany, ebony, brass
The Putnam Dana McMillan Fund, 83.1

JONATHAN BOROFSKY
American, 1942–
Hammering Man, 1981
Wood and metal
Gift of funds from the Regis
Corporation, the Aimee Mott Butler
Foundation and the Christina N. and
Swan J. Turnblad Fund. 84.120

ALEXANDER CALDER
American, 1898–1976
Ahab, 1953 (detail)
Painted metal
Gift of Bruce B. Dayton and Mr. and
Mrs. Gerald A. Erickson, by exchange,
83.77

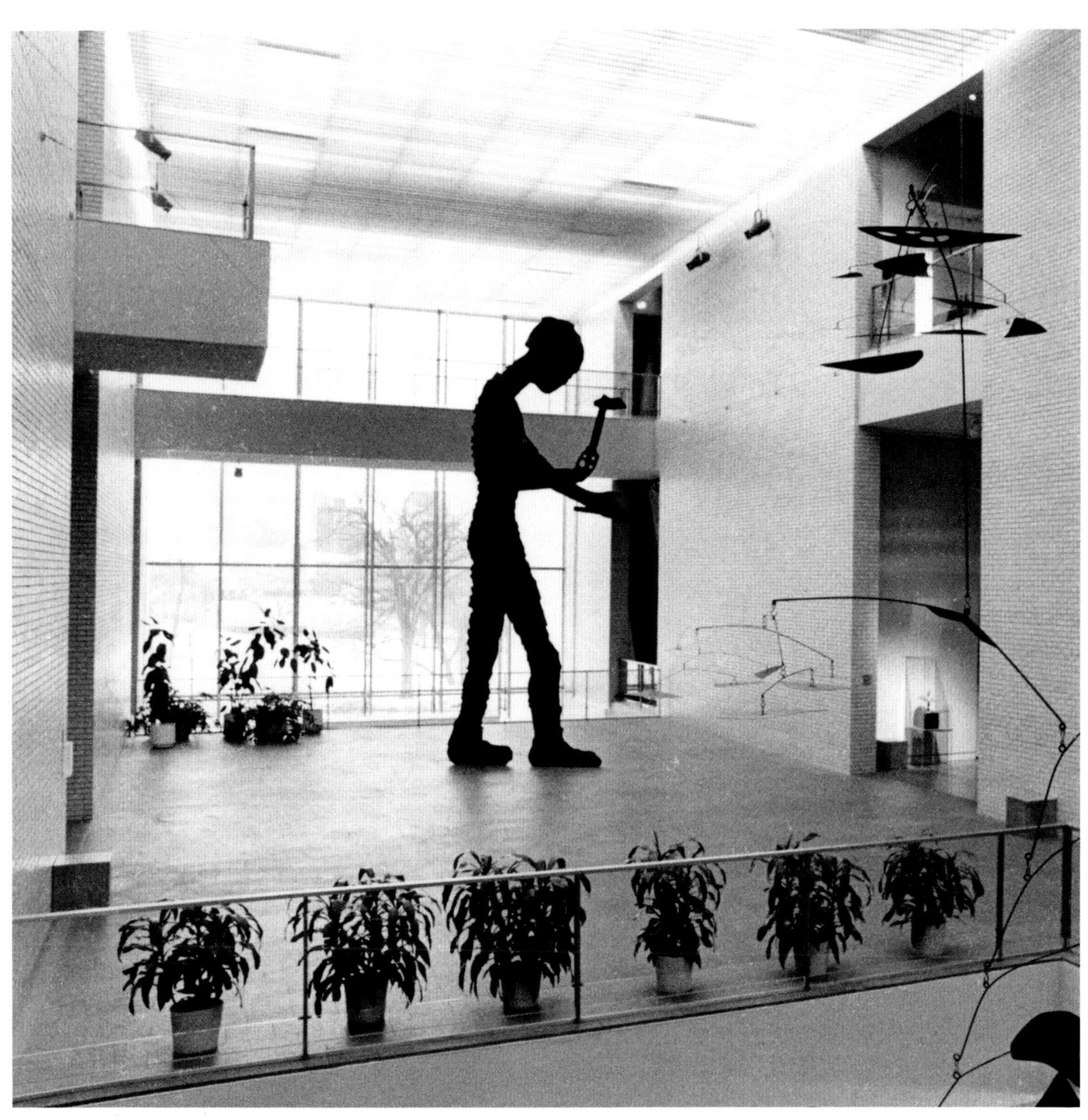

Department of

P A I N T I N G S

An American civic art museum such as The Minneapolis Institute of Arts attempts to provide an encyclopedic survey of the artistic traditions of Western and non-Western cultures. In Minneapolis, this goal was set by the first director, Joseph H. Breck (1914-17). Breck had been at the Metropolitan Museum of Art as curatorial assistant to Wilhelm Valentiner, who in turn had trained under Wilhelm von Bode, director of the Prussian State museums in Berlin, a leading authority on Italian Renaissance art, and the foremost museum director of his generation. From Valentiner, Breck adopted Bode's approach to encyclopedic museum collecting, and the policies Breck established in Minneapolis were carried out by Russell Plimpton during his long tenure as director (1921-56).

The origins of the paintings collection, however, go back even earlier. The railroad magnate James J. Hill had assembled a large and distinguished collection of French nineteenth-century romantic and realist paintings which included masterpieces by Corot, Courbet, Delacroix, and Millet. Although Hill himself presented but a single painting from his collection to The Minneapolis Institute of Arts (Courbet's splendid *Deer in the Forest*), many of the paintings in his collection have been bequeathed or given to the museum by his descendants. As a result, Minneapolis is particularly strong in French painting from about 1830 to 1865 and ranks as one of the richest museums in the country in this area of nineteenth-century European painting.

Hill's remarkable collection informed the taste of other Minnesota collectors. Not only did they buy Barbizon and French realist paintings, but certain collectors, like T. B. Walker, acquired American nineteenth-century landscapes that were a further reflection of the community's interest in the realist tradition. An appreciation of contemporary turn-of-the-century American paintings was fanned by the directors of the Society of Fine Arts's art school, Douglas Volk and Robert Koehler. Some of the earliest American paintings in our collection were impressionist pictures such as those that formed the Martin B. Koon Memorial Collection, e.g. John Twachtman's *White Bridge* and Childe Hassam's *Isle of Shoals.* With this local appreciation for contemporary or nearly contemporary French and American works, it is not surprising that the first painting purchased by the museum, in 1915, was Eugène Boudin's *On the Beach at Trouville* of 1860, which constituted one of the earliest acquisitions by an American museum in the field of French *plein-air* painting.

The Minnesota collections mentioned above helped to form the foundation of the museum's collection upon which Russell Plimpton subsequently built. Following the example of the great German museums, and their American counterparts already established in New York, Boston, and Philadelphia, Plimpton began assembling comprehensive collections. His interest in American painting, however, related almost exclusively to the museum's period rooms, which were installed during his directorship. This focus had two fateful consequences. First, since all the American period rooms belonged to the eighteenth century, Plimpton did not buy American paintings of the nineteenth and early twentieth centuries at a time when they could have been purchased for a modest outlay. And secondly, the pictures acquired for these eighteenth-century rooms were, for the most part, undistinguished portraits.

Plimpton devoted far more energy to the European schools, making acquisitions in all areas. He was especially interested in Italian gold-ground pictures of the fourteenth and fifteenth centuries and in Dutch seventeenth-century and French and English nineteenth-century masters. His aim in buying was to obtain a wide range of pictorial types and subjects highlighted by a small number of masterpieces. Thus in 1924 he acquired El

JACOPO TINTORETTO
Italian, 1518–94
The Raising of Lazarus, about 1558–59
Oil on canvas
Gift of an anonymous donor, 83.74

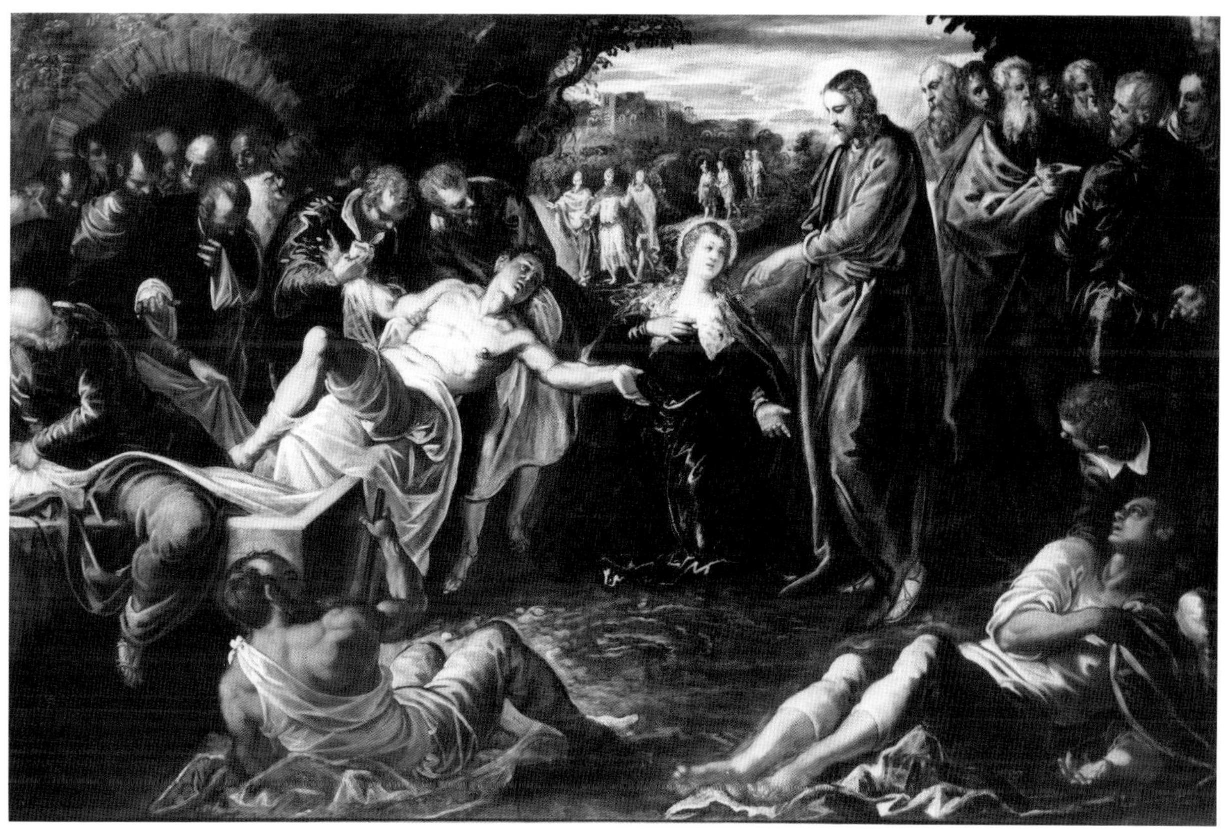

Greco's *Christ Driving the Money Changers from the Temple.* He bought paintings by Pieter Claesz, Bartolomeus van der Helst, Meindert Hobbema, Salomon van Ruysdael, Peter Paul Rubens, and Gustave Courbet. And, late in his directorship, he acquired Goya's *Self-Portrait with Dr. Arrieta* and Chardin's *Attributes of the Arts.* Several notable late nineteenth- and early twentieth-century French paintings also entered the Institute's collection during Plimpton's last years as director—our pictures by Cézanne, Delaunay, Seurat, and Van Gogh; Gauguin's *Tahitian Landscape*; Léger's *Table and Fruit*; and Matisse's *Boy with Butterfly Net* and *White Plumes.*

Plimpton stressed breadth rather than depth when adding to the collection. For him, the major challenge was to secure a single characteristic example of a given master's work. With this philosophy and the modest scale of private collecting in the Twin Cities, the Institute would not assemble multiple holdings of Old Masters like Van Dyck, Rembrandt, or Rubens, or the great French impressionist and post-impressionist painters, who are often abundantly represented in the museum collections of larger American cities.

In striving to be encyclopedic, Plimpton sought to buy works by the most important artists in the history of art. Like the acquisitions of many museums of the time, some of his purchases associated with famous names—the Master of Flemalle, Van Goyen, Murillo, Palma Vecchio, Parmigianino, Ruisdael, Tiepolo, Veronese, Wilson, and Zurbaran—unfortunately bore optimistic attributions, however. Others were either modest examples by well-known artists or pictures whose condition presented serious problems. Among the latter was Titian's *Temptation of Christ*, acquired in 1925. This work proved to be Plimpton's most controversial purchase, and its position within Titian's oeuvre is still a subject of lively debate. The documents pertaining to its acquisition reveal his concern over what the

authorities of the time, including Bode in Berlin, thought of this painting. Despite the approbation of Plimpton's informed colleagues, the Titian caused some controversy in the United States press and prompted an article in the *New York Herald Tribune* that may have discouraged Plimpton from making comparable forays into the marketplace for other celebrated Old Masters.

Russell Plimpton was succeeded as director by his chief curator, Richard Davis (1956-59), whose main interest was European paintings, especially of the late nineteenth and twentieth centuries. The most controversial personality ever associated with The Minneapolis Institute of Arts, Davis radically redirected the aims of the museum with regard to acquisitions. He saw the need to secure masterpieces for the permanent collection, and his buying program gave the collection a stamp of quality with idiosyncrasies that are evident to this day. Selecting areas of European painting that were progressive, that were not fully understood in the United States, that were undervalued—late Monet, pointillism, fauvism, and German and Austrian expressionism—Davis bought aggressively and well, and he cultivated a group of private collectors, including John Cowles, Putnam Dana McMillan, Samuel Maslon, and Donald Winston, whose munificent gifts have tremendously enhanced the museum's collection.

For Davis, the aesthetic quality and effect of the individual work was paramount. In his quest for masterpieces, he rejected Plimpton's policy of gathering a wide range of representative pictorial types and saw no need to retain paintings in the collection that did not meet his own rigorous aesthetic standards. Having persuaded like-minded trustees to support this position, he instituted an ambitious deaccessioning policy that unraveled the character of the collection as developed by Plimpton. In many fields of the museum Davis's aggressive deaccessioning was unfortunate, but in adding to the collection he

JAN VAN GOYEN
Dutch, 1596–1656
*River Landscape (Pellekussenpoort near
Utrecht),* 1648
Oil on panel
Gift of Bruce B. Dayton, 83.84

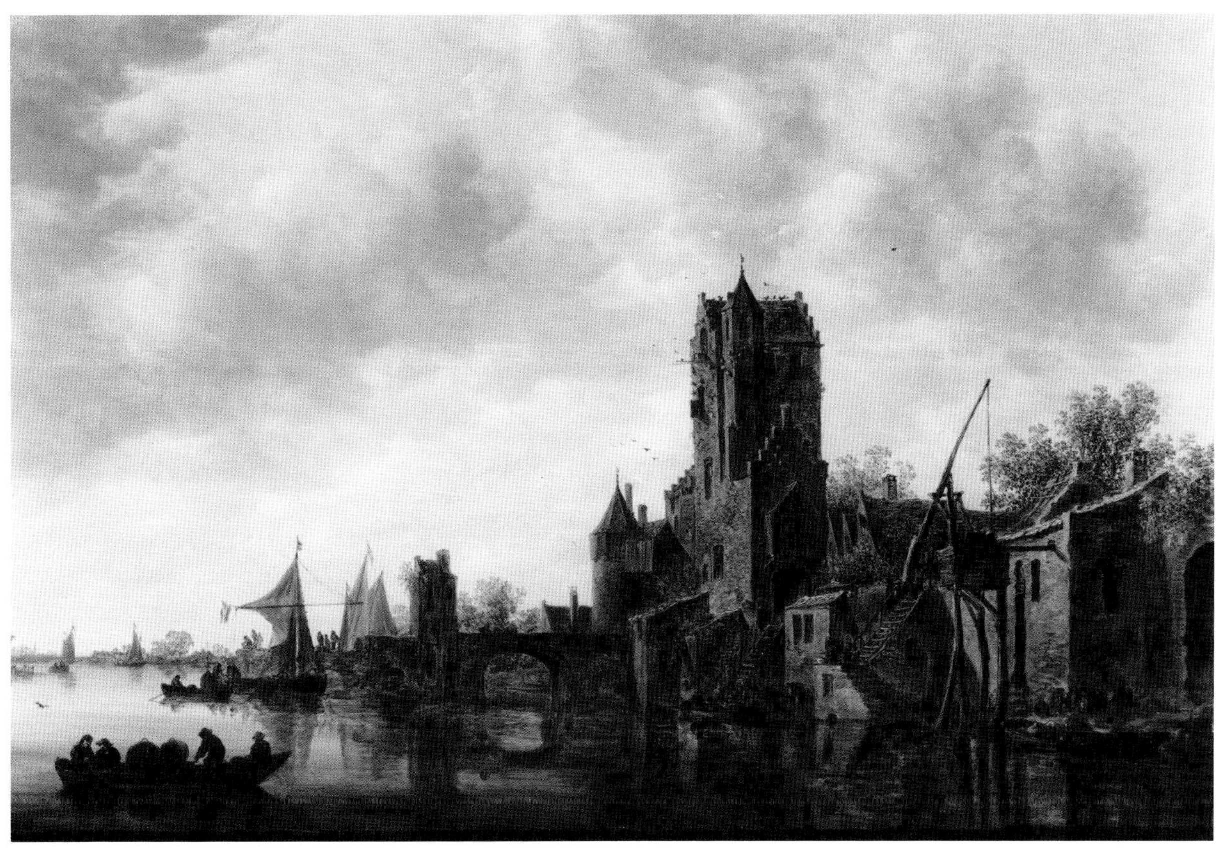

59

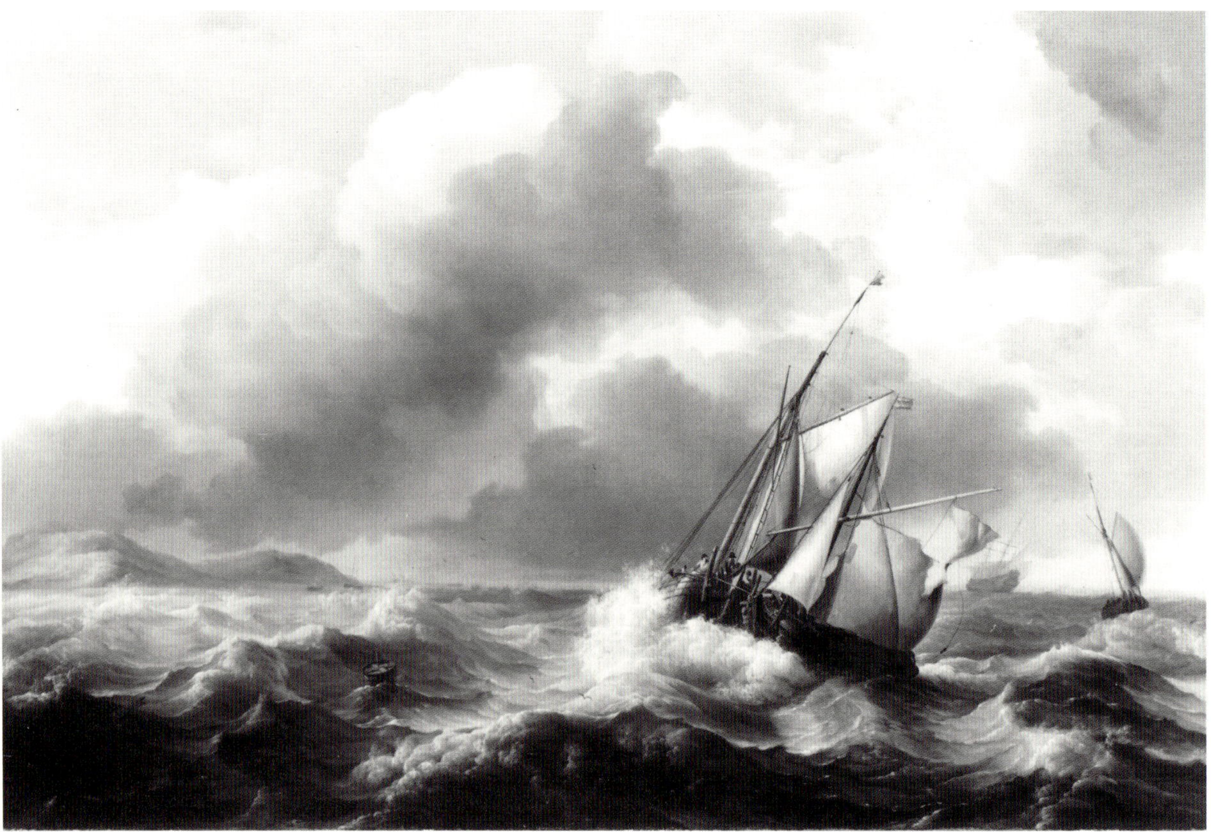

acquired objects of major significance, objects that are now recognized as some of the Institute's finest works of art.

Following the brief tenure of Carl Weinhardt, Jr. (1961-63), the next director, Anthony M. Clark (1963-73), pursued a policy of museum growth that was both distinguished and personal. Clark was attracted by the last great epoch of Italian art—the late seventeenth and eighteenth centuries, particularly in Rome, Naples, Turin, and central Italy, but excluding Venice. He recognized the importance of this art before it was commonly accepted and before it became fashionable on the art market.

In buying against the art market, Clark embraced not only later Italian painting and decorative arts but also neoclassical painting in Europe and nineteenth-century sculpture. For small sums of money he was able to assemble a sizable and representative collection of Italian baroque painting capped by several outstanding accessions: the Castiglione and the Cortona, to name two. He also acquired major Italian baroque pictures to replace comparable examples by Guido Reni and Guercino sold from the collection during the previous decade. The Prud'hon, the Girodet-Trioson, and the Thorvaldsen, all purchased by Clark, form the core of our small but choice neoclassical collection.

Samuel Sachs II (1974-85) pursued a similar policy as director, in seeking major accessions. Sachs, like Clark, chose to buy against the market, acquiring in areas unfashionable at the time, but now highly valued. Certain aspects of impressionism, French academic painting, and British nineteenth-century Olympian and Pre-Raphaelite work are now represented by notable examples by Bazille, Caillebotte, Balthus, Tissot, Millais, and Lord Leighton.

The history of the paintings collection includes some turbulent chapters and abrupt shifts in policy. It is history marked by great passion and deeply held convictions — indicators of a vitality that continues to the present day. Against this background I shall try to elucidate my own philosophy of buying, relating it to the permanent collection as it exists after more than seventy years of history.

Of course, the aim of the department of paintings is to secure works of art that illustrate the diversity of European and American painting with objects whose qualities as masterpieces stimulate the imagination and satisfy the intellect. Currently it is fashionable to interpret museum objects principally as artifacts, but this approach fails to address the broader issue of the museum as a public repository offering inspiration to the viewer seeking the beauty as well as the meaning of artistic achievement. The visual arts are a powerful means of transmitting aesthetic ideas from one generation to another and of maintaining the past as a living experience. For this reason, The Minneapolis Institute of Arts must continue to add paintings of consummate beauty and intellectual substance to its already distinguished collection. Each acquisition must excite interest by meeting the highest aesthetic standards, and must be in the best possible condition.

During the past three years, we have focused on acquiring seventeenth-century paintings, for several reasons. Under the directorship of Anthony Clark, The Minneapolis Institute of Arts concentrated on buying in the Italian school of the seventeenth and eighteenth centuries, and this attention to later Italian painting overlooked opportunities for acquisitions in the Northern

European schools. First-rate Dutch and Flemish seventeenth-century paintings are still available on the art market, providing an excellent opportunity to build a truly distinguished and representative holding. Through the generosity of the museum's greatest benefactor, Bruce Dayton, The Minneapolis Institute of Arts acquired Jan van Goyen's *River Landscape*, one of the most important and best-preserved Dutch landscape paintings in North America. In 1981 Mrs. Charles Sweatt gave a one-half interest in her magnificent painting by Philips Wouwerman, *Festive Peasants before a Panorama*. A significant example of a landscape replete with genre elements, this is generally considered the finest work by Wouwerman in North America. Mrs. Sweatt also gave the Institute Pieter de Hooch's *Asparagus Vendor*, a work from the artist's later years.

The Minneapolis Institute of Arts also has been able to enrich its holdings of Dutch seventeenth-century paintings by upgrading the collection. Using funds principally from the deaccessioning and sale of twenty-five paintings by the British marine painter Montague Dawson, we bought two major marine paintings, strikingly different from one another, by Ludolph Backhuysen and Abraham Storck. Backhuysen's exhilarating depiction of storm-tossed seas under a dramatic cloud canopy is the essence of exuberant baroque art, whereas Storck's naval battle captures the intensity and fury of an event that shaped the course of European history. In our collection of European paintings, *Four Days' Battle* is the earliest representation of a famous event contemporary with the artist.

The Institute has upgraded its collection by trading certain works towards others of better and more appropriate quality. We possess one of Meindert Hobbema's masterpieces, *Wooded Landscape with a Watermill*, and we also owned a second landscape by Hobbema which had a condition problem and was not of museum quality. The department sold this unexhibitable work at public auction and put the substantial proceeds toward the early seventeenth-century *Landscape with a Courtly Procession* of 1619 by Esaias van de Velde, one of the pioneers of Dutch landscape realism.

While the Institute has recently concentrated on seventeenth-century Dutch works, it has not overlooked its obligations in other fields. Fulfilling these responsibilities has been difficult, however. We lack a major fifteenth-century Tuscan panel painting, and although we have searched for an appropriate example, their rarity may preclude our ever securing a picture of the requisite quality. Important works of the fifteenth-century Netherlandish and German schools are also hardly available, but the Institute should acquire selected sixteenth-century Flemish and German

pictures, which though scarce and expensive are still to be had. In 1982 the museum did obtain an excellent example of gold-ground Swabian painting, the charming *Elevation of the Magdalene* by the Master of Messkirch (lately identified as Peter Strüb the Younger).

Until recently the museum lacked an important Venetian sixteenth-century mannerist painting, and Tintoretto's *Raising of Lazarus*, datable to the later 1550s, fills a huge lacuna. It is a bold and wonderful example of the *alla prima* oil painting technique for which the Venetian artists of the cinquecento were renowned. Moreover, its mannerist composition and strident Roman Catholic Counter-Reformation subject matter express the intellectual ferment of sixteenth-century Europe with extraordinary power.

While we already have mentioned a number of

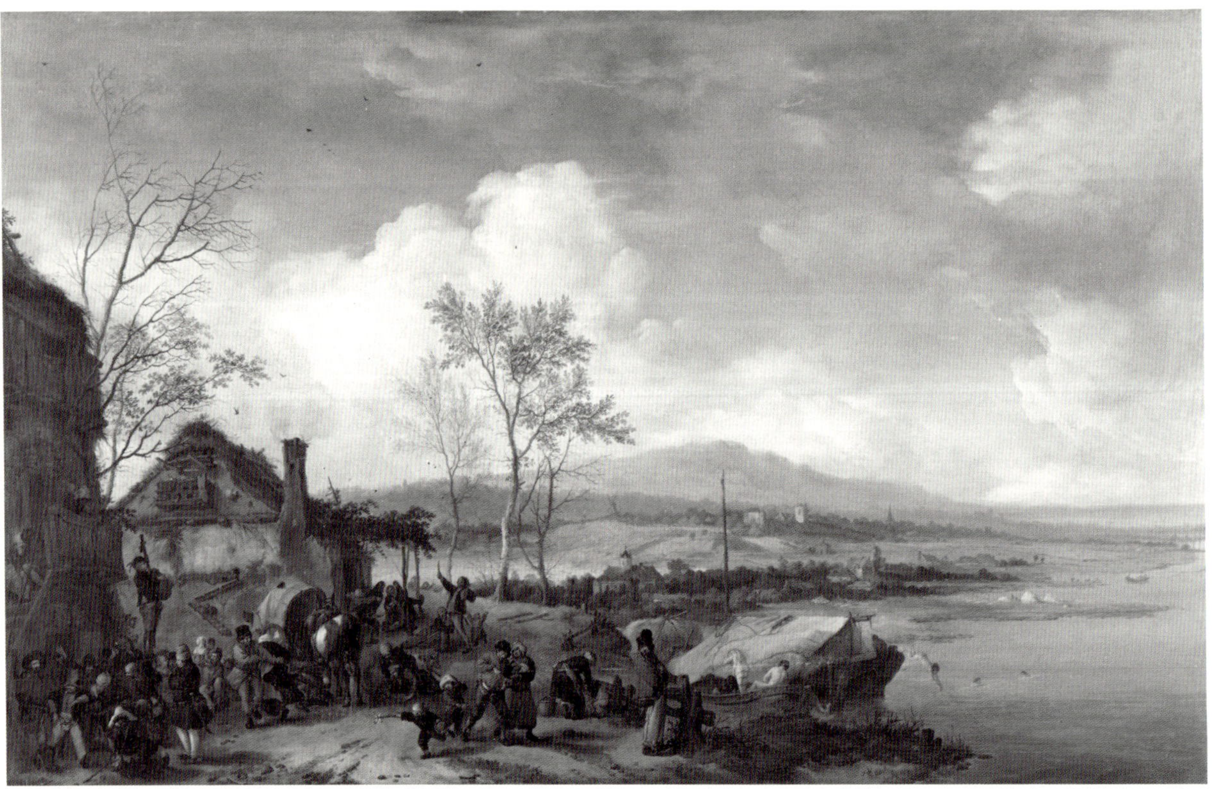

PHILIPS WOUWERMAN
Dutch, 1619–68
Festive Peasants before a Panorama,
1653
Oil on canvas
Gift of Margaret L. Sweatt, 81.107

ABRAHAM STORCK
Dutch, 1635–1710?
The Four Days' Battle, 1666
Oil on canvas
Gift of John B. Hawley, by exchange,
the Walter H. and Valborg P. Ude
Memorial Fund, the Christina N. and
Swan J. Turnblad Memorial Fund, and
the Ethel Morrison Van Derlip Fund,
84.31

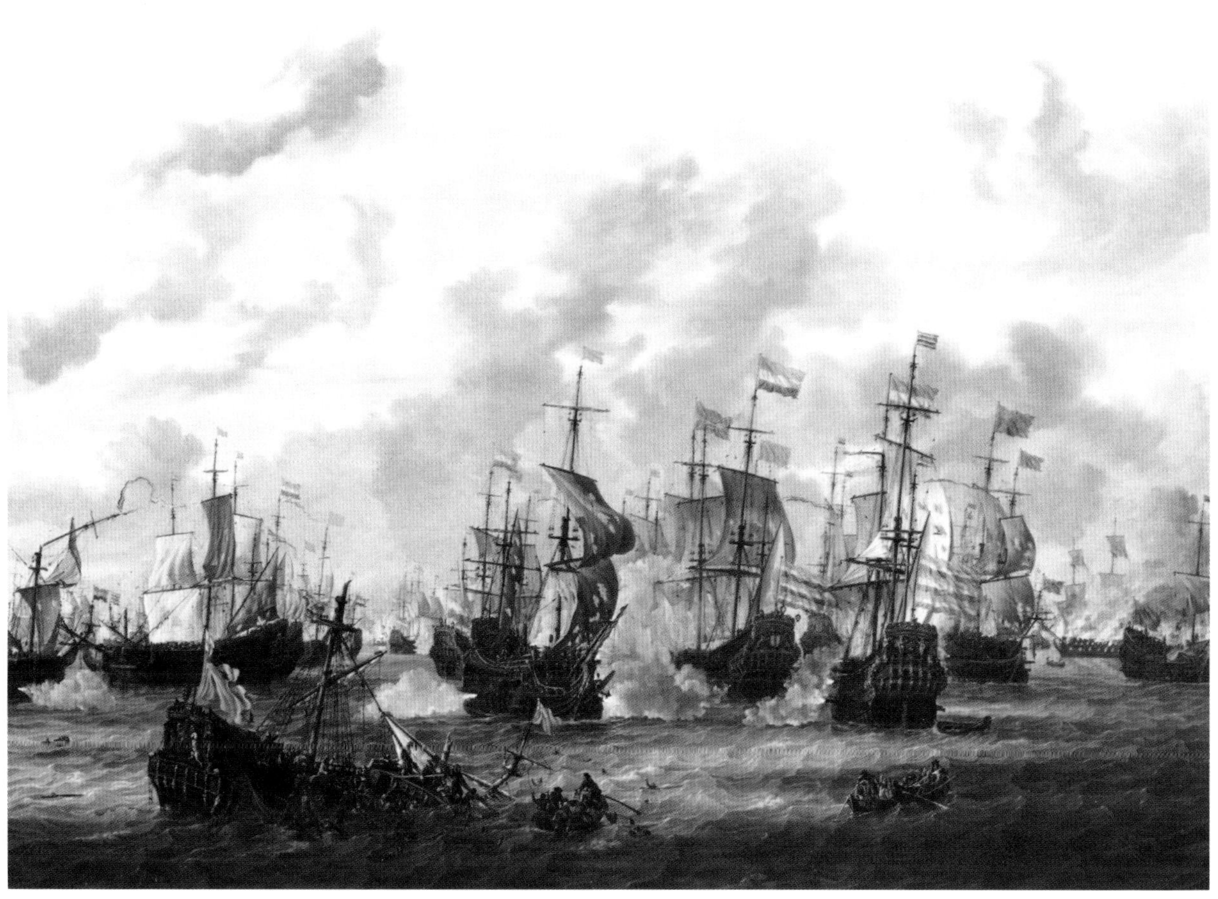

Dutch baroque painting acquisitions, many gaps remain in the seventeenth-century collection. Major paintings are fortunately still available, but our needs are significant. We lack a landscape by Claude Lorrain, a French Caravaggesque subject, and a large-scale French classicizing devotional painting. We have no Flemish still-lifes or portraits and do not own a work by Jacob Jordaens. The Spanish school of the seventeenth century also is thinly represented. However, *The Penitent Magdalene* by Bartolomé Esteban Murillo, one of the masters of the golden age of Spanish painting, was purchased recently with funds provided by Bergmann Richards.

In general the eighteenth century requires a great deal of attention. The French school is highlighted by a notable selection of neoclassical paintings, the finest of them bought by Anthony Clark. But the museum lacks an early eighteenth-century *fête galante* subject, and the European rococo style is poorly represented. We have, for example, no major works by Gianbattista Tiepolo or his school. In 1985 we were able to add a late eighteenth-century English work, a characteristic nocturnal landscape by Joseph Wright of Derby. This is a welcome addition to the collection of British pictures.

One of the Institute's great strengths is French

romantic and realist paintings of the nineteenth century, largely from the extraordinary collection assembled by James J. Hill almost a century ago. Many of Hill's descendants have given the museum works from his collection, with the result that we now boast a formidable array of major paintings by Corot, Diaz, Dupré, Delacroix, Fromentin, Millet, Rousseau, and Troyon. Miss Mary Boeckmann and Mrs. Peter ffolliott, two of Hill's descendants, have enriched our nineteenth-century holdings with gifts of Théodore Rousseau's *Path in a Forest (St. Jean de Paris)* and the first painting by Frits Thaulow to enter the collection. Our collection of French impressionists has always lacked a Monet of the 1870s or '80s, but in 1984 Mrs. Anne Pierce Rogers presented a rare and distinguished Claude Monet *Still-Life with Pheasants and Plovers*, an extraordinarily beautiful and unusual work by this artist.

Georges Braque's *Viaduct at L'Estaque* of 1907, a seminal picture documenting the transition from fauvism to early cubism, has been the greatest single addition to the twentieth-century European collection. Surrealism is not well represented in the museum, but Salvador Dali's *Portrait of Juan de Pareja*, a recent gift from Mrs. John Pillsbury, Sr., is an important addition in this early twentieth-century field. Our significant collection of early German expressionism has been enhanced by the addition of E. L. Kirchner's *Dance Training*, given in 1980 by Mrs. Charles Meech. In the area of American painting, where we have many needs, we recently purchased two important twentieth-century works: Georgia O'Keeffe's *City Night* and Grant Wood's *Birthplace of Herbert Hoover*, the latter owned jointly with the Des Moines Art Center.

We are all aware that the widespread interest in art has become a fashionable preoccupation of the late twentieth century. Sensational blockbuster exhibitions and the public's fascination with the astronomical prices paid for master-pieces, publicized by auction houses and the popular press, focus attention on the art world without addressing fundamental aesthetic issues. While the excitement in the press has generated public interest in art, the meaning of art and its role in the tradition of Western culture remain elusive. Art has the capacity to transmit the aesthetic values of a culture from one generation to another. It presents profound insights into the artistic intellect and creativity of past civilizations. One of the important functions of a museum like The Minneapolis Institute of Arts is to continue to reinforce a public awareness that the value of art is eternal and transcends the bounds of financial sensationalism and fashion. Through the masterworks in a museum's collection we can inspire an awareness of the value of art in our culture. The curator's and trustee's primary responsibility is to continue to acquire such works, works which will remain the ultimate gauge of the museum's greatness.

George S. Keyes
Curator of Paintings

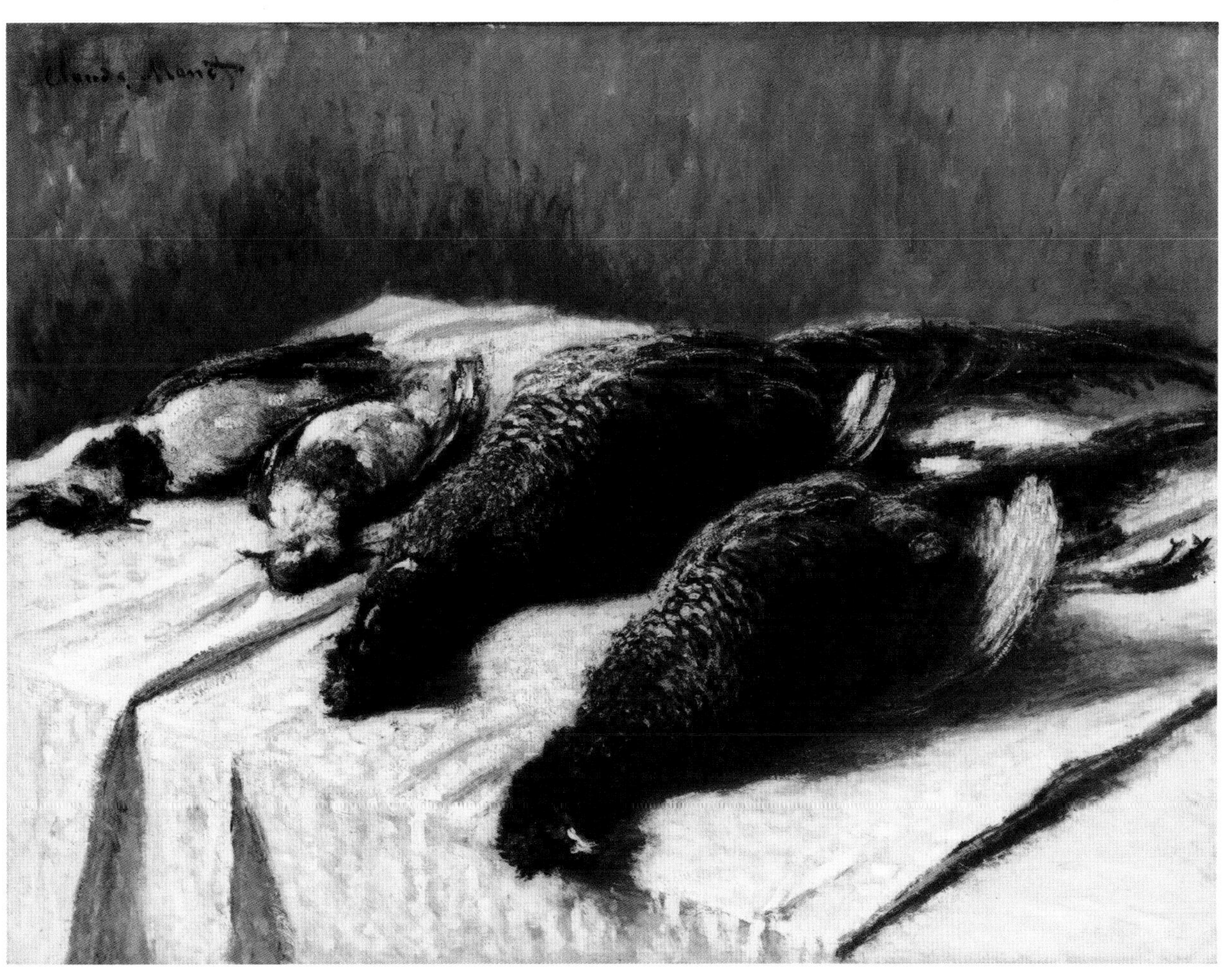

CLAUDE MONET
French, 1840–1926
Still Life with Pheasants and Plovers,
1879
Oil on canvas
Given by Anne Pierce Rogers in
memory of John DeCoster Rogers,
84.140

Department of

PAINTINGS

LUDOLPH BACKHUYSEN
Dutch, 1631–1708
Fishing Vessels Offshore in a Heavy Sea,
1684
Oil on canvas
Gift of John Hawley, by exchange, 82.84

ALBERT BIERSTADT
American, 1830–1902
The Merced River in Yosemite, 1868
Oil on canvas
Given in memory of Douglas Atherton
Bean, 81.6

CAMERON BOOTH
American, 1892–1980
Sombrous #4, 1959
Oil on canvas
Estate of Mrs. Cameron Booth, 84.54

GEORGES BRAQUE
French, 1882–1963
The Viaduct at L'Estaque, 1907
Oil on canvas
The John R. Van Derlip Fund, the
Fiduciary Fund and gift of funds from
Mr. and Mrs. Patrick Butler and various
donors, 82.22

EANGER IRVING COUSE
American, 1866–1936
Indian Painter
Oil on canvas
Gift of Mr. and Mrs. Peter M. Butler,
80.30

DOMENICO DUPRA
Italian, 1689–1770
Portrait of Michel de Launay des Isles,
1673–1731
Oil on canvas
Gift of Karl and Rosamond deLaittre,
83.8

JAN VAN GOYEN
Dutch, 1596–1656
*River Landscape (Pellekussenpoort near
Utrecht),* 1648
Oil on panel
Gift of Bruce B. Dayton, 83.84

PIETER DE HOOCH
Dutch, 1629–84
The Asparagus Vendor, 1675–80
Oil on canvas
Gift of Mrs. Margaret L. Sweatt, 82.46

VASSILY KANDINSKY
Russian, 1866–1944
Nymphenburg, 1904
Oil on canvasboard
Gift of Mr. and Mrs. Donald Winston,
81.106.1

ERNST LUDWIG KIRCHNER
German, 1880–1938
Dance Training, 1910–11
Oil on canvas
Gift of Mrs. Charles Meech, 80.27

SIR EDWIN LANDSEER
English, 1803–73
The Cat's Paw, 1824
Oil on panel
Given in memory of Agnes Lynch
Anderson by Dr. Roger L. Anderson,
82.47

ALESSANDRO MAGNASCO
Italian, 1667–1749
Monks Praying in a Grotto
Oil on canvas
Gift of Mr. and Mrs. Theodore Bennett,
83.6.3

CLAUDE MONET
French, 1840–1926
Still Life with Pheasants and Plovers,
1879
Oil on canvas
Given by Anne Pierce Rogers in
memory of John DeCoster Rogers,
84.140

BARTOLOME ESTEBAN MURILLO
Spanish, 1617–82
Penitent Magdalene, about 1660
Oil on canvas
In memory of my devoted and beloved
wife, Marguerite Sexton Richards, and
in appreciation of the warmth and
cordiality of the reception given me by
the people of Minneapolis. The
Bergmann Richards Memorial Fund,
82.23

STUART NIELSEN
American, 1947–
Large Butterfly Screen, 1978
Five shaped fiberglass segments with
applied pigments
Gift of Cowles Media Company/
Minneapolis Star and Tribune, 84.55

GEORGIA O'KEEFFE
American, 1887–
City Night, 1926
Oil on canvas
Gift of the Regis Corporation, Mr. and
Mrs. W. John Driscoll, the Beim
Foundation, the Larsen Fund and by
public subscription, 80.28

SIR JOSHUA REYNOLDS
English, 1723–92
Mrs. Froude, nee Phyllis Hurrell, 1762
Oil on canvas
Gift of the F. K. and Vivian O'Gara
Weyerhaeuser Foundation, 84.36

WILLIAM TROST RICHARDS
American, 1833–1905
Quiet Seascape, 1883
Oil on canvas
Gift of Mr. and Mrs. W. John Driscoll,
80.67

CHARLES M. RUSSELL
American, 1865–1926
Buffalo Hunt, 1891
Oil on canvas
Gift of Mr. and Mrs. George R. Steiner
in memory of Frank M. Steiner, a friend
and admirer of Charles and Nancy
Russell, 83.149

CHARLES M. RUSSELL
American, 1865–1926
The Death Song of Lone Wolf, 1901
Oil on canvas
Gift of Mr. and Mrs. George R. Steiner,
in memory of Frank M. Steiner, a friend
and admirer of Charles and Nancy
Russell, 85.107

GIROLAMO DA SANTACROCE
Italian, 1503–56
The Annunciation
Oil on panel
Gift of Mr. and Mrs. Theodore Bennett,
83.6.1

ABRAHAM STORCK
Dutch, 1635–1710?
The Four Days' Battle, 1666
Oil on canvas
Gift of John B. Hawley, by exchange,
the Walter H. and Valborg P. Ude
Memorial Fund, the Christina N. and
Swan J. Turnblad Memorial Fund, and
the Ethel Morrison Van Derlip Fund,
84.31

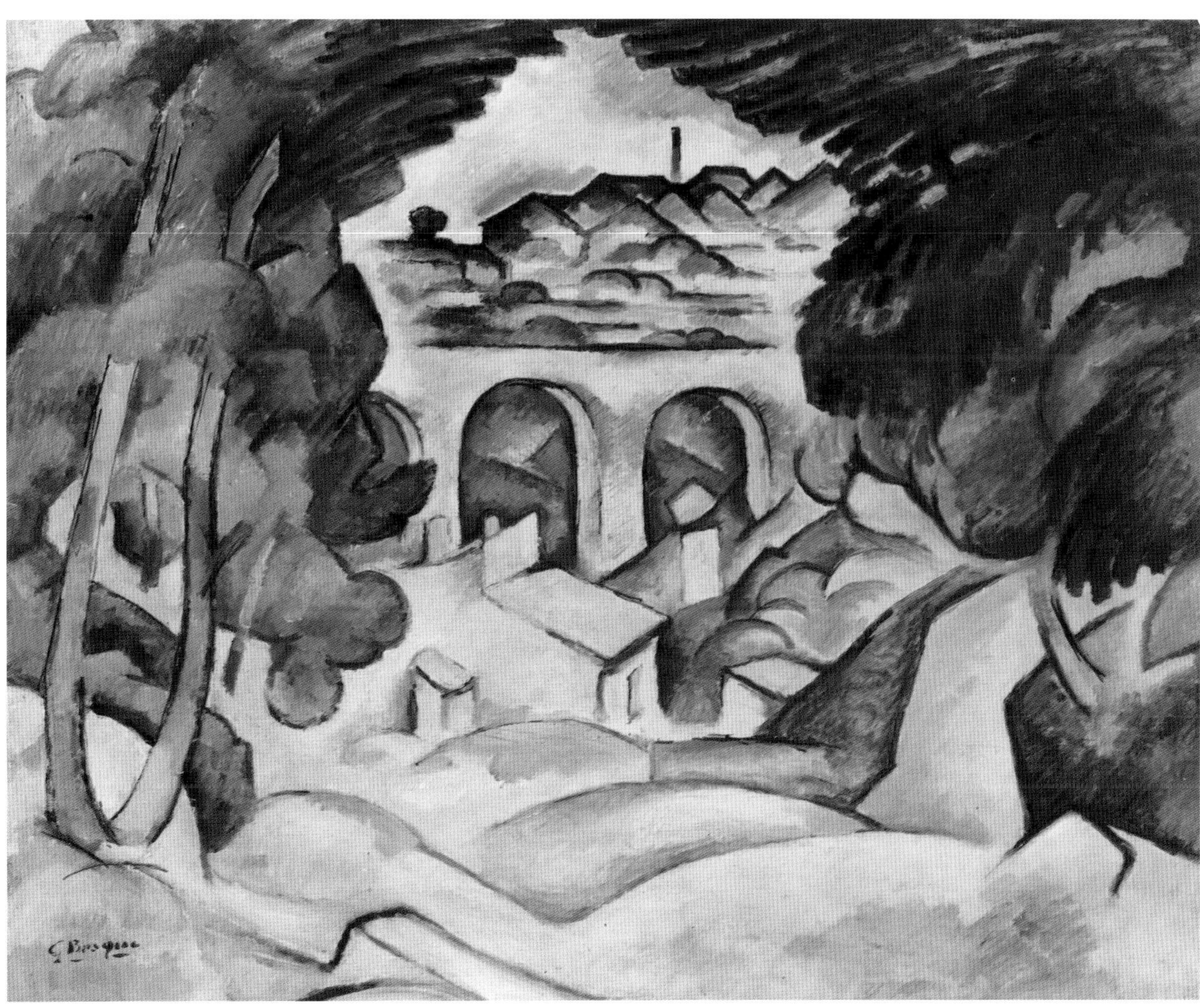

PETER STRUB THE YOUNGER
(MASTER OF MESSKIRCH)
German, active 1530–43
The Elevation of the Magdalene
Tempera on panel
The Bergmann Richards Memorial Fund
and the Fiduciary Fund, 82.83

JACOPO TINTORETTO
Italian, 1518–94
The Raising of Lazarus, about 1558–59
Oil on canvas
Gift of an anonymous donor, 83.74

ESAIAS VAN DE VELDE
Dutch, 1590–1630
Landscape with a Courtly Procession
1619
Oil on canvas
The Ude Fund and bequest of Tessie
Jones, by exchange, 83.122

PHILIPS WOUWERMAN
Dutch, 1619–68
Festive Peasants before a Panorama,
1653
Oil on canvas
Gift of Margaret L. Sweatt, 81.107

JOSEPH WRIGHT OF DERBY
English, 1734–97
A Cottage on Fire, about 1787
Oil on canvas
The Putnam Dana McMillan Fund and
bequest of Lillian Malcolm Larkin, by
exchange, 84.53

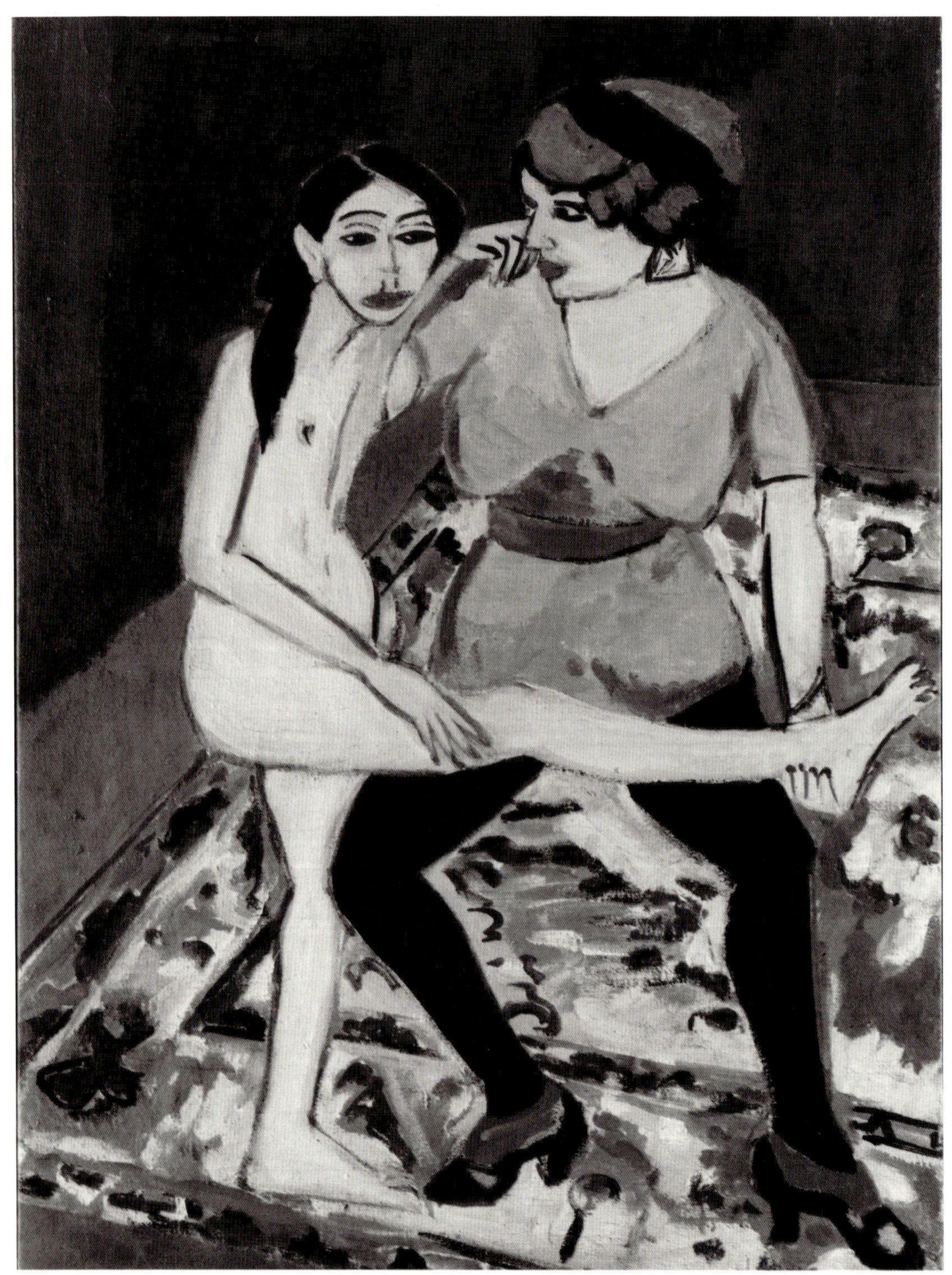

ERNST LUDWIG KIRCHNER
German, 1880–1938
Dance Training, 1910–11
Oil on canvas
Gift of Mrs. Charles Meech, 80.27

GEORGIA O'KEEFFE
American, 1887–
City Night, 1926
Oil on canvas
Gift of the Regis Corporation, Mr. and
Mrs. W. John Driscoll, the Beim
Foundation, the Larsen Fund and by
public subscription, 80.28

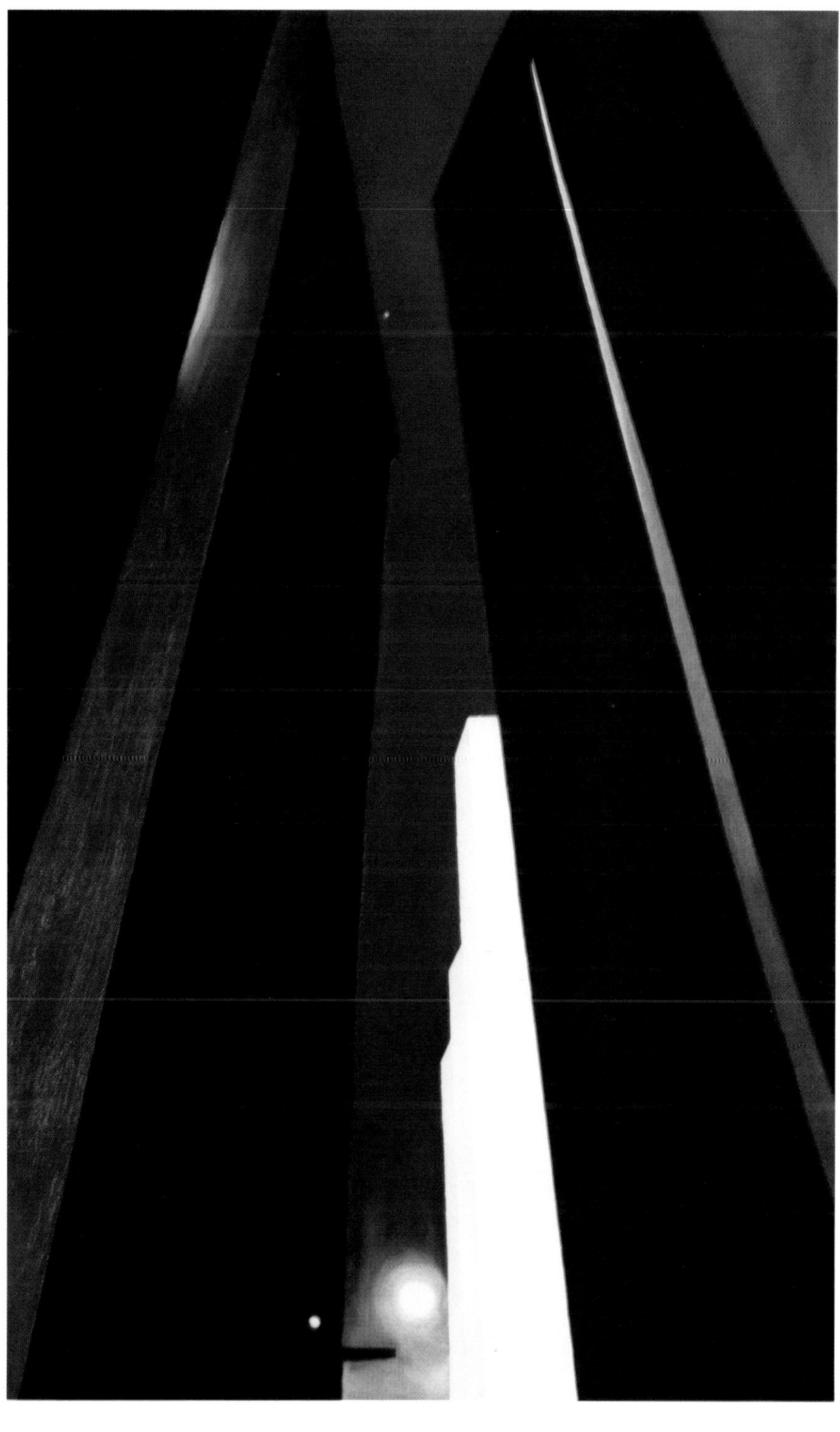

PHOTOGRAPHY

Like most American art museums, The Minneapolis Institute of Arts did not recognize photography as an appropriate field of collecting activity until about ten years ago. Although the battle for the acceptance of photography as an artistic medium was fought, by the pioneering artist Alfred Stieglitz among others, in the teens and twenties, curators and collectors schooled in more traditional fields have often found photography hard to accept as a valid means of artistic expression, preferring to employ it as an archival and reference tool only.

There were, however, a small number of museums that formed early collections of photography as art. The Albright-Knox Gallery in Buffalo acquired its small group of photographs as a result of a 1910 exhibition organized for the museum by Alfred Stieglitz. The Boston Museum of Fine Arts was next to establish a collection, in 1924, also through Stieglitz's efforts. In 1933 Stieglitz gave his collection of photography by members of the Photo Secession to the Metropolitan Museum. When the Museum of Modern Art opened in 1932, it included photography in both its exhibitions and collections.

Exhibitions of serious amateur photography proliferated in the 1930s in the United States and Europe. The Minneapolis Institute of Arts was widely noted for its annual photography salon exhibitions that featured prominent local amateurs alongside internationally renowned mentors like Max Thorek and Adolf Fassbender. Begun in 1932, the exhibitions reached their zenith in the forties and then, in the mid-1950s, were discontinued. Many reasons can be found for their decline, but it is more important to note that from these large and diverse exhibitions no photographs were retained for the museum's collections.

The Minneapolis collection began to take shape in 1972, when Anthony Clark, encouraged by the interest and support of Kate and Hall J. Peterson, formed a curatorial department. In the past decade the Petersons' example has generated further support for the department and greater activity in the local community of collectors. The photography collection now includes nearly 3,500 images, and continues to grow.

Any collection worthy of being so called—unless it is merely an agglomeration — has an internal coherence. Certain objects, for reasons of beauty, eloquence and artistic presence, surpass and highlight the collection as a whole. The secondary, but nevertheless important, other works that form the main body provide the aesthetic texture, the variations and digressions, that enhance our interest and understanding. The character of a collection is found in the tone, the resonances and nuances that serve to bridge and unify the separate objects in a harmonious group. In private collections the philosophy, and therefore the tone of the collection, is that of one person and one point of view, however catholic or narrow that viewpoint may be. The idiosyncracies of these collections are frequently the source of their strength and interest.

Most public museum collections have been assembled by various directors, curators, and donors over long periods of time. While it is possible to single out those pictures and objects that entered the collections at the instigation of one or another director, the overall tone is more varied than that of private collections. More often than not, museum collections are art-historical in texture and tone.

The Minneapolis collection, however, has been until very recently the work of one curator. It is a collection that has grown and flourished, especially in the area of photography since 1940. While any number of photographs — primarily of a historical nature — have not entered the collection for want of funds, a great many others have been acquired both through purchase and donation. The museum's acquisition policy makes no distinction between gifts and purchases; gifts are

ROBERT FRANK
American (b. Switzerland), 1924–
Parade—Hoboken, New Jersey, about
1955
Gelatin silver print
Robert C. Winton Fund, 84.104

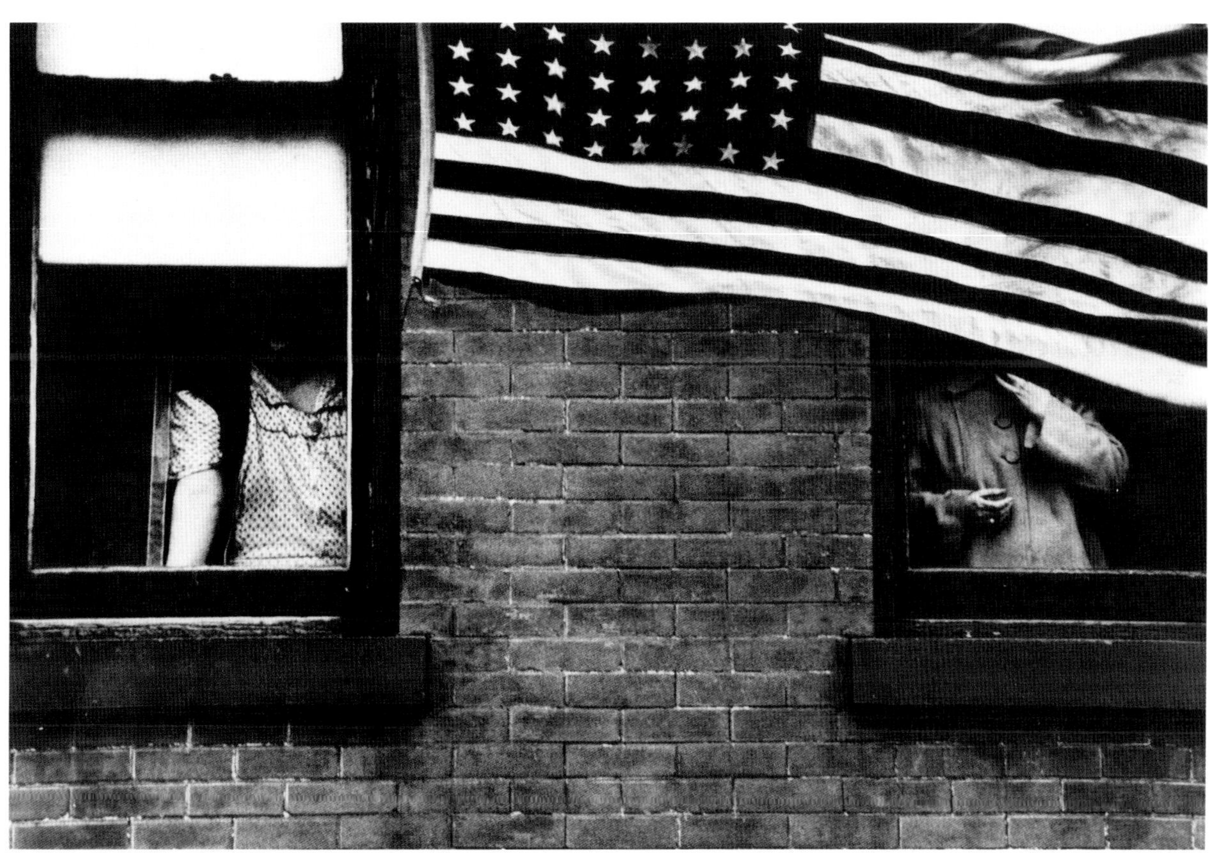

subject to the same standards of curatorial judgment that apply to purchases. The collection has been guided, selected and is presented according to a considered and tangible set of criteria, based on three fundamental assumptions:

(1) Photography as it has been practiced since the late nineteenth century has had as one of its several applications the production of camera-made images for expressive artistic purposes. Such pictures are appropriate to the collections of an encyclopedic art museum like The Minneapolis Institute of Arts.

(2) The history of photography is parallel to the history of modern art. While there are clear technical factors that have served in part to shape its special character, photography as an art has been the product of the same cultural and socio-political influences that have formed the other visual arts. A full account and understanding of photography as an art form is attainable only within the context and study of the development and history of the visual arts from the last century to the present — not separately.

(3) Contemporary photography, like all contemporary art, exists and is practiced, consciously or unconsciously, within a continuum. Individual images are self-sufficient, but at the same time can be seen as standing in relation to other works by the same artist and contemporaries as well as to the history and traditions that precede it.

The living artist attempts to depart from and advance beyond what is known: the work of a teacher, the work of the previous decade or century. The safeguards of art historical precedent are not very useful or even applicable if we are to engage and meet working artists on their own terms. A curator cannot be confident of the staying power of a newly minted picture in the same way that one can be sure of the endurance of a well-documented Japanese print or an impressionist painting.

Curators who purchase and exhibit contemporary art are frequently asked, "How can you tell what is good; don't you just rely on your personal taste, likes and dislikes, in your decisions?"

There is no simple answer to this question. Each work must be approached and assessed in its own terms, i.e., those laid down by the artist. That is not to say that objective and separate criteria do not apply, rather that the objects themselves must be respected and responded to — judged — very largely according to their own dictates and authority. It is essential to be aware of one's biases and predispositions, lest those subjective responses bear unwittingly upon critical facilities.

There are, alas, no strict formulas or rules, no yardstick of artistic excellence. The recipe is simply the one stated above: be attuned to the full range of your responses, your knowledge, your powers of discrimination and your intelligence.

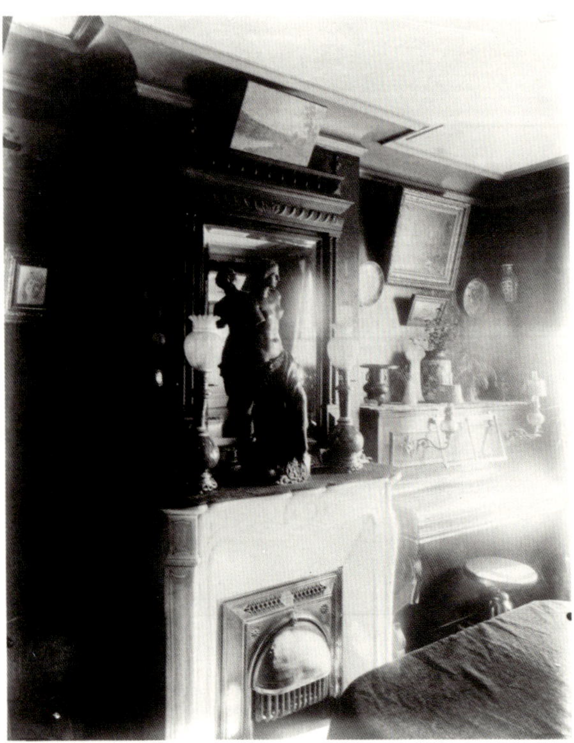

JEAN-EUGENE-AUGUSTE ATGET
French, 1857–1927
*Intérieur d'un employé aux magasins
du Louvre,* 1910
Albumen print
Gift of John A. Rollwagen, 83.150

ALFRED STIEGLITZ
American, 1864–1946
The Steerage, 1907
Photogravure from "291,"
September–October, 1915
Gift of Myron Kunin, 84.37.6a

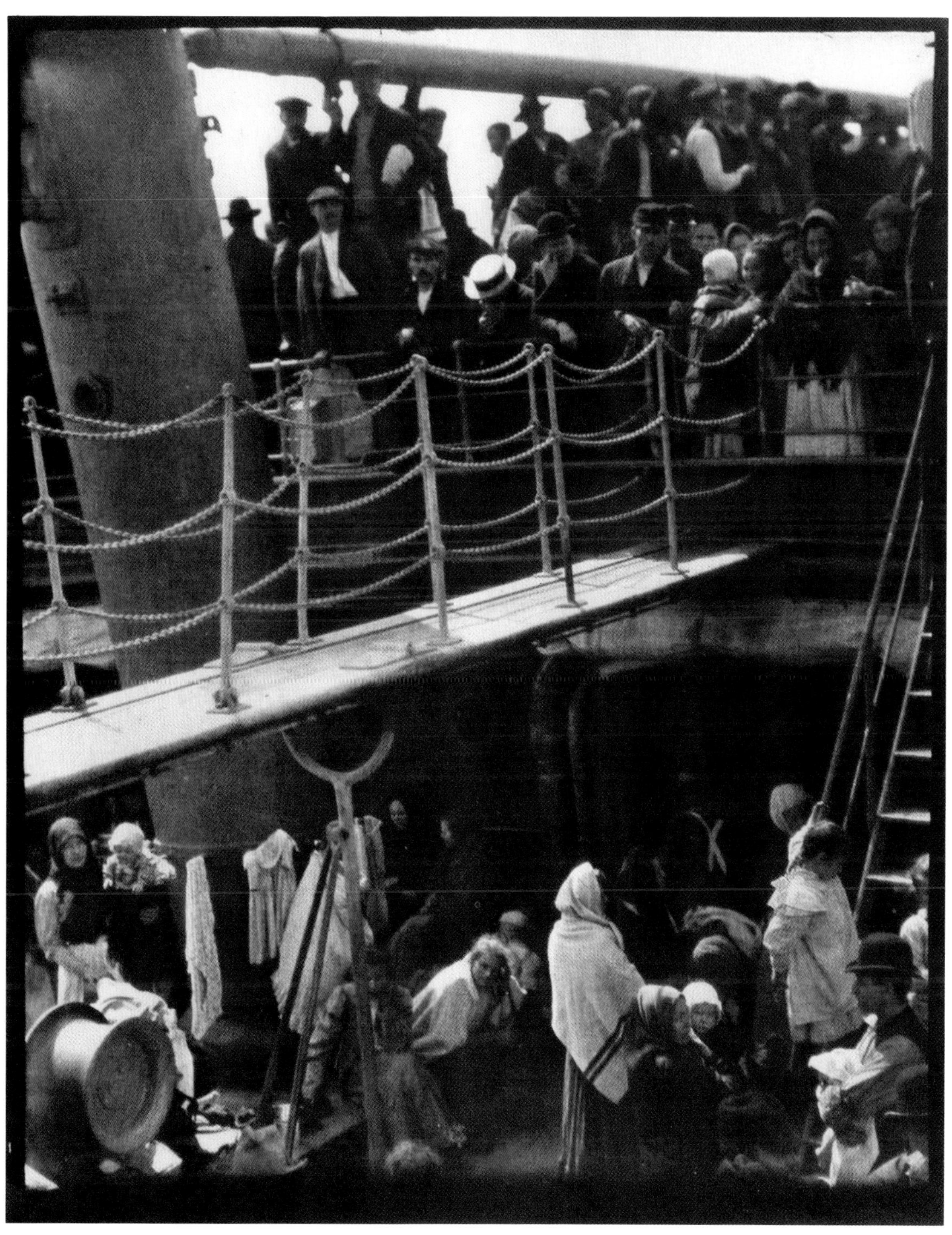

Curators are often thought to acquire works for the collection because they "like" them, and to reject those they dislike. In practice, pictures are often purchased that are difficult, controversial, sometimes contrary to one's taste or favor. A curator may decide that a problematic picture is needed because it serves to explain, elucidate or counterpoint other pictures. Moments like this — and they are not infrequent — keep things lively, to say the least. It sometimes seems like a clear case of sophistry when a curator defends a proposed acquisition known to be outside or contrary to his or her "taste" or "liking."

Yet if a collection were to grow only according to the tastes and biases of the curator's personal inclinations, unmediated by opposing considerations and values, the balance and diversity so essential to a public collection would be unattainable. The odd or eccentric work of art is a vital ingredient. If it grates and irritates, all the better. If it provokes and stimulates further debate, wonderful. If the pictures we buy serve merely to confirm and reassure us of the comfortable verities, they may just as well be passed over.

In evaluating photographs for the collection, I pose the following questions:
(1) Does the photograph engage and hold me visually, emotionally and intellectually? This first encounter is highly subjective, and is subject to later amendment as other information and insights accrue. This is essentially the way we refine and advance our knowledge in general. But at this earliest point, the question is how the image affects me.

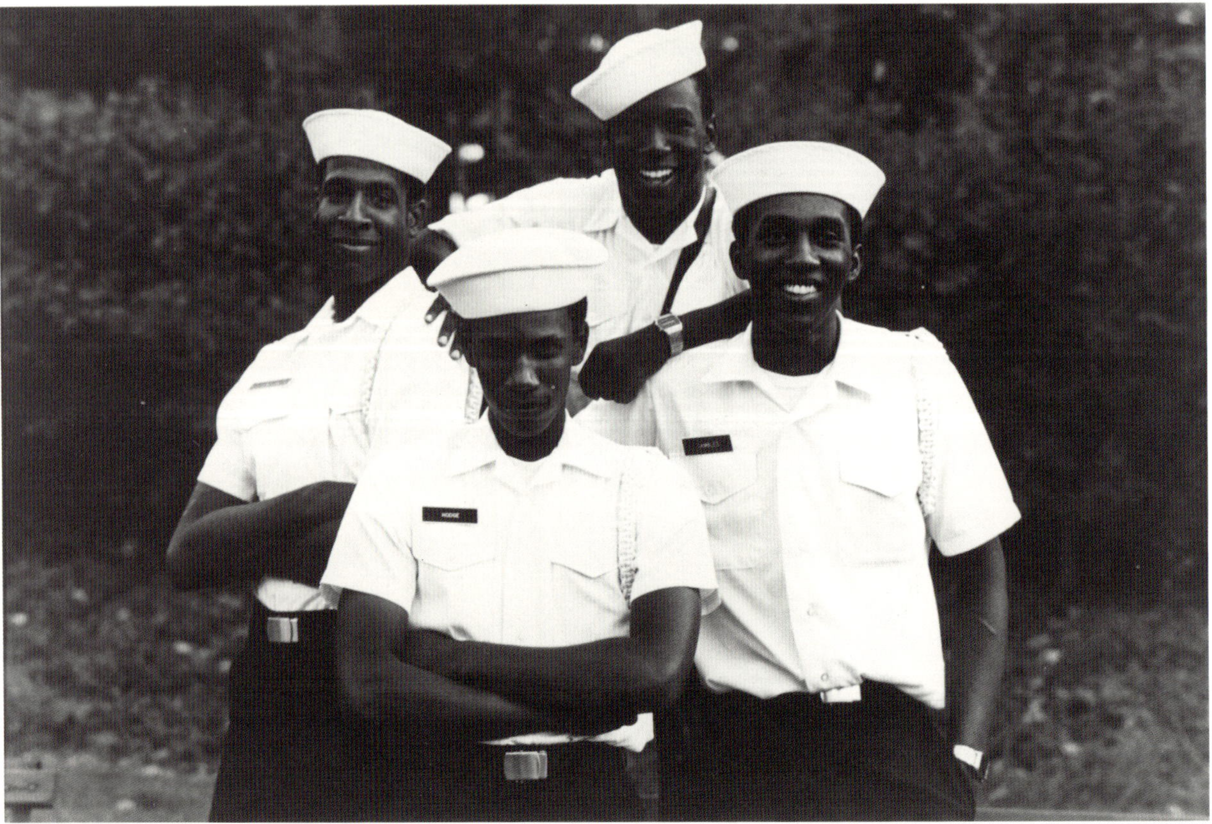

THOMAS F. ARNDT
American, 1944–
*Four Coast Guard Cadets, Great
America Amusement Park, Chicago,*
1981
Gelatin silver print
Gift of Martin Weinstein, 84.125.9

 WILLIAM MORTENSEN
American, 1897–1965
Human Relations, 1932
Bromoil transfer print
The Christina N. and Swan J. Turnblad
Memorial Fund, 84.100.2

(2) Is the picture familiar to me; where have I seen it before; and am I acquainted with the photographer's work from exhibitions, publications, or reputation? In itself, this is not an aesthetic consideration. It does lead to useful comparisons, however.

(3) Does the collection have other work by this photographer? If so, is this one important to add? Is it a variation on one we have? Is it a better print?

(4) Would having this picture strengthen the collection in a demonstrable way? Does it advance and explain the history and aesthetics of photography? How?

(5) Is money available to purchase this photograph? Or will this expenditure prevent the purchase of a more important work?

(6) Is there a collector or donor whose taste is inclined toward this kind of picture or artist? If so, would that person (or corporation) be likely to provide the money for the purchase, or would they buy it themselves with a view toward future donation to the collection?

All of these questions, or variations on them, occur naturally in considering an addition to the collection. These several points will also be the outline of the argument the curator will employ in presenting the picture to the director, the other curators and, ultimately, to the accessions committee.

I have tried to describe above the history and philosophy of the photography collection; it is perhaps equally revealing to look at its goals for the future. All curators keep formal or informal wish lists, and this category of hoped-for acquisi-

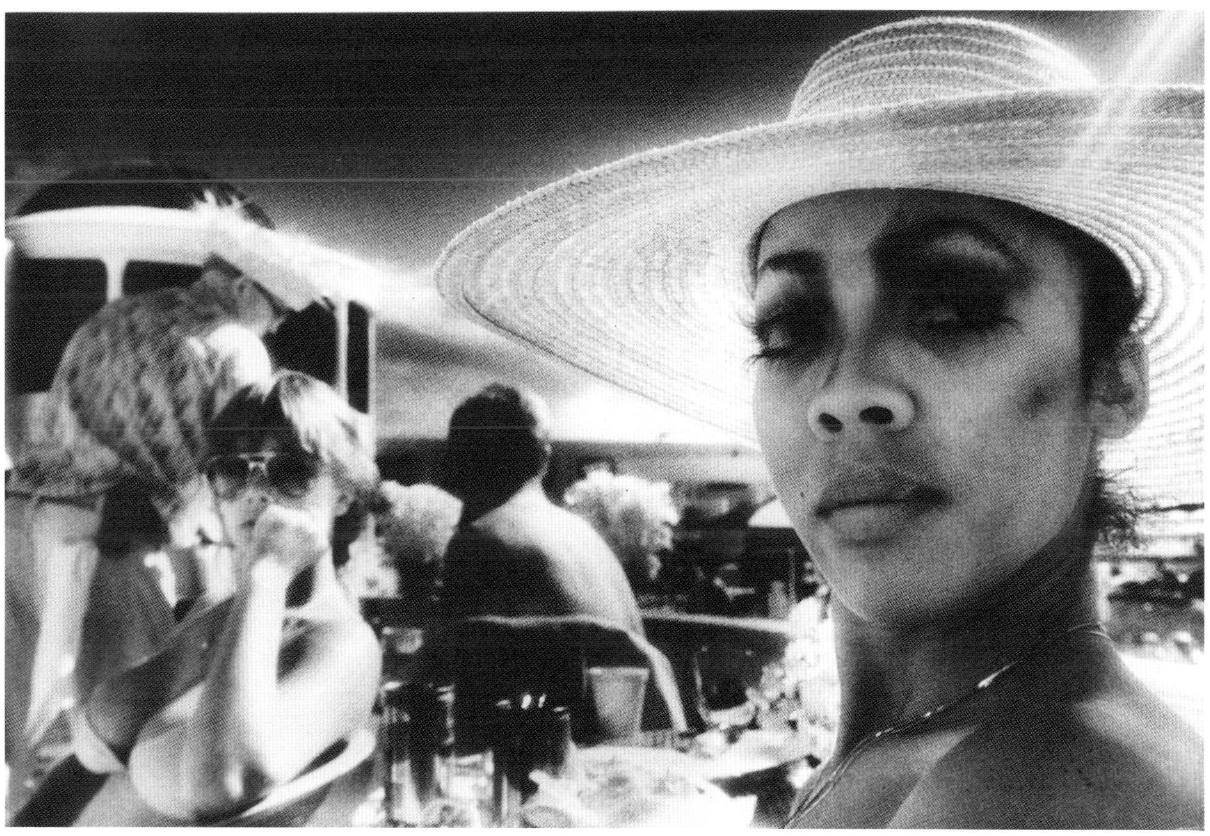

tions presents a clear sense of the curator's ideal philosophy.

The wish list is not altogether fantasy or dream. It is more often than not made up of known or possible purchase opportunities. These pictures, if brought into the collection, would enliven and strengthen the collection as it stands.

Of the numerous photographers that might be listed who are underrepresented, or, in embarrassingly large numbers, not represented at all, for want of sometimes as little as $500 or $1,000, some are major figures in the history of photography, and such works fill our wish list.

Another and possibly more important wish list is made up of those photographers who are working in relative obscurity. Continuous and diligent detective work is required to recognize artists in

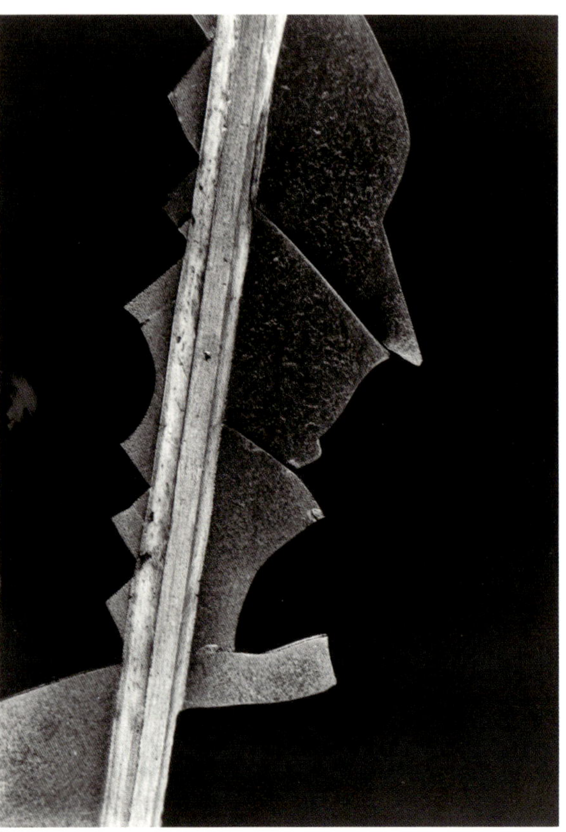

other parts of the country and in Europe and the East whose work has not been published or exhibited. Without exception, each visit to New York, or Detroit, Los Angeles, Düsseldorf or Tokyo results in the discovery of a photographer (most often several) whose work would be a superb addition to the collection. Seeking and acquiring new work is exhilirating, slightly dangerous (it is, after all, someone else's money you are spending), but is finally the most positive way in which to fulfill the museum's mission and responsibility to the art of our time.

It is often stated that The Minneapolis Institute of Arts led the way for other museums in collecting fine photographs. In an important sense this has been true. We began early and ambitiously, and other museums of comparable size followed our example in dramatic ways. What once was a bold beginning has been exceeded handily by many other museums of our size. Although we retain a national reputation for strength and progressiveness, our preeminence may soon become a myth as we compete with the growing interest of collectors and other museums. If we are serious, decisive, and adequately funded, however, we can continue to set a pace and tone of historical strength as well as innovation.

Carroll T. Hartwell
Curator of Photography

AARON SISKIND
American, 1903–
New York City (Window 3), 1947
Gelatin silver print
Gift of Robert and Joyce Menschel,
84.96.5

FRANK W. GOHLKE
American, 1942–
*Grain Elevators and Lightning,
La Mesa, Texas,* 1975
Gelatin silver print
Gift of Martin Weinstein, 84.125.12

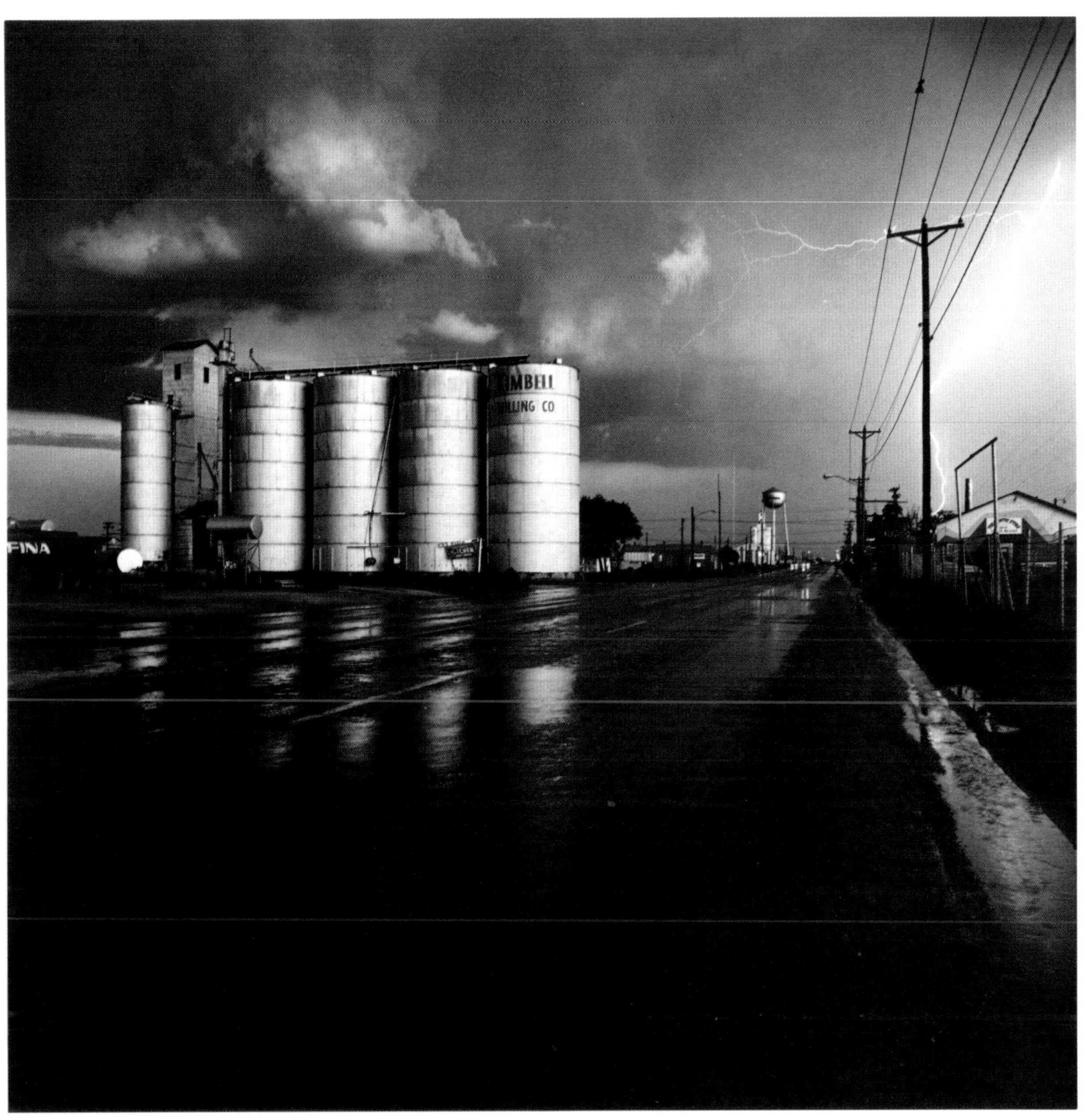

Department of

PHOTOGRAPHY

THOMAS F. ARNDT
American, 1944–
Subway, Brooklyn, 1980
Gelatin silver print
The Mr. and Mrs. Julius E. Davis Fund,
81.19.1

THOMAS F. ARNDT
American, 1944–
*Four Coast Guard Cadets, Great
America Amusement Park, Chicago,*
1981
Gelatin silver print
Gift of Martin Weinstein, 84.125.9

JEAN-EUGENE-AUGUSTE ATGET
French, 1857–1927
Hotel Lambert, Ile St. Louis, Paris, 1900
Albumen print
Gift of Virginia M. Zabriskie, 83.154.8

JEAN-EUGENE-AUGUSTE ATGET
French, 1857–1927
*Intérieur d'un employé aux magasins
du Louvre,* 1910
Albumen print
Gift of John A. Rollwagen, 83.150

RICHARD AVEDON
American, 1923–
Jimmy Durante, Comedian, 1953
Gelatin silver print
The Christina N. and Swan J. Turnblad
Memorial Fund, 81.94.3

RICHARD AVEDON
American, 1923–
Ezra Pound, Poet, 1958
Gelatin silver print
The Christina N. and Swan J. Turnblad
Memorial Fund, 81.94.8

PIERRE BOUCHER
French, 1908–
Untitled, 1937
Gelatin silver print
Gift of Virginia M. Zabriskie, 83.154.21

BILL BRANDT
English, 1905–83
Hampstead, London, 1945
Vintage gelatin silver print
Mr. and Mrs. Patrick Butler Fund, 85.88

HARRY CALLAHAN
American, 1912–
Chicago, about 1952
Dye transfer print
Gift of Emanuel E. Brotman, 80.69.5

HARRY CALLAHAN
American, 1912–
Florence, 1957
Dye transfer print
Gift of Emanuel E. Brotman, 80.69.11

HARRY CALLAHAN
American, 1912–
Untitled, 1978
Color coupler print
Gift of the American Telephone and
Telegraph Company, 81.120.7

CARL CHIARENZA
American, 1935–
Noumenon 119, 1984
Gelatin silver print
Gift of funds from Kate and Hall J.
Peterson, 85.85

WILLIAM CHRISTENBERRY
American, 1936–
*Church Between Greensboro and
Marion, Alabama,* 1973
Color coupler print
Gift of Virginia M. Zabriskie, 83.154.9

WILLIAM CLIFT
American, 1944–
*Santa Fe River Gorge from Cerro
Seguro,* 1978
Gelatin silver print
Gift of the American Telephone and
Telegraph Company, 81.120.10

PIERRE CORDIER
Belgian, 1933–
Hommage a Nonyme, 1972
Chemigram
The Ethel Morrison Van Derlip Fund,
84.12.1

PETER DELORY
American, 1948–
Formentera Bicycle Ride, 1976
Gelatin silver print
Gift of Frank Kolodny, 82.126.3

LOUIS FAURER
American, 1916–
Family Times Square, 1948
Gelatin silver print
The Ethel Morrison Van Derlip Fund,
81.98.2

LOUIS FAURER
American, 1916–
Tulips on Broadway, about 1948
Gelatin silver print
Gift of Mr. and Mrs. Paul N. Rifkin,
82.124.11

LOUIS FAURER
American, 1916–
Woman with Umbrella, Times Square,
about 1948
Gelatin silver print
Gift of Mr. and Mrs. Paul N. Rifkin,
82.124.5

LARRY FINK
American, 1941–
Debutante Ball, Hotel Pierre, 1978
Gelatin silver print
Gift of Mr. and Mrs. Paul N. Rifkin,
82.124.28

ROBERT FRANK
American (b. Switzerland), 1924–
Parade—Hoboken, New Jersey, about
1955
Gelatin silver print
Robert C. Winton Fund, 84.104

ROBERT FRANK
American (b. Switzerland), 1924–
Motorama, Los Angeles, 1956
Gelatin silver print
William Hood Dunwoody Fund, 81.96

LEE FRIEDLANDER
American, 1934–
Diane and Amy Arbus, 1963
Gelatin silver print
Mr. and Mrs. Patrick Butler Fund,
85.91.6

LEE FRIEDLANDER
American, 1934–
Mary Frank, 1967
Gelatin silver print
Mr. and Mrs. Patrick Butler Fund,
85.91.2

LEE FRIEDLANDER
American, 1934–
Jean Genet, 1968
Gelatin silver print
Mr. and Mrs. Patrick Butler Fund,
85.91.1

LEE FRIEDLANDER
American, 1934–
John Szarkowski, 1976
Gelatin silver print
Mr. and Mrs. Patrick Butler Fund,
85.91.12

LEE FRIEDLANDER
American, 1934–
John Coplans, 1983
Gelatin silver print
Mr. and Mrs. Patrick Butler Fund,
85.91.7

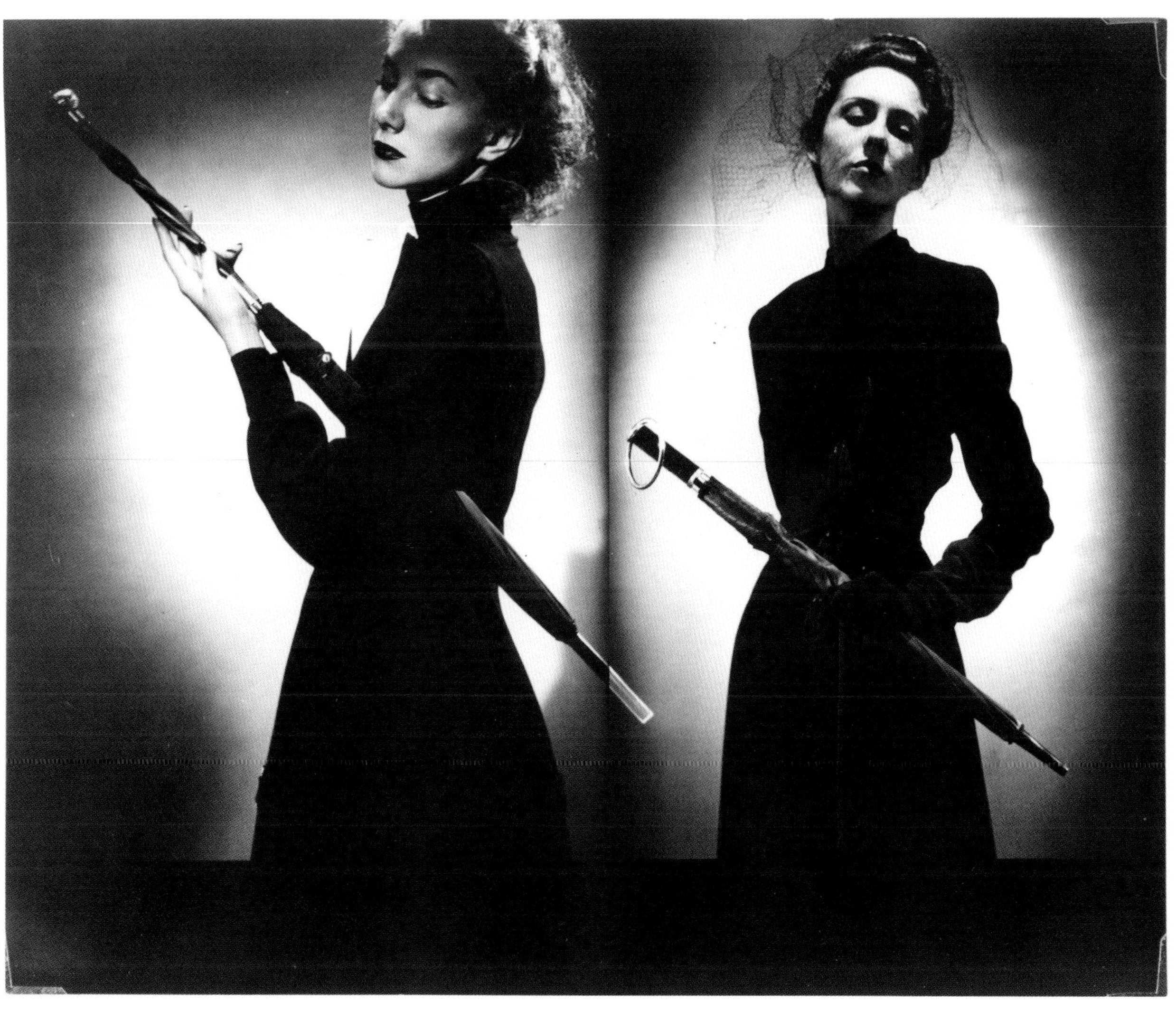

FRANÇOIS KOLLAR
French (b. Czechoslovakia), 1904–
Untitled, 1939
Gelatin silver print
Gift of Virginia M. Zabriskie, 83.154.18

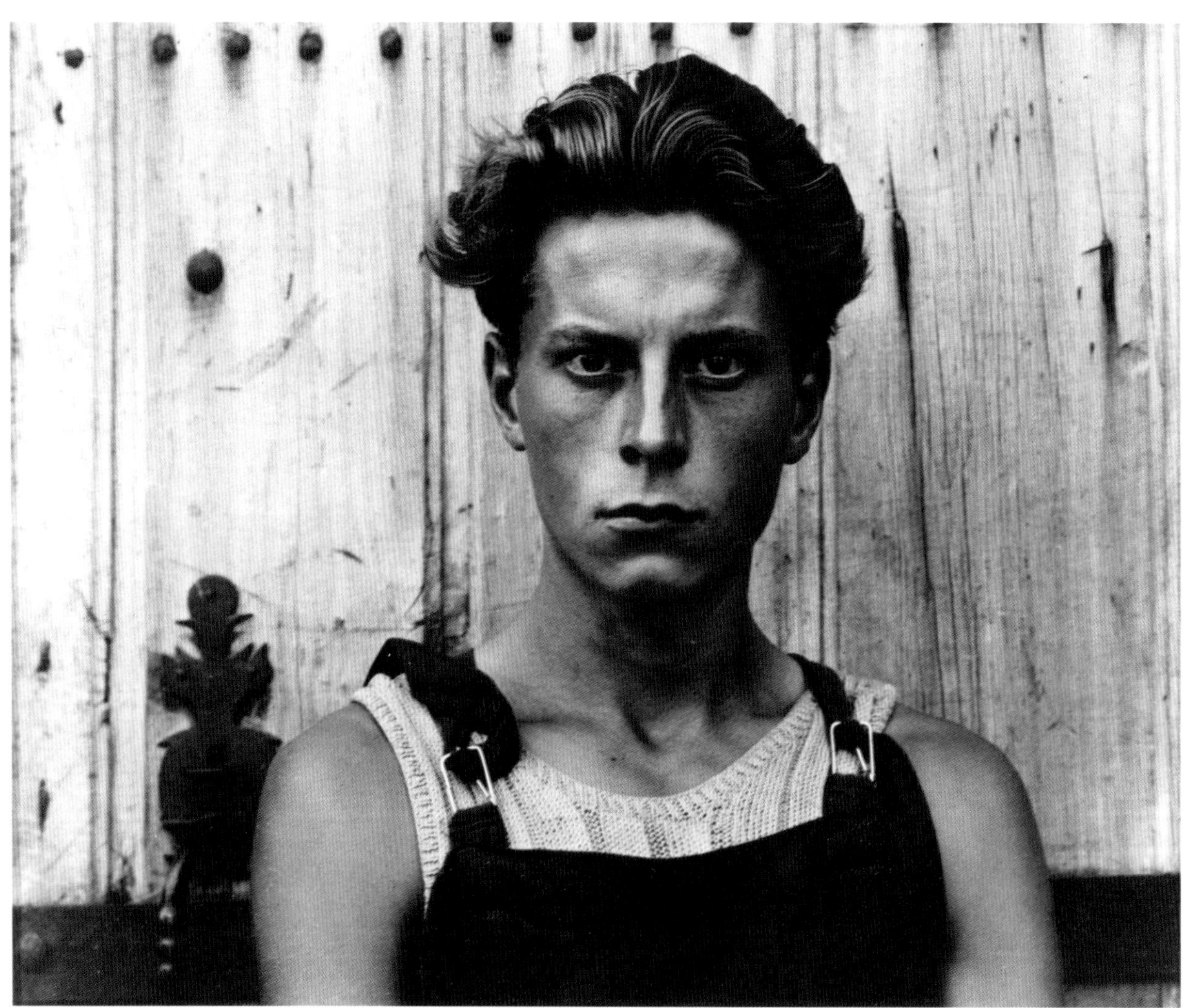

PAUL STRAND
American, 1890–1976
Young Boy, Gondeville, France
Gelatin silver print
Gift of John A. Rollwagen and Beverly J.
Baranowski, 85.118

ARNOLD GENTHE
American (b. Germany), 1869–1942
Untitled, n. d.
Gelatin silver print
Gift of Virginia M. Zabriskie, 83.154.4

FRANK W. GOHLKE
American, 1942–
*Grain Elevators and Lightning,
La Mesa, Texas*, 1975
Gelatin silver print
Gift of Martin Weinstein, 84.125.12

FRANK GOHLKE
American, 1942–
View of Bay Bridge, San Francisco,
1979
Gelatin silver print
Gift of Martin Weinstein, 84.125.13

E. O. GOLDBECK
American, 20th century
Red Square and the Kremlin, Moscow,
1967
Gelatin silver print
Gift of an anonymous donor, 85.109

SERGE HAMBOURG
American (b. France), 1936–
Flower Market, Pescia, Italy, 1981
Dye bleach color print
Ethel Morrison Van Derlip Fund, 85.2.2

SERGE HAMBOURG
American (b. France), 1936–
La Régence, Trouville, 1982
Dye bleach color print
Ethel Morrison Van Derlip Fund, 85.2.1.

LEWIS W. HINE
American, 1874–1940
*General Utility Boy at Lumber
Company, Orange, Texas*, 1913
Gelatin silver print
Gift of Virginia M. Zabriskie, 83.154.1

LEN JENSHEL
American, 1949–
Coe Estate, Oyster Bay, 1982
Color coupler print
Gift of funds of the Photography
Council, 82.130.2

WILLIAM KLEIN
American, 1926–
Bikini, Moscow, 1959
Gelatin silver print
Mr. and Mrs. Patrick Butler Fund,
85.91.17

WILLIAM KLEIN
American, 1926–
*Yablonchkima, Russian Sarah
Bernhardt, Moscow*, 1961
Gelatin silver print
Mr. and Mrs. Patrick Butler Fund,
85.91.15

WILLIAM KLEIN
American, 1926–
Hand, Lebanon, 1963
Gelatin silver print
Mr. and Mrs. Patrick Butler Fund,
85.91.16.

STUART D. KLIPPER
American, 1941–
Oak Meadows, Scott County, Minnesota,
1981
Color coupler print
Gift of the artist, 85.4.1

STUART D. KLIPPER
American, 1941–
*Corn Cribs, Freeborn County,
Minnesota*
From *The World in a Few States* series,
1983
Color coupler print
Gift of the artist, 85.4.10

STUART D. KLIPPER
American, 1941–
Brooklyn Bridge, 1984
Color coupler print
Gift of Martin Weinstein, 84.125.14.1

STUART D. KLIPPER
American, 1941–
Brooklyn Bridge, 1984
Color coupler print
Gift of Martin Weinstein, 84.125.14.2

JAMES KNIPE
American, 1942–
Hankey's Trees, 1982
Albumen print
Gift of the artist, 84.26.3

JAMES KNIPE
American, 1942–
Boats along Mississippi, 1983
Albumen print
Gift of the artist, 84.25.2

FRANÇOIS KOLLAR
French (b. Czechoslovakia), 1904–
Untitled, 1939
Gelatin silver print
Gift of Virginia M. Zabriskie, 83.154.18

TIMOTHY LAMB
American, 1951–
Untitled, n.d.
Dye bleach color print
Gift of Martin Weinstein, 83.41

ALEN MACWEENEY
American (b. Ireland), 1939–
Little Tinker Child, 1965–66
Gelatin silver print
Gift of Ivor Massey, 82.127.26

ALEN MACWEENEY
American (b. Ireland), 1939–
White Horse, Donegal, 1965–66
Gelatin silver print
Gift of Ivor Massey, 82.127.16

RICHARD MISRACH
American, 1949–
Hawaii I, 1978
Color coupler print
Gift of the American Telephone and
Telegraph Company, 81.120.51

TINA MODOTTI
Mexican (b. Italy), 1896–1942
Hand of the Puppeteer, 1926
Gelatin silver print
Mr. and Mrs. Patrick Butler Fund, 85.87

BARBARA MORGAN
American, 1900–
Martha Graham, Lamentation, 1935
Gelatin silver print
Gift of Virginia M. Zabriskie, 83.154.10

WILLIAM MORTENSEN
American, 1897–1965
Human Relations, 1932
Bromoil transfer print
The Christina N. and Swan J. Turnblad
Memorial Fund, 84.100.2

JOAN MOSS
American (b. Canada), 1931–
Caesar's Palace, Las Vegas, 1980
Gelatin silver print
Gift of the Photography Council,
82.129.2

NICHOLAS NIXON
American, 1947–
New Orleans, 1978
Gelatin silver print
Gift of the American Telephone and
Telegraph Company, 81.120.52

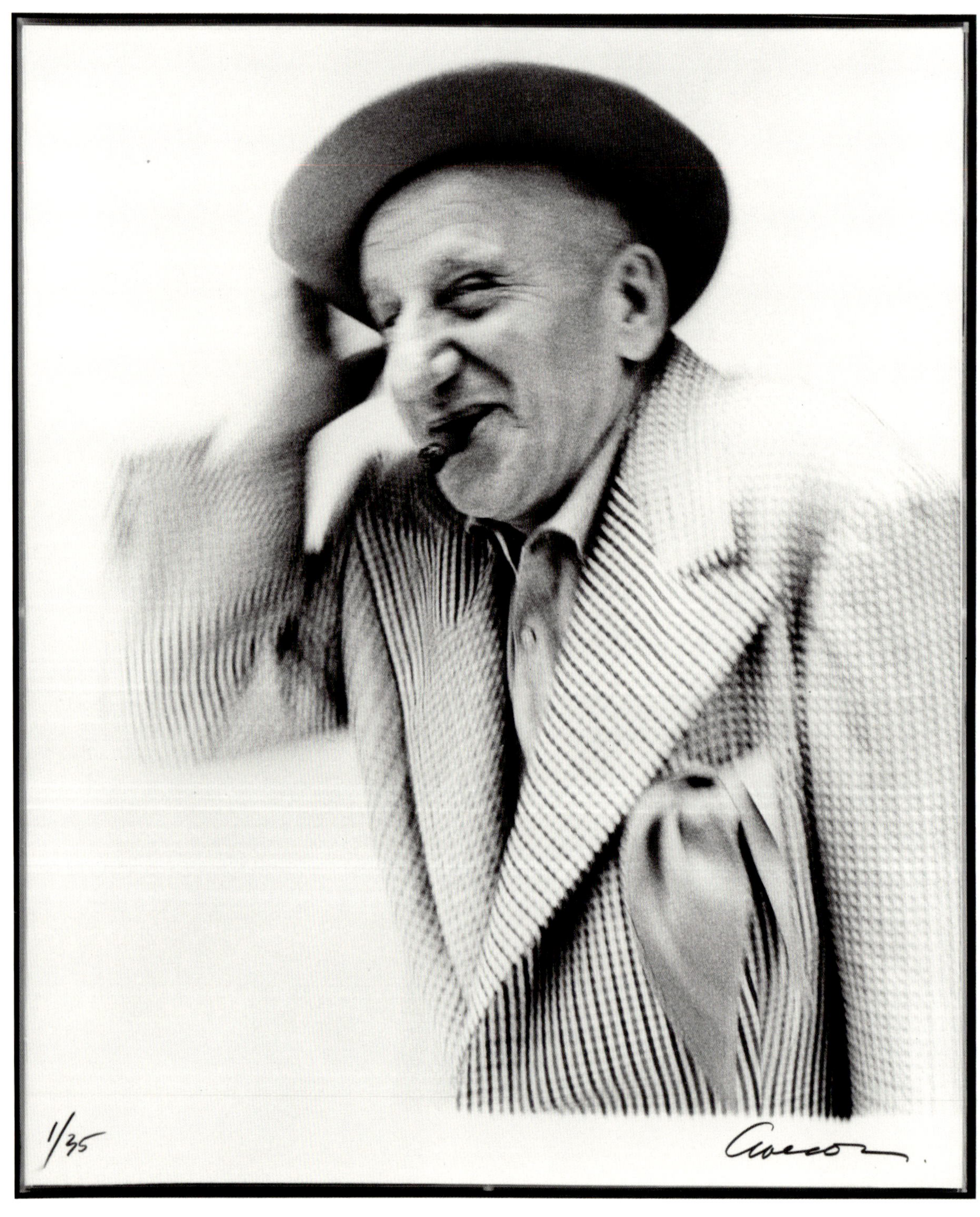
1/35

RICHARD AVEDON
American, 1923–
Jimmy Durante, Comedian, 1953
Gelatin silver print
The Christina N. and Swan J. Turnblad
Memorial Fund, 81.94.3

JOSE ORTIZ-ECHAGUE
Spanish, 1898–
Lino de Duelo, 1932
Fresson print
Mr. and Mrs. Patrick Butler Fund, 85.90

TOD PAPAGEORGE
American, 1940–
Central Park, 1980
Gelatin silver print
The Ethel Morrison Van Derlip Fund,
82.37.2

JOHN SCHLESINGER
American, 20th century
Untitled (fugitive), 1984
Gelatin silver print
The Ethel Morrison Van Derlip Fund,
85.3

NEIL SELKIRK
English, 1947–
Charles Colson, 1973
Gelatin silver print
The Ethel Morrison Van Derlip Fund,
80.47.5

NEIL SELKIRK
English, 1947–
H. E. Mr. Peter Jay and Mrs. Jay, 1978
Gelatin silver print
The Ethel Morrison Van Derlip Fund,
80.47.2

RAGUBIR SINGH
Indian, 1942–
*Village Well in Dusty Winds, Jodhpur
District, India,* about 1981
Dye transfer print
Gift of Martin Weinstein, 84.125.1

AARON SISKIND
American, 1903–
New York City (Window 3), 1947
Gelatin silver print
Gift of Robert and Joyce Menschel,
84.96.5

AARON SISKIND
American, 1903–
Martha's Vineyard, 1948
Gelatin silver print
Gift of Robert and Joyce Menschel,
84.96.1

EVE SONNEMAN
American, 1946–
Window, Camera, Chicago, 1978
Two dye bleach color prints
Gift of Estelle Schwartz, 83.104.1, 2

ALFRED STIEGLITZ
American, 1864–1946
The Steerage, 1907
Photogravure from "291,"
September–October, 1915
Gift of Myron Kunin, 84.37.6a

ALFRED STIEGLITZ
American, 1864–1946
Equivalent, 1929
Gelatin silver print
Gift of Harry Drake, 83.152

ALFRED STIEGLITZ
American, 1864–1946
From the Shelton, West, 1935
Gelatin silver print
Gift of Harry Drake, 83.151

PAUL STRAND
American, 1890–1976
Young Boy, Gondeville, France
Gelatin silver print
Gift of John A. Rollwagen and Beverly J.
Baranowski, 85.118

STEPHANIE B. TORBERT
American, 1945–
Terrell Lucius, 1980
Dye bleach color print
The Ethel Morrison Van Derlip Fund,
84.27

GEORGE UPHAM
American, 1946–
Untitled, n.d.
Color coupler print
Gift of the artist, 85.86

JOANN VERBURG
American, 1950–
Dine Drawing, 1982
Five gelatin silver prints
The Ethel Morrison Van Derlip Fund,
82.131.1–5

JOHN VONG
American, 1950–
Untitled, about 1974
Gelatin silver print
Gift of the artist, 84.59.29

DIANA WALKER
American, 1942–
Court Jester (Queen Elizabeth II and
Ronald Reagan), San Francisco, 1983
Color coupler print
Gift of the artist, 84.99

DIANA WALKER
American, 1942–
Walter Mondale, 1984
Color coupler print
Gift of the artist, 84.60.2

TODD WEBB
American, 1905–
Avenue of the Americas, New York City,
1948
Gelatin silver print
Gift of Martin Weinstein, 84.125.4

Department of
PRINTS AND DRAWINGS

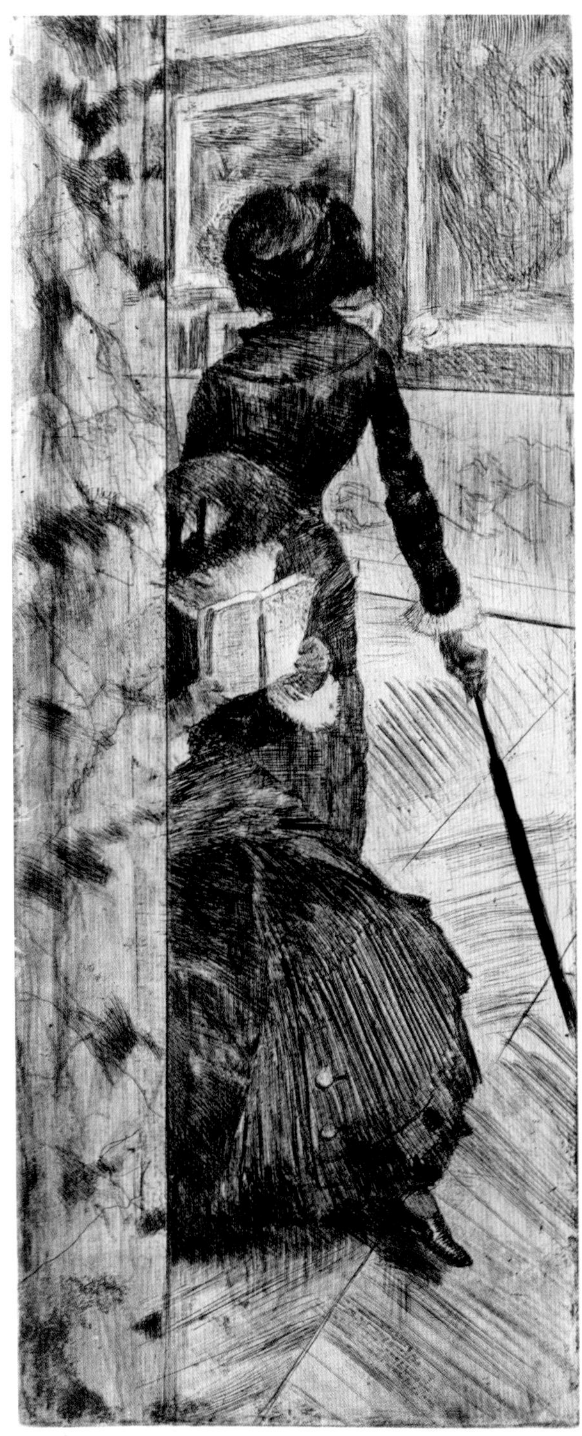

At present the collections housed in the Department of Prints and Drawings are numerically the largest in the museum, consisting of more than forty thousand prints, about two thousand drawings and several hundred illustrated books. The disproportionate ratio of prints to drawings is an indication of the relative importance placed on these two categories by past curators and directors at the Institute since its beginnings in 1915.

While it is true that the first director, Joseph Breck, initially purchased a small group of prints and an equal number of drawings, his stated goal was to form an encyclopedic collection of prints at the museum, and he seems not to have entertained similar ambitions for a drawings collection. This inequity in Breck's collecting policy is not as strange as it seems at first glance, if one considers the circumstances at the time of World War I when the new building first opened its doors. At that time most European art treasures, including Old Master drawings, seemed securely placed either in such institutional settings as national and ecclesiastical museums or in the collections of aristocratic families. A fledgling museum in the midwest could only aspire to first-rate examples of drawings from the recent past or the present. Prints, on the other hand, offered a wider scope for collecting: since they exist in multiple impressions, a new museum could form a collection of fine prints which might include great examples by the Old Masters, as well as more recent works. In fact, Breck realized his hopes for just such an encyclopedic collection of prints the very next year when one of the museum's founding trustees, Herschel V. Jones, presented the Institute with the William M. Ladd Collection of five thousand prints dating from the fifteenth to the twentieth century. With this gift the Institute joined the ranks of the older public print collections on the east coast, and managed to surpass every midwestern civic museum except the Art Institute of Chicago.

EDGAR DEGAS
French, 1834–1917
Au Louvre: La Peinture (Mary Cassatt),
1879-80
Etching and drypoint
The Putnam Dana McMillan Fund,
P.82.13

PIET MONDRIAN
Dutch, 1872–1944
Chrysanthemum, 1906
Pencil and watercolor
Gift of Bruce B. Dayton, 83.162

The gift of such a large number of original works of art affected the museum in several ways. Because the collection required the supervision of a trained specialist, the museum's first separate curatorial department was established in 1916, with Marie C. Lehr at its head. (The Department of Prints and Drawings remained the only specialized curatorial division within the museum for more than fifty years.) It became Miss Lehr's task to catalogue the collection and to supervise the study room where the prints and drawings were available to the public. More significantly, at a time when the museum's nascent collection of paintings, sculpture and decorative arts was very small, the size and scope of the Ladd Collection made it an extremely important resource during the next decades for a series of changing exhibitions organized by the first curator.

Over the next forty years Mr. Jones's gift of the Ladd Collection influenced the pattern of collecting prints and drawings by the museum in two significant ways. First, the existence of a rich and varied collection of prints apparently precluded purchases in this field, with the result that only a handful of prints were bought by Miss Lehr before her retirement in 1941, or by the second director, Russell Plimpton, during his tenure from 1921 until 1956. Fortunately the collection continued to receive gifts from private collectors, including Herschel Jones. During the decade before his death in 1928, Mr. Jones took advantage of the unexpected availability of wonderful examples of Old Master prints from European collections dispersed after the war. Mr. Jones presented half of his collection of five hundred Old Master prints during his lifetime; the remaining half, including many great masterpieces, came to the museum in 1968 after the death of his daughter, Tessie Jones.

The presence of the Ladd Collection also seems to have stifled the growth of the drawings collection, in spite of the growing availability of older works. In the early days, under Breck's director-

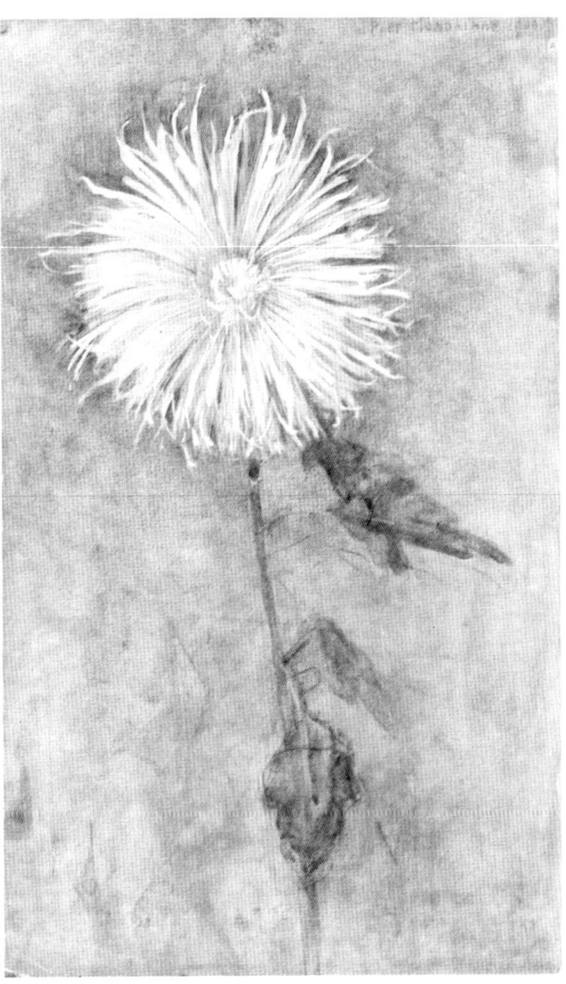

ship, over one hundred drawings had been bought with museum funds, although ninety percent of these were contained in a sketchbook by Burne-Jones. In the 1920s Mrs. Horace Ropes established a fund in memory of her father, John De Laittre, which allowed Russell Plimpton to purchase another hundred drawings for the museum. Some of these drawings were venturesome acquisitions of works by the new generation of modern European artists, including Picasso and Matisse, but most were by artists who are little known today. At the same time, gifts of drawings to the Institute were relatively few in number, for there was no local collector of drawings comparable in stature to Herschel Jones.

In 1956 the collecting activity of the entire museum changed dramatically with the appointment of Richard Davis as director. That same year witnessed the revival of the Department of Prints and Drawings, which had been left without a curator since Miss Lehr's retirement in 1941. With a generous donation of funds from Herschel Jones's son and daughter-in-law, Mr. and Mrs. Carl W. Jones, the museum was able to lure Harold Joachim away from the Art Institute of Chicago where he was second-in-command of the Department of Prints and Drawings. Before returning to Chicago in 1958 to become head of the department, Joachim charted a new course for collecting prints in Minneapolis. Not only did he work closely with local collectors, laying the groundwork for many future gifts, but with Davis's encouragement he also used endowment funds for buying masterpieces in the field of prints on a regular basis. Among the notable impressions bought at this time may be cited Dürer's *Adam and Eve*, Rembrandt's *Christ Crucified Between Two Thieves* ("The Three Crosses"), and Blake's monotype *Nebuchadnezzar*, all among the museum's greatest treasures.

In addition, Joachim allowed his own interest in graphic arts of the late nineteenth and early twentieth century to dictate some of his purchases, including important prints by Degas, Redon, Vuillard and Cézanne. At a time when buying German Expressionist works had yet to become fashionable for most American museums and collectors, Joachim purchased a small but choice group of prints in this field, acquisitions which mirrored the director's acquisition of Expressionist paintings during the same period.

Under the directorship of Anthony Clark the museum's acquisition policies became even broader in scope. Davis's focus on the single great work of art was maintained, but increasingly the most impressive purchases were made in areas that had been overlooked by most other museums of our standing. In light of this new philosophy of acquisitions, it is not surprising that trustees supported the purchase of the Minnich Collection, an extraordinary group of eight thousand prints documenting the history of botanical, zoological, and fashion illustrations from the fifteenth through the nineteenth centuries. This accession not only added a dimension to the print collection not frequently encountered in American museums, but it also preserved intact one of the most distinctive collections ever formed in Minnesota. Clark encouraged Edward Foster, the new curator of prints and drawings, to follow an acquisition policy of similar breadth. Consequently, when Foster began to strengthen the holdings of German Expressionist prints, he bought works by lesser known artists such as Meidner and Felixmüller as well as master prints by Beckmann and Kirchner.

In the 1960s many of the best young American artists began working at one or another of a growing number of print workshops, with the result that printmaking in this country began to enjoy a new respect. Foster, interested in this development, became the first curator of the department for whom the acquisition of contemporary art was a primary goal. At a time when some aspects of modern American art were highly controversial, he bought prints by Rauschenberg and drawings by Johns and Lichtenstein, which form the cornerstone of the department's contemporary American holdings.

For the first time as well, a concerted effort was made to buy drawings in a wide variety of fields of interest to Clark, Foster, and other scholars on the staff: eighteenth-century Dutch, French and Italian, nineteenth-century English, and early twentieth-century German and Austrian. The purchase of many of these drawings was made possible by the donation of specially designated

GIOVANNI BATTISTA TIEPOLO
Italian, 1696–1770
Vari Capricci
Suite of ten etchings
The Herschel V. Jones Fund, by
exchange, P.81.2.1–10

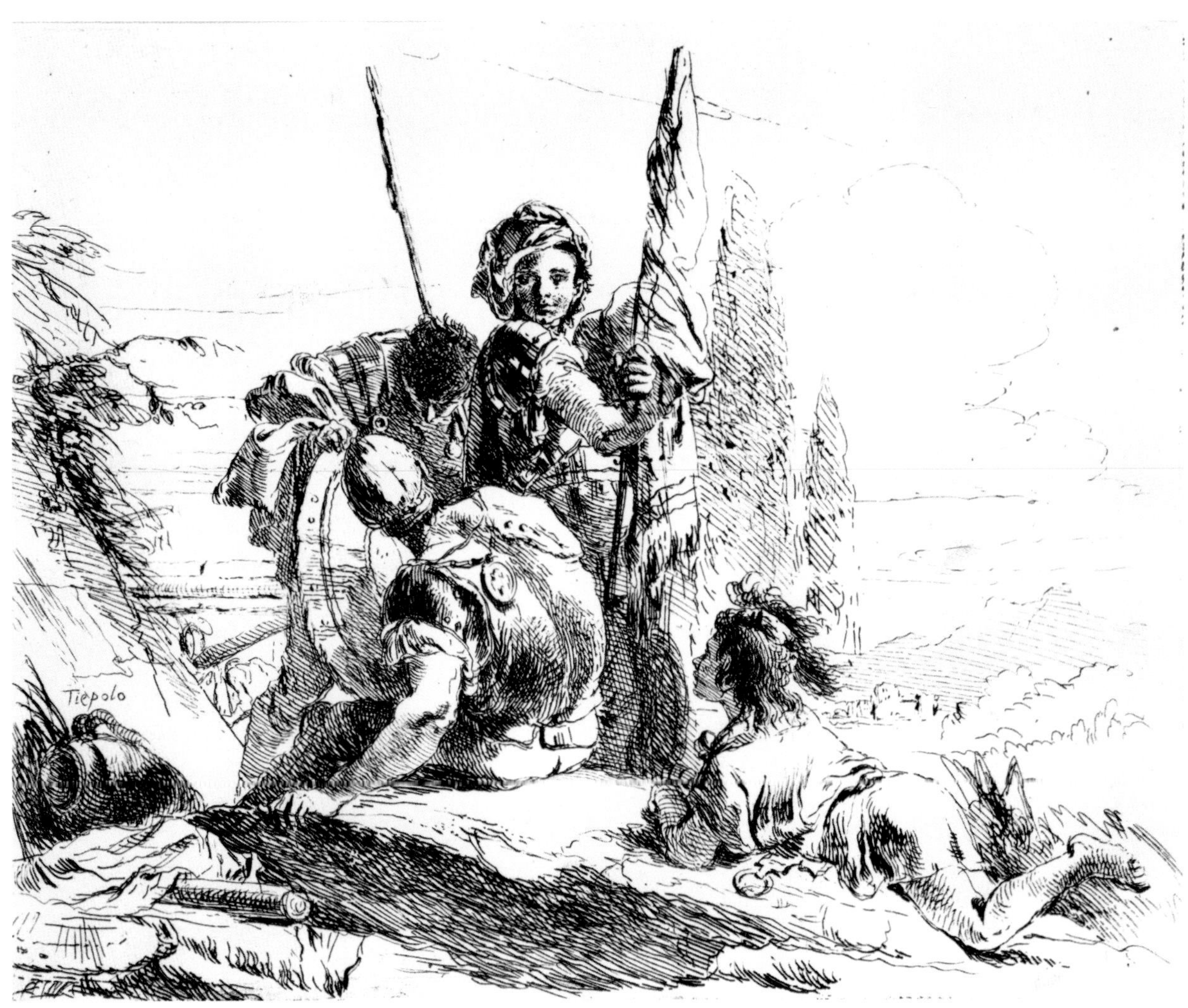

funds from several patrons, including David M. Daniels, Hall and Kate Peterson and the Henfield Foundation.

Since joining the staff in 1972, two years before Samuel Sachs was appointed director, I have concentrated on adding works by major artists, while continuing to strengthen the collection by buying works by lesser known artists as well. Because the curators in charge of the collection have always been print specialists, we took the opportunity in 1982 to add to the staff Richard Campbell, a draw-ing specialist, so that this aspect of the collection would receive the attention it deserves.

The works of art on view in the prints and draw-ings galleries give some indication of the collect-ing activities in the department in recent years. Curators like nothing better than to be able to make significant additions to an underdeveloped area of the collection, especially when that area has been overlooked by the public as well so that collecting opportunities abound at a devalued rate. Most of the eighteenth-century French prints on exhibit were bought in this way, although the market for such prints has risen considerably, in a very short space of time. Debucourt's *Promenade Publique*, 1792, the latest addition in this category, is undoubtedly one of the greatest color prints made in France during the eighteenth century, a period of notable importance for the development of this medium.

For a museum that prides itself on its paintings and decorative arts from eighteenth-century Italy, it was regrettable that the print department could only boast first-rate etchings by one of the three great Italian printmakers of the period. Our set of Canaletto etchings is exceptional, and it had long been our hope to add works by Tiepolo and Piranesi of comparable quality. We achieved our goal by acquiring early impressions of a set of four fantasy designs of Piranesi, the *Grotteschi*, as well as the suite of ten etchings by Tiepolo known as the *Vari Capricci*.

As might be expected in a collection as good as ours, our holdings of prints by Dürer and Rembrandt are very fine and include magnificent proofs of some of their greatest works. Nonetheless, we are always delighted when this core of the collection can be further enriched. Two very early impressions of woodcuts by Dürer were added, *St. John the Baptist and St. Onuphrius* of about 1506 and the charming *Holy Family with Anna and Joachim*, 1511. The latter print was acquired by exchanging a duplicate impression of another woodcut of the same date and similar subject that is no longer thought to have been designed by Dürer. Since this new acquisition means that we now own examples of both prints, we are exhibiting them together so that the viewer can see the superior quality of the Dürer design.

We also were able to increase the number of Rembrandt's etchings in the museum by four, including a brilliant impression of the portrait of *Clement de Jonghe* which was bought at auction. This fourth-state impression with the dramatic

chiaroscuro of its rich drypoint offers a marked contrast to the sensitive first state in pure etching which was already in the collection. Seen together the two versions demonstrate something of Rembrandt's creative process as he developed his portrait through successive stages.

The third great master in the history of printmaking is Goya, and until recently our collection of his prints was extensive but undistinguished. Our centennial acquisition program in 1983 enabled us to remedy this situation with the purchase of a set of eighty aquatints, the *Caprichos*, which is one of the earliest to have been printed from Goya's plates. Subsequently, we have bought several impressions from later editions of one of the prints from the *Caprichos*, and when they are exhibited next to each other, the extraordinary richness of the early set can be readily appreciated.

The centennial year was the occasion for a successful bid at auction on a beautiful drawing by Fragonard. This is the most important drawing to have been bought by the museum in more than a decade, and one which we hope will set a standard for future purchases of drawings.

While it is gratifying to review our accomplishments in buying so many remarkable works of art for the department in competition with other museums and collectors, it is important to take note of the broad range and exceptional quality of the prints, drawings, and artists' books that have come to the museum as gifts. Without the generous support of so many private collectors who have enriched the collection with gifts of purchase funds and works of art, our collections would be greatly diminished.

John Ittmann
Curator of Prints and Drawings

FRANCISCO JOSE DE GOYA Y LUCIENTES
Spanish, 1746–1828
Los Caprichos
Presentation copy before the first edition of 1799. Set of 80 etchings with aquatint in the original binding.

Gift of Mr. and Mrs. John T. Adams, Dr. and Mrs. David Bradford, Mr. and Mrs. Benton J. Case, Mr. and Mrs. W. John Driscoll, Mr. and Mrs. Reuel Harmon, and the William Hood Dunwoody Fund, by exchange, P.83.57.1–80

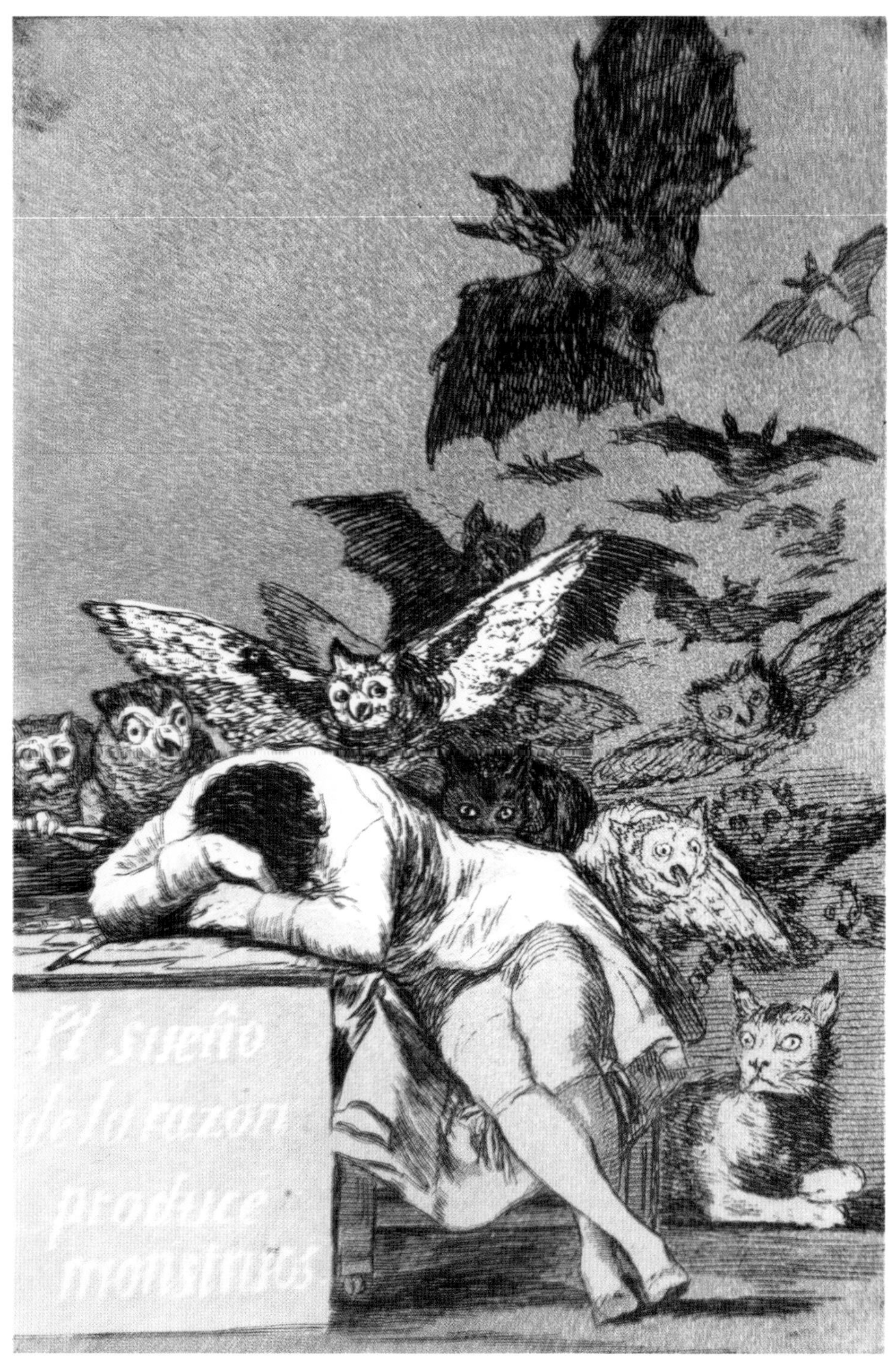

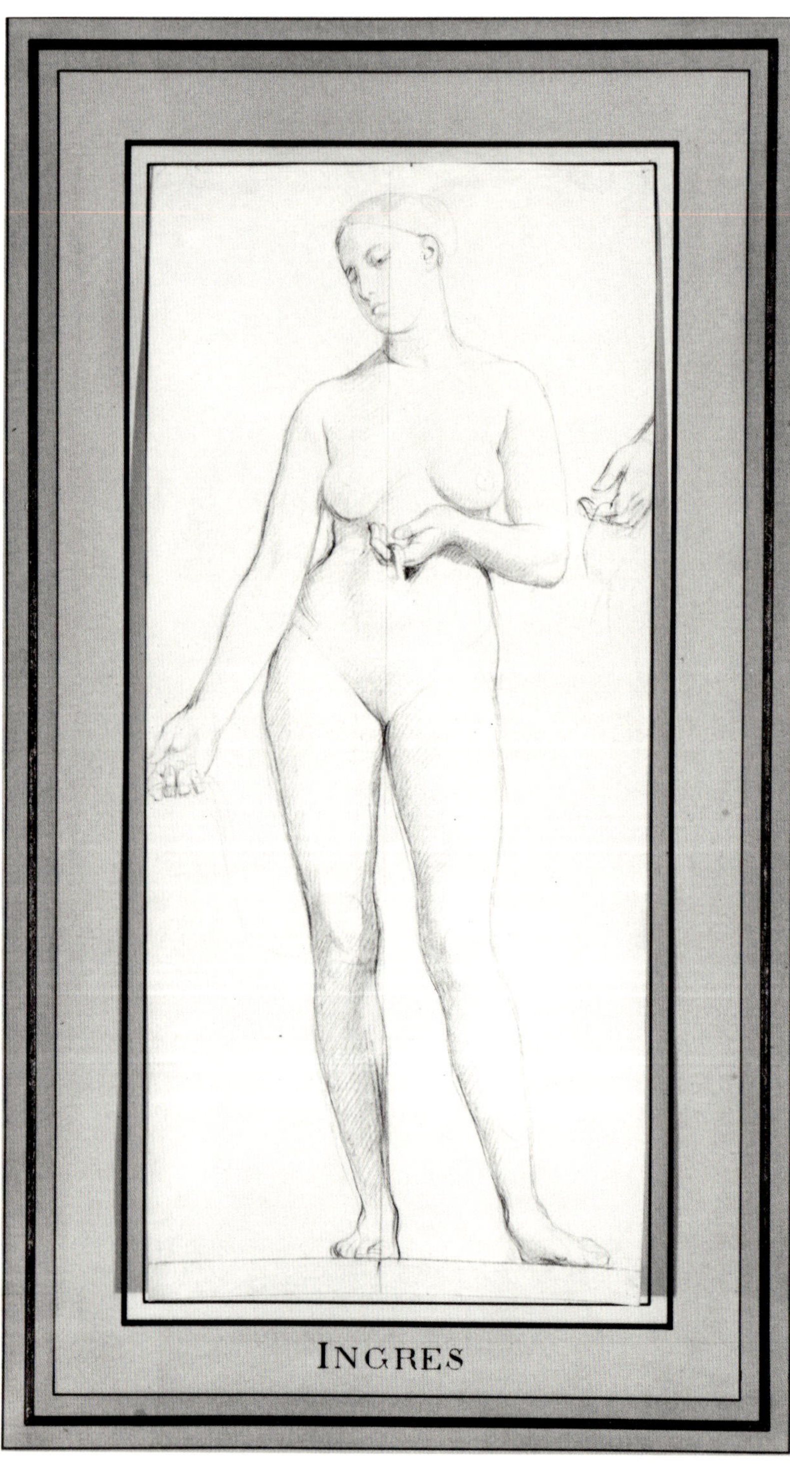

PRINTS

ADOLPHE APPIAN
French, 1818–98
Entreé du village d'Artemare, 1880
Etching
The Ethel Morrison Van Derlip Fund,
P.85.9

WILLIAM BAILEY
American, 1930–
Untitled (Still life), 1983
Etching
Gift of Martin Weinstein, P.84.37

GEORG BASELITZ
German, 1938–
Eagle Blue, 1974
Color woodcut, hand painted
The Ethel Morrison Van Derlip Fund,
P.82.25

ED BAYNARD
American, 1940–
Snow Flower, 1979
Aquatint
The Ethel Morrison Van Derlip Fund,
P.80.17

JACOB BINCK
German, about 1500–69
Portrait of Lucas Gassel, Painter, 1529
Engraving
The Fiduciary Fund, P.80.23

PIERRE BONNARD
French, 1867–1947
Child with Lamp, about 1897
Color lithograph printed in five colors
Bequest of Dorothy Millett Lindeke,
P.84.22

PIERRE BONNARD
French, 1867–1947
Quelques aspects de la vie de Paris,
1899
13 color lithographs
Gift of Mrs. John S. Pillsbury, Sr.,
P.80.57.1–13

FRANÇOIS BONVIN
French, 1817–87
La Tisserande, 1861
Etching
The Ethel Morrison Van Derlip Fund,
P.82.29

RICHARD BOSMAN
American, 1944–
Man Overboard, 1981
Woodcut
The William Hood Dunwoody Fund,
P.81.52

JEAN-AUGUSTE-DOMINIQUE INGRES
French, 1780–1867
*Standing Female Nude with Restudy of
Left Hand*
Black chalk
The John R. Van Derlip Fund, 80.7

FISKE BOYD
American, 1895–
Concept, 1951 (U.N. Building, N.Y.)
Woodcut
Gift of funds from June 1 Gallery,
Miscellaneous Purchase Fund and the
Ethel Morrison Van Derlip Fund,
P.84.31

RODOLPHE BRESDIN
French, 1822–85
Rocky Landscape, 1880
Etching
Gift of funds from an anonymous donor,
P.82.1

JULES CHERET
French, 1836–1931
Palais de Glace, Champs Elysées, 1894
Color lithograph
Gift of Bruce B. Dayton, P.85.5

HOWARD NORTON COOK
American, 1901–
Hudson River Bridge, 1930
Drypoint
The Ethel Morrison Van Derlip Fund,
P.80.94

THOMAS COX
American, 1948–
Ziggurat, 1984
Color woodcut and lithograph
Gift of the Print and Drawing Council,
P.84.65

PHILIBERT-LOUIS DEBUCOURT
French, 1755–1832
La Promenade publique, 1792
Etching, engraving and aquatint printed
in yellow, blue, red, and black from
four plates
The William Hood Dunwoody Fund,
P.85.32

EDGAR DEGAS
French, 1834–1917
Au Louvre: La Peinture (Mary Cassatt),
1879-80
Etching and drypoint
The Putnam Dana McMillan Fund,
P.82.13

GILLES-ANTOINE DEMARTEAU
French, 1750–1806
Head of a Woman, about 1792
Chalk manner engraving
Gift of the Shepherd Gallery, P.82.39

CHARLES MELCHOIR DESCOURTIS
French, 1753–1826
Les Espièglés
Aquatint with etching and engraving
The Ethel Morrison Van Derlip Fund,
P.81.62

JEAN-LOUIS DESPREZ
French, 1742–1804
Chimère de M. Desprez, about 1778–80
Etching
Gift of funds from the Print and
Drawing Council, P.84.7

WERNER DREWES
American (b. Germany), 1899–1985
Elevated, 1931
Woodcut
Gift of Kemper E. Kirkpatrick, P.85.3

ALBRECHT DURER
German, 1471–1528
St. John the Baptist and St. Onuphrius,
about 1504
Woodcut
Gift of Mr. and Mrs. Peter Butler,
P.81.44

ALBRECHT DURER
German, 1471–1528
*Holy Family with Anna and Joachim
Under a Tree,* 1511
Woodcut
Gift of Mr. and Mrs. Harrison R.
Johnson, Jr., by exchange, and the Ethel
Morrison Van Derlip Fund, P.81.54

JAMES ENSOR
Belgian, 1860–1949
Musiciens fantastiques, 1888
Etching
Gift of Mr. and Mrs. David Tunick in
honor of Samuel Sachs II, P.84.67

MARIANO FORTUNY Y DE MADRAZO
Italian, 1871–1949
Rio a Venezia, 1896
Etching and aquatint
The Ethel Morrison Van Derlip Fund,
P.84.38

HELEN FRANKENTHALER
American, 1928–
Cedar Hill, 1983
Color woodcut
Gift of First Bank, St. Paul, P.84.1

CHARLES GARABEDIAN
American, 1923–
The Vampire, 1975
Color lithograph
Gift of Mr. and Mrs. Benton Case, Jr.,
P.83.17

ARNAUD-ELOI GAUTIER D'AGOTY
French, 1745–83
Flayed Skeleton, 1773
Color mezzotint and etching, printed
from four plates
Gift of the Print and Drawing Council,
P.84.8

HENDRIK GOLTZIUS
Dutch, 1558–1617
Josina Hamels, 1580
Engraving
Jacques de la Faille, 1580
Engraving
Gift of Mr. and Mrs. Harrison R.
Johnston, Jr., P.80.31.1–2

HENDRIK GOLTZIUS
Dutch, 1558–1617
The Judgment of Midas, 1590
Engraving
Gift of David M. Daniels, P.80.53

FRANCISCO JOSE DE GOYA Y
LUCIENTES
Spanish, 1746–1828
Los Caprichos
Presentation copy before the first
edition of 1799, bound set of 80
etchings with aquatint in the original
binding. Gift of Mr. and Mrs. John T.
Adams, Dr. and Mrs. David Bradford,
Mr. and Mrs. Benton J. Case, Mr. and
Mrs. W. John Driscoll, Mr. and Mrs.
Reuel Harmon, and the William Hood
Dunwoody Fund, by exchange,
P.83.57.1–80

FRANCISCO JOSE DE GOYA Y
LUCIENTES
Spanish, 1746–1828
Al Conde Palatino, first edition, 1799,
plate 33, from *Los Caprichos*
Etching, drypoint, aquatint and burin,
brown ink
Gift of funds from Barbara Kaerwer,
Ann and Louis Zelle, anonymous donors
and the Print and Drawing Council
in memory of Harold Joachim,
P.84.5

Department of

PRINTS AND DRAWINGS

FRANCISCO JOSE DE GOYA Y
LUCIENTES
Spanish, 1746–1828
Al Conde Palatino, second edition,
about 1855, plate 33, from *Los
Caprichos*
Etching, drypoint, aquatint, and burin
Gift of the Print and Drawing Council,
P.85.53

FRANCISCO JOSE DE GOYA Y
LUCIENTES
Spanish, 1746–1828
Al Conde Palatino, tenth edition,
1918–28, plate 33, from *Los Caprichos*
Etching, drypoint, aquatint and burin,
brown ink
Gift of funds from Barbara Kaerwer, Ann
and Louis Zelle, anonymous donors and
the Print and Drawing Council in
memory of Harold Joachim, P.84.6

MICHAEL GRAVES
American, 1934–
Domestic Landscape, 1984
Color woodcut
Gift of members of the Print and
Drawing Council's Chicago tour, P.84.40

ISIDORE STANISLAS HELMAN
French, 1743–1806 or 1809
N'Ayez pas peur, ma bonne amie, 1776,
after Moreau le Jeune
Etching and engraving
Gift of funds from the Print and
Drawing Council, P.83.70

DAVID HOCKNEY
English, 1937–
Celia in a Wicker Chair, 1974
Color etching and aquatint
The Ethel Morrison Van Derlip Fund,
P.81.45

RICHARD HOUSTON
Irish, 1722–75
Portrait of James Sayre (after Johann
Zoffany), 1772
Mezzotint
The Fiduciary Fund, P.80.22

FRANÇOIS JANINET
French, 1752–1813
The Difficult Confession, 1787
Aquatint
The Ethel Morrison Van Derlip Fund,
P.81.63

JASPER JOHNS
American, 1930–
Target II, 1967–68
Etching and aquatint, second of two
states
Gift of the Betty Parsons Foundation,
P.85.12

FERNAND KHNOPFF
Belgian, 1858–1921
Un Masque, 1899
Drypoint
Gift of funds from the Print and
Drawing Council, P.84.9

FERNAND KHNOPFF
Belgian, 1858–1921
Gesture of Offering
Drypoint
Gift of funds from Mr. and Mrs. Lauress
V. Ackmann, P.84.10

FERNAND KHNOPFF
Belgian, 1858–1921
Sire Hallwyn
Drypoint
Gift of funds from Mr. and Mrs. Lauress
V. Ackmann, P.84.11

BERNARD LEPICIE
French, 1699–1755
The Provider, 1742, after Chardin
Etching and engraving
The Ethel Morrison Van Derlip Fund,
P.81.15

JEAN-BAPTISTE LE PRINCE
French, 1734–81
Le Repos, 1771
Etching and aquatint, from an album of
137 prints by Le Prince
Gift of Herschel V. Jones, by exchange,
P.85.35

ARTHUR ALLEN LEWIS
American, 1873–1957
Spring (illustration for Petronius),
about 1927
Color woodcut
The Ethel Morrison Van Derlip Fund,
P.80.37

ARTHUR ALLEN LEWIS
American, 1873–1957
Spring
Color woodcut
The Ethel Morrison Van Derlip Fund,
P.80.38

ROY LICHTENSTEIN
American, 1923–
Brushstrokes, 1967
Color lithograph
Gift of Rev. Richard Hillstrom in
memory of Edward and Irene Hillstrom,
P.84.42

EDVARD MUNCH
Norwegian, 1863–1944
The Kiss, 1902
Color woodcut
The Herschel V. Jones Fund, by
exchange, P.79.59

GIUSEPPE DE NITTIS
Italian, 1846–84
Woman with a Fan, about 1873–75
Etching and drypoint
The Putnam Dana McMillan Fund,
P.82.33

MIMMO PALADINO
Italian, 1948–
Fantasma, 1980
Color softground etching
The Ethel Morrison Van Derlip Fund,
P.82.26

PABLO PICASSO
Spanish, 1881–1973
Taureau de profil, 1945
Crayon transfer lithograph
Gift of Darwin Reedy, P.81.69

GIOVANNI BATTISTA PIRANESI
Italian, 1720–78
Grotteschi
Suite of four etchings
The Ethel Morrison Van Derlip Fund,
P.81.26.1–4

GIOVANNI BATTISTA PIRANESI
Italian, 1720–78
Imaginary View of a Prison, plate 14
from the *Carceri d'Invenzione*
Etching
Anonymous gift, P.84.70

CAMILLO PROCACCINI
Italian, about 1551–1629
The Transfiguration
Etching, first of two states
Gift of W.L. Tenney and Alice Tenney
Mitchell, by exchange, P.85.10

PHILIBERT-LOUIS DEBUCOURT
French, 1755–1832
La Promenade publique, 1792
Etching, engraving and aquatint printed
in yellow, blue, red, and black from
four plates
The William Hood Dunwoody Fund,
P.85.32

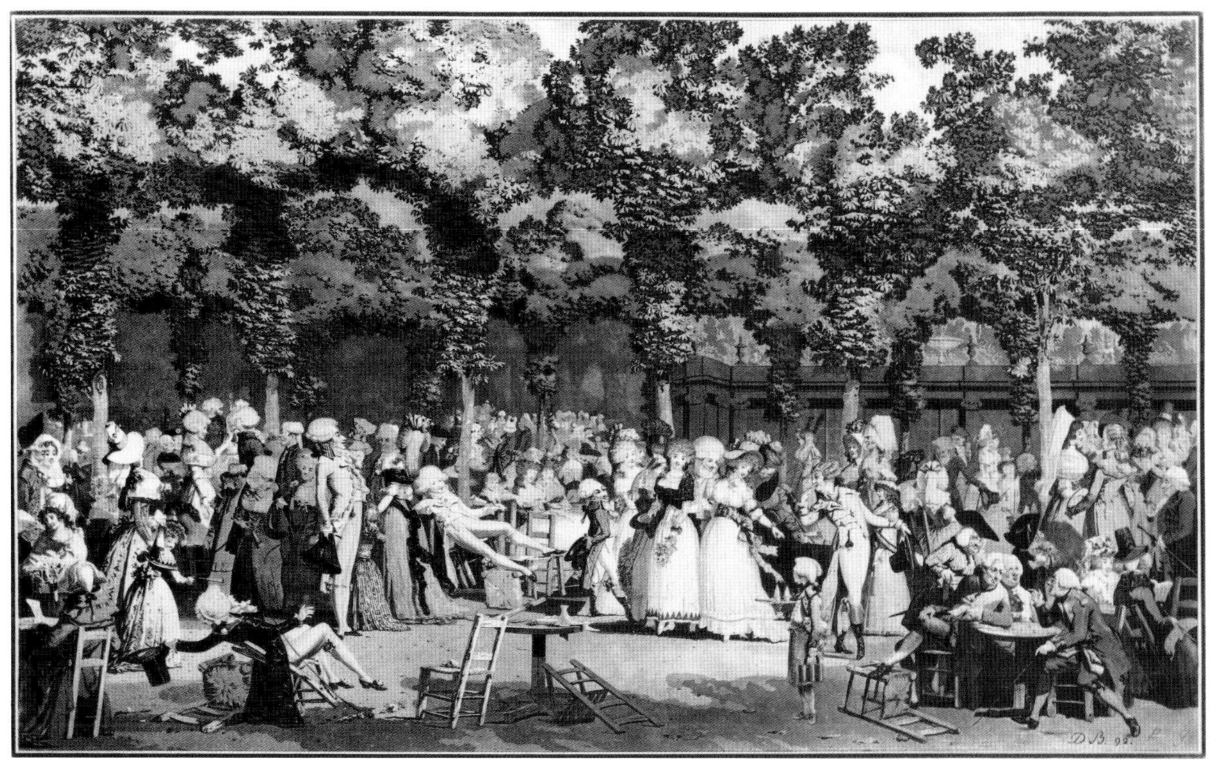

NICOLAS-FRANÇOIS REGNAULT
French, 1746–about 1810
Le Songe d'amour, 1791, after
Fragonard
Stipple engraving and etching
Gift of funds from the Print and
Drawing Council and Kemper E.
Kirkpatrick, P.83.71

REMBRANDT HARMENSZ VAN RIJN
Dutch, 1606–69
*Old Man Shading His Eyes with His
Hand,* about 1639
Etching
Gift of Mr. and Mrs. Harrison R.
Johnston, Jr., P.80.33

REMBRANDT HARMENSZ VAN RIJN
Dutch, 1606–69
The Triumph of Mordecai, about 1640
Etching
Gift of Mr. and Mrs. Harrison R.
Johnston, Jr., P.80.32

REMBRANDT HARMENSZ VAN RIJN
Dutch, 1606–69
Descent from the Cross, a Sketch, about
1642
Etching
Bequest of Harry Nord, P.83.11

REMBRANDT HARMENSZ VAN RIJN
Dutch, 1606–69
Clement de Jonghe, Printseller, 1651
Etching with drypoint, fourth of six
states
The Herschel V. Jones Fund, by
exchange, P.79.24

PIERRE AUGUSTE RENOIR
French, 1841–1919
The Hat Pin, 1897
Lithograph
Gift of Bruce B. Dayton, P.80.59

PIERRE-AUGUSTE RENOIR
French, 1841–1919
The Hat Pin, 1898
Color lithograph
Gift of Grace Bliss Dayton, P.83.81

HENRI RIVIERE
French, 1864–1951
Lavoir sous bois à Loguivy, 1894
Color woodcut on three sheets
The Ethel Morrison Van Derlip Fund,
P.81.41.1–3

ARNOLD RONNEBECK
American (born Germany), 1885–1947
Wall Street, about 1928–30
Lithograph
Gift of funds from the Hersey
Foundation, P.83.69

SUSAN ROTHENBERG
American, 1945–
Head and Bones, 1980
Woodcut
The Ethel Morrison Van Derlip Fund,
P.82.24

JAN SAENREDAM
Dutch, 1565–1600
The Expulsion from Eden, about 1604,
after Abraham Bloemaert
Engraving
The Ethel Morrison Van Derlip Fund,
P.84.60

AUGUSTIN DE SAINT AUBIN
French, 1736–1807
Au moins soyez discret
Etching and engraving
The Ethel Morrison Van Derlip Fund,
P.81.33

AUGUSTIN DE SAINT AUBIN
French, 1736–1807
Comptez sur mes sermens
Etching and engraving
The Ethel Morrison Van Derlip Fund,
P.81.34

STEVEN SORMAN
American, 1948–
The Singing Bridge, 1979
(Trial proof with notes)
Linocut, woodcut with hand dusted
gold, and blue pencil
The Vermillion Archives
(Inventory 144)
Gift of funds from the North Star
Foundation and the Hersey Foundation,
P.83.59.144

STEVEN SORMAN
American, 1948–
The Singing Bridge, 1980
Color woodcut, linocut, silkscreen,
etching with aquatint, and lithograph
with hand dusted gold
The Vermillion Archives (Inventory 80)
Gift of funds from the North Star
Foundation and the Hersey Foundation,
P.83.59.80

PIETER CLAESZ SOUTMAN
Dutch, about 1580–1657
The Betrayal of Christ, before 1620,
after Anthony Van Dyck
Etching touched with ink, wash, and
graphite
The Ethel Morrison Van Derlip Fund,
P.84.61

DONALD SULTAN
American, 1951–
Untitled, 1980
Aquatint
The Ethel Morrison Van Derlip Fund,
P.80.41

MICHIEL SWEERTS
Flemish, 1618–64
Old Man with a Long Beard, 1656
Etching
Gift of Mr. and Mrs. John E. Andrus III,
P.82.14

PIETRO TESTA
Italian, about 1611–50
*Achilles Plunged into Water from the
Styx*
Etching
Gift of the Print and Drawing Council,
P.85.8

GIOVANNI BATTISTA TIEPOLO
Italian, 1696–1770
Vari Capricci
Suite of ten etchings
The Herschel V. Jones Fund, by
exchange, P.81.2.1–10

HENRI DE TOULOUSE-LAUTREC
French, 1864–1901
La Troupe de Mlle. Eglantine, 1896
Color lithograph
Gift of Bruce B. Dayton, P.80.58

MOSES VAN UYTTENBROECK
Dutch, about 1595–about 1647
Shepherd with a Stick
Etching
The Ethel Morrison Van Derlip Fund,
P.84.59

WALLERANT VAILLANT
Dutch, 1623–77
The Young Draftsman, after Michiel
Sweerts
Mezzotint
The Ethel Morrison Van Derlip Fund,
P.83.83

JEAN-HONORE FRAGONARD
French, 1732–1806
The Sacrifice of the Rose, 1770–80
Black chalk and washes
Gift of Mr. and Mrs. Clinton Morrison,
83.109

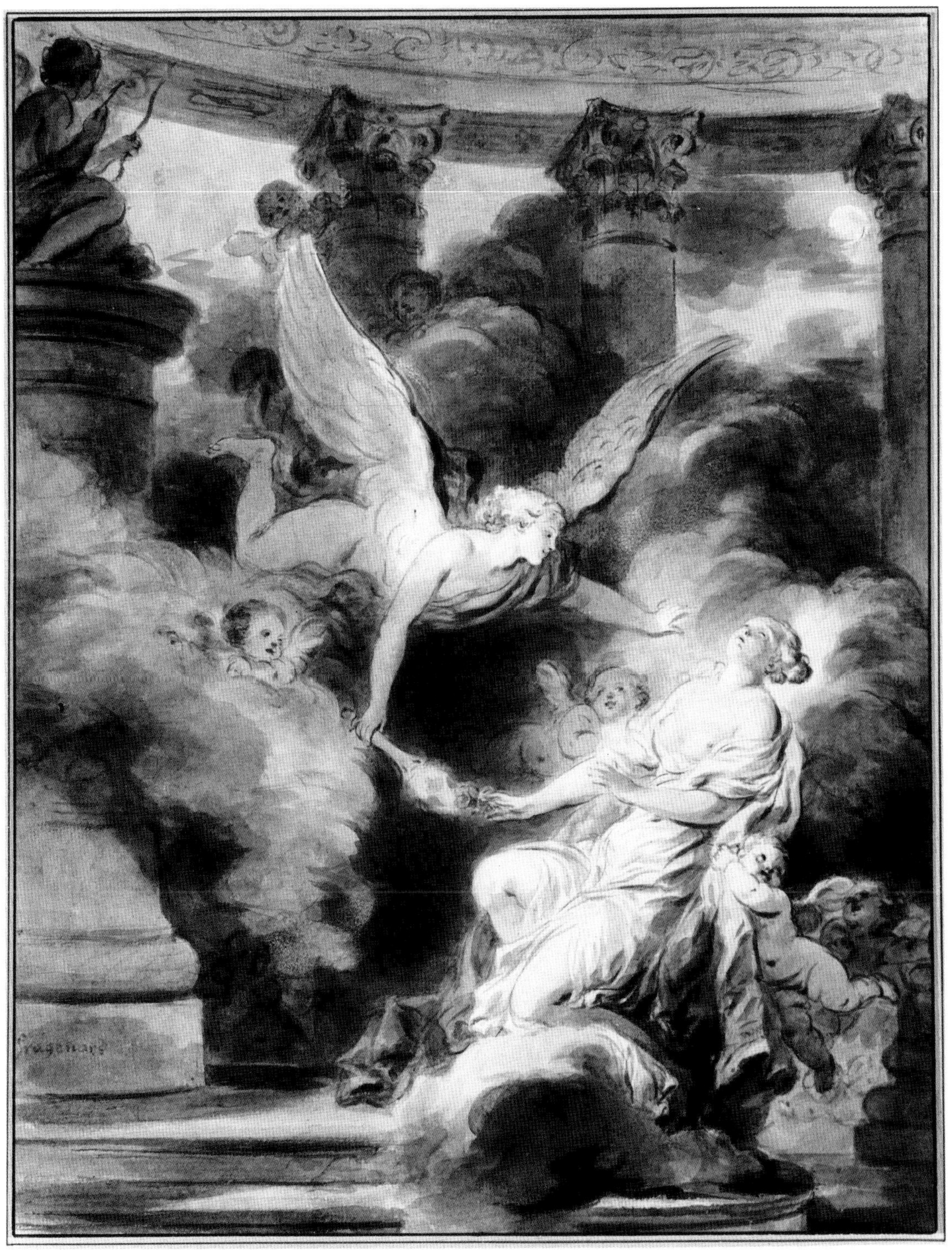

Department of

PRINTS AND DRAWINGS

STOW WENGENROTH
American, 1906–78
Milliken's House, 1931
Lithograph
The Ethel Morrison Van Derlip Fund,
P.82.27

TOM WESSELMAN
American, 1931–
Smoker, 1976
Embossed color lithograph, 35/75
Gift of Margey and Russell Cowles II,
P.83.24

JOHN WHESSELL
English, about 1760–after 1823
Head of a Woman
Etching
Gift of the Print and Drawing Council,
P.84.63

JAMES ABBOTT MCNEILL WHISTLER
American, 1834–1903
The Unsafe Tenement, 1858
Etching, second of four states
Gift of Mr. and Mrs. W. L. Tenney and
Alice Tenney Mitchell, by exchange,
P.85.11

JAMES ABBOTT MCNEILL WHISTLER
American, 1834–1903
The Storm, 1861
Drypoint
Gift of Mr. and Mrs. Edwin Stanton
Fetcher, P.83.84

GRANT WOOD
American, 1891–1942
In the Spring, 1939
Lithograph
Gift of Rev. Richard Hillstrom in
memory of Edward and Irene Hillstrom,
P.84.43

DRAWINGS

Italian, about 1780–90
*Alternative Designs for a Neoclassical
Interior*
Pencil, pen, ink, and watercolor
The Putnam Dana McMillan Fund, 82.19

NICOLAS AFRICANO
American, 1948–
*Sheriff I Deliver Ramerrez, the Highway
Man to your Charge, Justice Must Be Done*
Black ink on white paper
Gift of the National Endowment for the
Arts and the Patrick and Aimee Butler
Family Foundation, 83.14

GEORGE BELLOWS
American, 1882–1925
Nude Standing: Seen from Back, about
1923
Conté crayon and tuche
Gift of Dr. and Mrs. John E. Larkin, Jr.,
in memory of Harold Joachim, 83.166.3

GEORGE BELLOWS
America, 1882–1925
Study for a Young Man Standing
Conté crayon
Gift of Dr. and Mrs. John E. Larkin, Jr.,
83.166.2

EDME BOUCHARDON
French, 1698–1762
Dum Pelago Desaevit Hiems Marine,
1744
Red chalk medallion design
The Ethel Morrison Van Derlip Fund,
82.73

FRANÇOIS BOUCHER
French, 1703–70
Lovers Surprised, about 1765
Brown and black chalks
A gift of many generous friends of
Samuel Sachs II in honor of his service
to The Minneapolis Institute of Arts,
85.61

RODOLPHE BRESDIN
French, 1822–85
Fishing Village, about 1852
Pen and black ink
Gift of David P. Becker in memory of
Philip W. Pillsbury, Mary Pillsbury Lord,
Katharine Pillsbury McKee and Helen
Pillsbury Becker, 85.62

FELIX BUHOT
French, 1847–98
Grand guignol
Black, brown and white chalk
Gift of Edward A. Foster, 80.77

THOMAS COUTURE
French, 1815–79
Recumbent Female Nude
Black and white chalks
Gift of John deLaittre and the Ethel
Morrison Van Derlip Fund, 84.70

CHARLES FRANÇOIS EUSTACHE
French, 1820–70
The Eustache Estate near Cherbourg,
about 1865
Charcoal and white chalk
Anonymous gift of funds, 83.127

MARIANO JOSE FORTUNY Y CARBO
Spanish, 1838–74
A Young Lady in a Blue Dress, 1866
Watercolor and white gouache
The Hadlai A. Hull and David Draper
Dayton Funds, 84.20

JEAN-HONORE FRAGONARD
French, 1732–1806
The Sacrifice of the Rose, 1770–80
Black chalk and washes
Gift of Mr. and Mrs. Clinton Morrison,
83.109

CLEMENT HAUPERS
American, 1900–
Night Club Dancers, 1928
Pen, brush, and ink
Gift of Dr. and Mrs. John E. Larkin, Jr.,
83.166.12

JEAN-AUGUSTE-DOMINIQUE INGRES
French, 1780–1867
*Standing Female Nude with Restudy of
Left Hand*
Black chalk
The John R. Van Derlip Fund, 80.7

ALEXIS-VICTOR JOLY
French, 1798–1894
Landscape with Ruins of a Château,
about 1825–30
Brown ink and wash
Gift of funds from the Print and
Drawing Council, 83.165

YASUO KUNIYOSHI
American, 1893–1953
Rotting Away in Sand
Graphite
Gift of Dr. and Mrs. John E. Larkin, Jr.,
83.166.13

HENRI LAURENS
French, 1885–1954
Female Nude, 1924
Gouache on board
Anonymous gift, 80.65.4

JEAN-JACQUES FRANÇOIS
LE BARBIER, THE ELDER
French, 1738–1826
An Offering to Venus, about 1780
Pen, black ink and wash, and watercolor
Gift of funds from the Print and
Drawing Council, 83.164

FERNAND LEGER
French, 1881–1955
Untitled
Pencil and ink
Anonymous gift, 80.65.2

96

RENE MAGRITTE
Belgian, 1898–1967
Le 16 Septembre, about 1955
Gouache
Gift of Marguerite and Russell Cowles II
in memory of Russell Cowles, 80.78

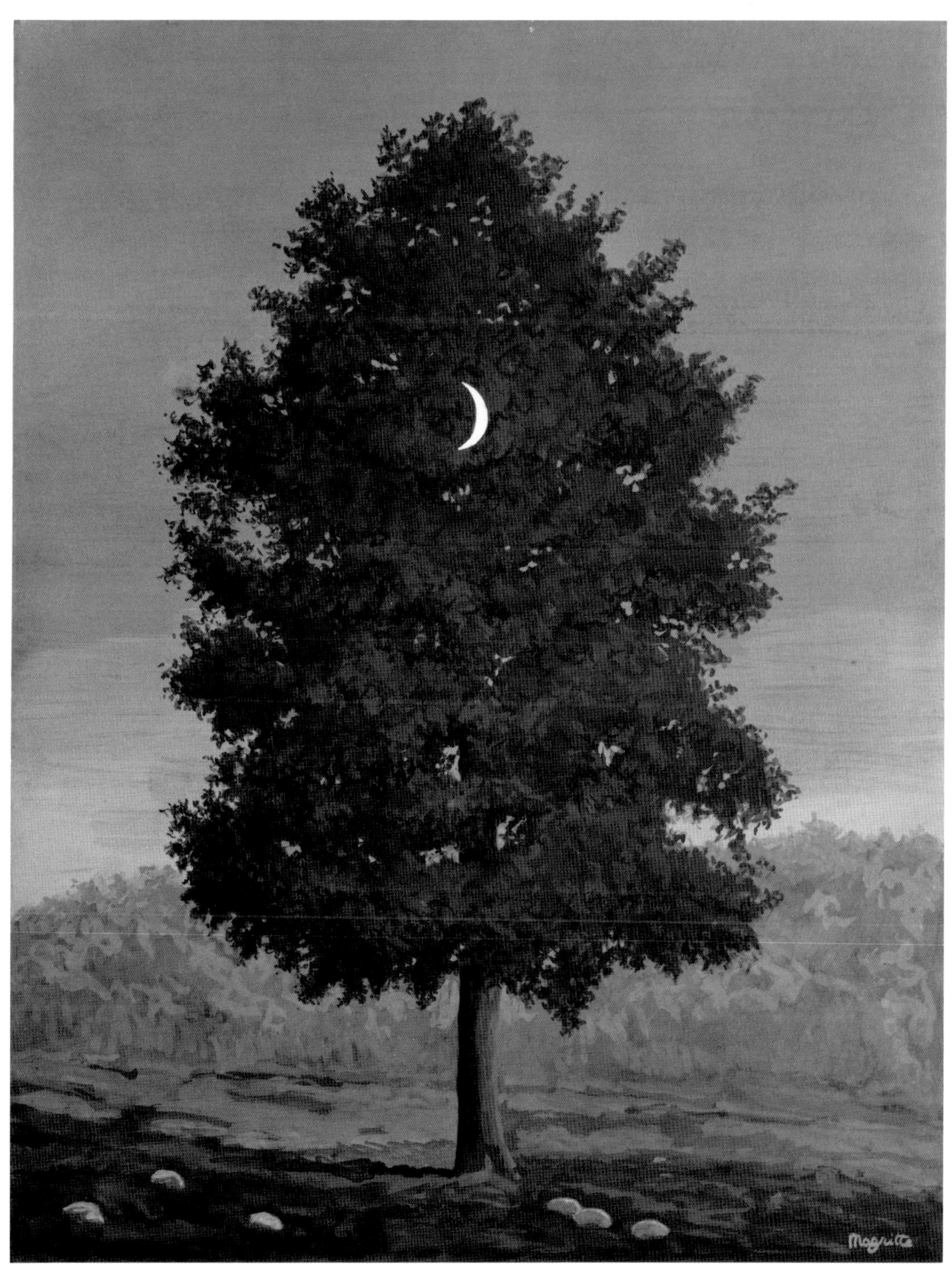

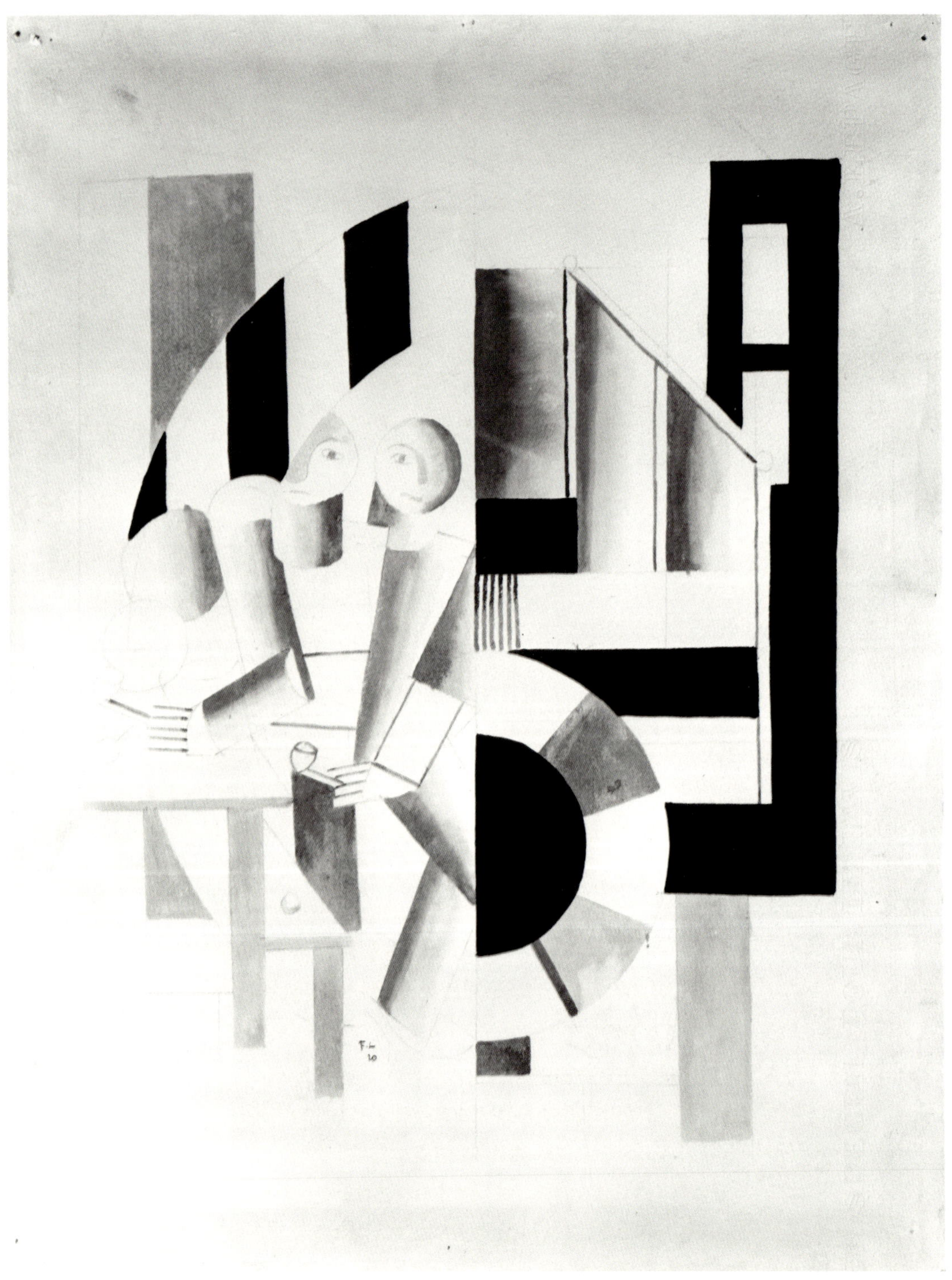

FERNAND LEGER
French, 1881–1955
Untitled
Pencil and ink
Anonymous gift, 80.65.2

NICOLAS-BERNARD LEPICIE
French, 1735–1784
The Difficult Move, about 1781
Pen, ink, gray wash, and watercolor
A gift of many generous friends of
Samuel Sachs II in honor of his service
to The Minneapolis Institute of Arts,
85.60

RENE MAGRITTE
Belgian, 1898–1967
Le 16 Septembre, about 1955
Gouache
Gift of Marguerite and Russell Cowles II
in memory of Russell Cowles; 80.78

REGINALD MARSH
American, 1898–1954
Coney Island Bathers, about 1946
(same on verso)
Chinese ink and watercolor
Bequest of Felicia Meyer Marsh,
82.103.1

DAVID MIDDAUGH
American, 1954–
Snake, Rattle and Roll, 1981
Prismacolor (pencil) on white paper
Gift of the National Endowment for the
Arts and Mr. and Mrs. John E. Andrus III,
83.20

MICHAEL MOGAVERO
American, 1950–
Untitled, 1981
Ebony pencil on white paper
Gift of the National Endowment for the
Arts and Mr. and Mrs. Milton L. Bullock,
83.22

JEAN-GUILLAUME MOITTE
French, 1746–1810
Bacchanalian Frieze, 1787–90
Pen, black ink and wash, green wash,
and white gouache
Gift of funds from the Print and
Drawing Council, John deLaittre, Dr.
and Mrs. John E. Larkin, Jr., Mr. and
Mrs. DeCourcy McIntosh, Andrea Bond,
Charles Skrief and three anonymous
donors, 83.71

PIET MONDRIAN
Dutch, 1872–1944
Chrysanthemum, 1906
Pencil and watercolor
Gift of Bruce B. Dayton, 83.162

EDUARDO PAOLOZZI
English, 1924–
Two untitled drawings
Brush and black ink
Gift of Mr. and Mrs. Howard B. Marks,
83.107.1, 2

JEAN PILLEMENT
French, 1728–1808
Landscape with a Cottage and Peasant
Black chalk
The Ethel Morrison Van Derlip Fund,
anonymous gift of funds, and gift of
funds from the Lutheran Brotherhood,
85.29

ISIDORE-ALEXANDRE-AUGUSTIN PILS
French, 1813–75
The Hunting Party
Graphite, ink, and watercolor
The David Draper Dayton Fund, 81.24

LARRY RIVERS
American, 1923–
Berdie, 1953
Pastel, charcoal, and graphite
Gift of the Maslon Foundation, 82.18.2

GEORGES ROUAULT
French, 1871–1938
Circus Girl, 1906
Watercolor and ink
Given in memory of Alice O'Brien,
81.127

BEN SHAHN
American, 1898–1969
Boy's Day
Brush and black ink
Anonymous gift, 84.142

PAUL SIGNAC
French, 1863–1935
Fishing Boats in La Rochelle, 1919–21
Graphite, watercolor, and opaque white
Gift of Nancy Speert Slater in memory
of Marion K. and Albert E. Heller,
83.108

TERRY WINTERS
American, 1949–
Botanical Subjects
Charcoal and pencil on white paper
Gift of the National Endowment for the
Arts and an anonymous donor, 83.27

GRANT WOOD
American, 1892–1942
The Sentimental Yearner, 1936–37
Crayon, pencil and gouache
Gift of Alan Goldstein, 80.91

THEO WUJCIK
American, 1936–
Robert Rauschenberg: Captive Light,
1979
Silverpoint on off-white paper
Gift of the National Endowment for the
Arts and the Patrick and Aimee Butler
Family Foundation, 83.28

ADJA YUNKERS
American (b. Russia), 1900–1984
Untitled, 1961
Oil on board
Gift of Martin G. Weinstein, 84.134

FRANCESCO ZUCCARELLI
Italian, 1702–88
View of a Terrace
Pen, brown ink, and gray wash
Bequest of Mrs. Margaret B. Hawks,
84.72

BOOKS

PIERRE BONNARD
French, 1867–1947
Parallèlement
Text by Paul Verlaine
Ambroise Vollard, Paris, 1900
109 lithographs and nine woodcuts
Gift of Bruce B. Dayton, B.85.1

JIM DINE
American, 1935–
*The Apocalypse, The Revelation of Saint
John the Divine*
Text from the King James Bible
Arion Press, San Francisco, 1982
29 woodcuts
Gift of Bruce B. Dayton, B.85.3

WASSILY KANDINSKY
Russian, 1866–1944
Klänge
Text by Wassily Kandinsky
R. Piper & Co., Munich, 1912
56 woodcuts (44 printed in black; 12 in
color)
Gift of Bruce B. Dayton, B.83.18

PABLO PICASSO
Spanish, 1881–1973
Vingt Poèmes
Text by Gongora
Les Grands Peintres Modernes et
le Livre, Paris, 1948
41 etchings and lift-ground aquatints
Gift of Bruce B. Dayton, B.81.4

Department of

T E X T I L E S

The growth of textile collections in most non-specialized American art museums has followed a recognizable pattern. The early textile acquisitions came as donations from private collectors and reflected individual taste and interests. Within the museum, they were placed under the care of the decorative arts department, and generally accumulated without a particular order or direction until they were sufficiently numerous to suggest the need for a textile specialist on the staff, not only to direct future acquisitions, but also to oversee storage, display, and conservation. The timetable of this developmental pattern has varied in different institutions depending upon the interests of the curatorial staff, the extent of

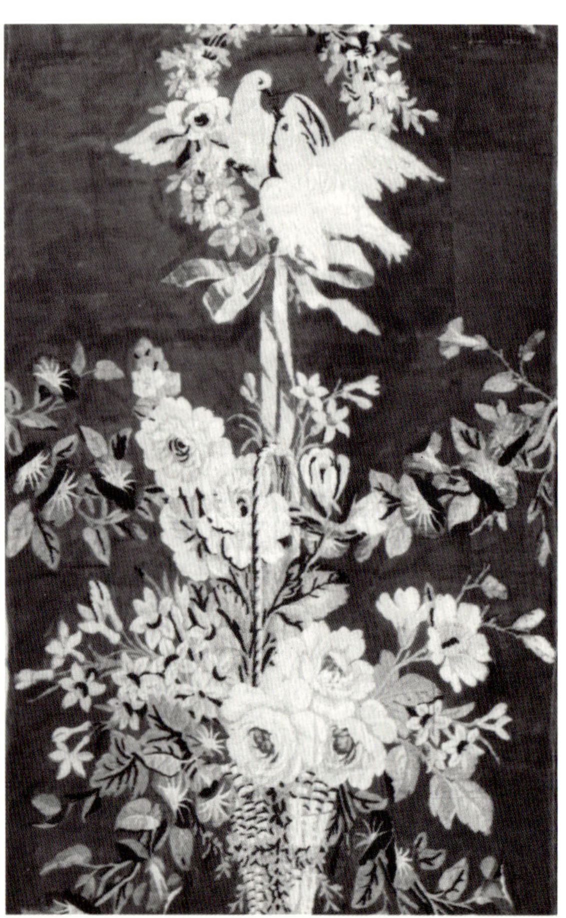

private collecting in the region, and the availability of museum-quality textiles. The establishment of a textile department and the implementation of an intelligent, purposeful purchasing program have historically been the foundation stones upon which the significant American textile collections, such as those at the Boston Museum of Fine Arts and the Metropolitan Museum, have been built.

Most of the major textile collections in this country are encyclopedic in nature, attempting to represent various techniques and cultural traditions. Although the size of an institution's holdings does not necessarily determine its rank, it is generally felt that "masterpieces," the rare, visually spectacular pieces which are a necessity to any significant textile collection, are better understood when they are supported by other first-class works of the same context. Thus the best museum collections are often those with the most extensive holdings.

Like the collections at Boston, the Metropolitan, the Cooper-Hewitt Museum and the Art Institute of Chicago, the Institute's textile collection is encyclopedic, encompassing such diverse techniques as tapestry and other woven structures, embroidery, various types of dyeing and basketry, from cultures as disparate as the late Roman world and twentieth-century Bhutan. The first textile acquisition, a Spanish sixteenth-century silk brocade, was purchased in 1913; the first director, Joseph Breck, working with Mrs. Charles Jarvis Martin, subsequently decided to pursue a first-class tapestry collection. Mrs. Martin continued to render assistance to the Institute while Russell Plimpton was director and by the end of the 1940s the museum had an outstanding collection of European tapestries, including *Esther* and *The Falconers*, two fifteenth-century Flemish works, *Dante at the Gates of Hell*, a sixteenth-century Italian piece, and many seventeenth- and eighteenth-century French tapestries.

PHILIPPE DE LASALLE
French, 1723–1803
Panel, 1770–75
Satin ground with discontinuous
supplementary weft patterning
Silk
The Groves Foundation Fund, 83.36

Egyptian, Coptic, 5th–7th century A.D.
Jewelled cross
Plain weave with tapestry patterning
Linen and wool
Gift of Aimee Mott Butler Charitable
Trust, Mr. and Mrs. John F. Donovan,
the Estate of Margaret B. Hawks, and
Eleanor Weld Reid, 83.126

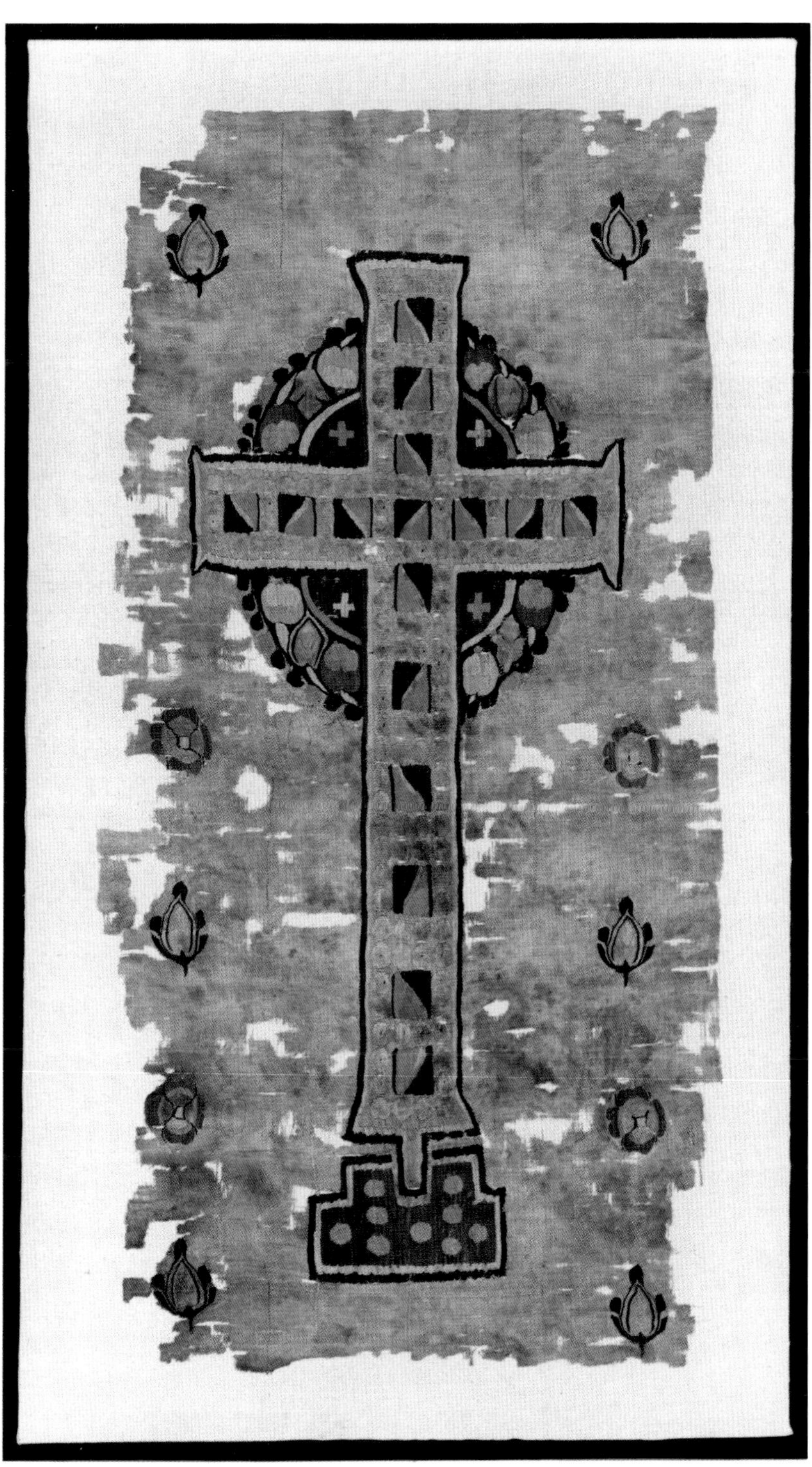

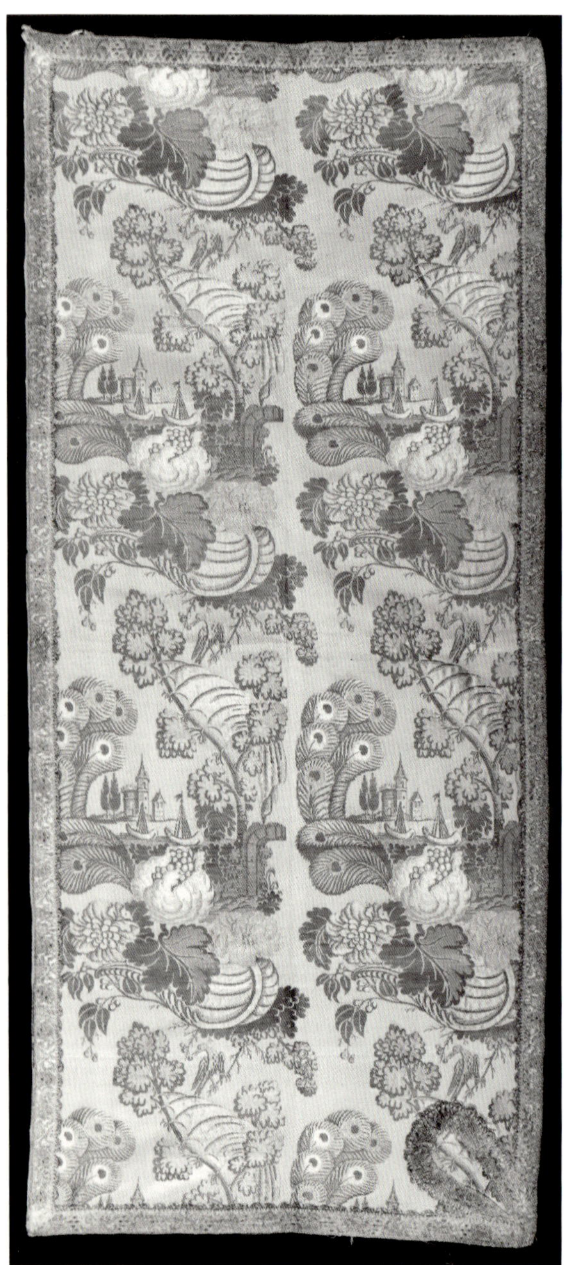

By traditional art-historical standards tapestries have always been considered the finest textiles, for the designs were frequently commissioned by royal courts from the famous painters of the day. This was a context fully understood by the directors, curators, and collectors of the first half of this century, and serious textile collecting tended to concentrate in this area. As more intense cultural and historical research has been done we are better able to understand and define objects in terms of the artistic and technical standards of their own time and place. This broader perspective permits us to collect knowledgeably in numerous areas, some of which formerly were not considered worthy of a museum's attention.

The growth of the Minneapolis collection in these new directions began early. Mrs. C. C. Bovey donated European silks, Kashmir shawls, and Navajo weavings in the early 1940s. In the 1920s and again in the forties private lace collections were added to the museum's holdings. By the late 1940s and the 1950s, private textile collecting was not particularly popular, and this was reflected in the sparse gifts to the Institute during those years. Since the late sixties, however, popular interest in handweaving, ethnic and archeological textiles, and collecting in the private sector has revived. In response to this reawakened interest the museum surveyed its collections and a special textile storage area was included in the 1972 expansion of the building. In 1979 the Textile Department was created, with the result that the textile holdings came to be viewed as a cohesive unit.

Although some art museums do collect costumes and other cut and sewn work, most of the Institute's textiles are flat in nature: panels, coverlets, quilts, carpets, and tapestries. Large costume collections are maintained at the University of Minnesota's Goldstein Gallery and at the Minnesota Historical Society, and the Institute has therefore not collected actively in this area. The few items of clothing we have are intended to demon-

French, 18th century
Panel
Satin ground with supplementary weft
patternings
Miscellaneous Funds, by exchange,
84.17.1

French, 18th century
Chasuble
Embroidered silk and metallic threads
The Christina N. and Swan J. Turnblad
Memorial Fund, 85.114

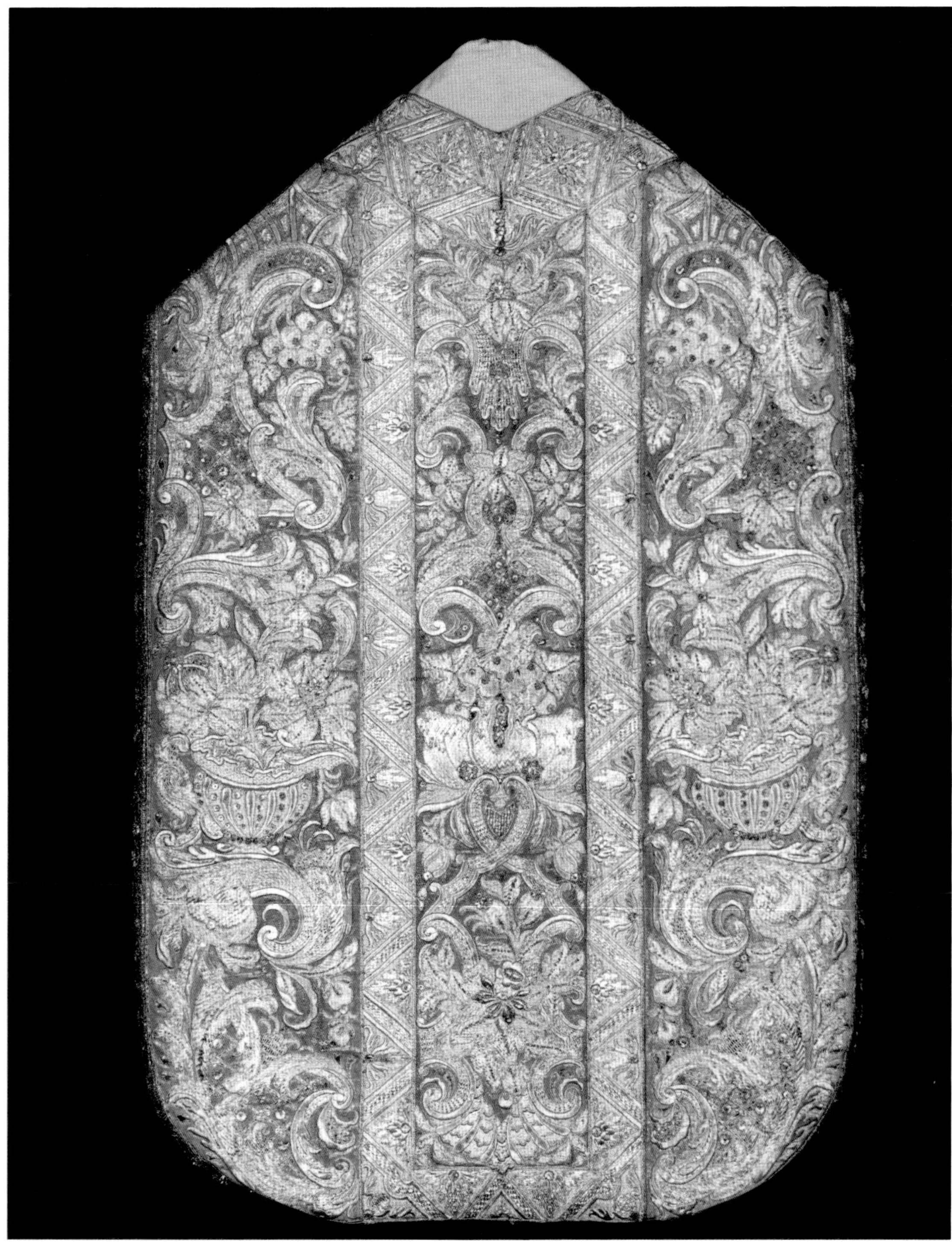

strate particular techniques or textile uses.

American and European museums frequently follow a pattern in which most textiles are cared for by a textile department with special expertise in technical aspects and physical care especially related to storage, conservation and exhibition installation needs. Some specialized holdings of textiles, however, may be under the care of specific departments with expertise on the cultural environment in which the fabrics were created. Thus the textile department here is responsible for all textiles in the museum with the exception of those from China, Japan, and Korea, which are cared for by the Department of Asian Arts.

At present the Minneapolis holdings can be divided into three categories: European, American, and non-Western or ethnic textiles. The practice of collecting European material is well established both for the museum as a whole and within the textile department. With the exception of the tapestries, however, the European textiles have been gathered in a somewhat random manner, without consideration of how the separate parts relate to each other. During the last five years a conscious effort has been made to fill in the stylistic and technical gaps. Particular attention has been paid to expansion in areas of the textile holdings corresponding to other strengths in the museum's collection, such as eighteenth-century France. Thus in 1981 and again in 1984 we made major purchase of textiles that demonstrate stylistic change in the famous French silk production of the eighteenth century. In addition the Groves Foundation, the Morse Foundation, and the Guilford Morse Memorial Fund helped us to add to the collection two major panels created by Phillipe de Lasalle, the foremost French silk designer of his time. We are also filling in gaps in other European areas, such as English embroidery; Italian, French and Flemish lace; and Italian and French velvets. Through the generous assis-

tance of Phyllis Lehmberg, Dr. and Mrs. David Bradford and individual members of the Textile Council, the department has been building over the last two years a collection of passementerie, or woven braids and fringes. As this area continues to grow, it will become one of the outstanding collections of its kind in the country.

In the future we plan to extend our already internationally known tapestry holdings by the addition of examples of English tapestry, presently unrepresented. In particular, we are looking for a fine Mortlake piece; we also hope to find in the future a Germanic "wildman" tapestry, as well as works by Frieda Hansen, a Norwegian weaver; the English designer William Morris, and Jean Lurçat of France, thus better representing Europe's great tapestry tradition.

As an American museum we have been rather neglectful of our own textile production, and we are now making an effort to develop this area. Carroll Simmons's donation of a remarkable American sampler and as the combined effort of several women in the community in 1983 to help us purchase a spectacular crazy quilt have advanced the cause, and we plan to continue growth in this area with the future acquisition of outstanding American samplers, quilts, coverlets, needlework, and printed textiles.

However, as Emerson said, "the sun also shines today," and American fiber artists are currently making significant contributions in the field. With the assistance of the Minnesota Quilters Guild, the Weavers Guild of Minnesota, Charles Senseman and the generous support of Ellen E. Wells, the department now has representative pieces from several internationally recognized contemporary artists: weaver/dyer Lyn Kline, quilter Jan Myers, sculptor Carol Ann Smith, weaver Gerhardt Knodel and designer-weaver Jack Lenor Larsen. In the future we hope to represent more fully contemporary textile expression in these fields, as well as in needlework and lace.

WILLIAM MORRIS
English, 1834–1896
Birds, 1879–80
Jacquard woven double cloth curtain panels
Wool
Gift of Mrs. Adele Roller, 84.66

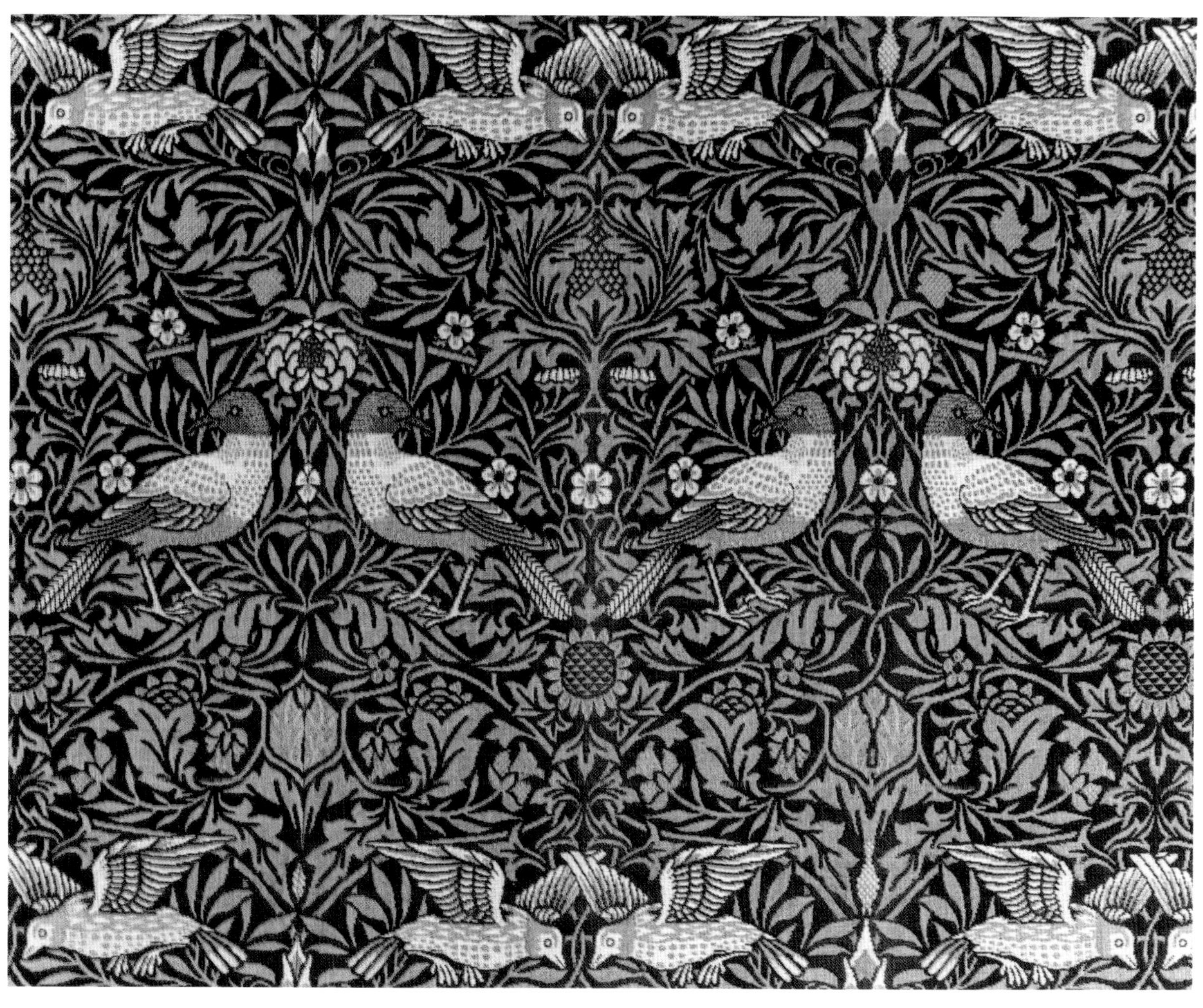

It is in the area of non-Western textiles that the museum's collecting pattern has been most erratic. Here, as elsewhere, these were not systematically collected until recently. With the assistance of several generous donors, however, we have concentrated in the last five years on three areas — the Uzbek ikats of Central Asia, the elaborate products of the body-tension looms of Bhutan, and the masterful and often fanciful embroidery and applique of the Hmong people, who have recently migrated in considerable numbers to Minnesota from their homeland in Laos.

Our most recently acquired ikat panel, a gift of Ellen and Sheldon Sturgis, not only gives greater dimension to the other pieces in the collection, but complements and allows for a fuller understanding of the Uzbek embroideries which are already a part of the museum's holdings. As additional pieces of this material become part of the collections we will have a better opportunity to study both the refined technique and the stylistic variations that reflect the cultural diversity of the Uzbek people.

In 1982 Bud Grossman made a gift of approximately forty textiles woven in Bhutan. These cotton and silk brocades are characteristically rich in color and elaborate in pattern. Even the most utilitarian items, such as garments and lap robes, make symbolic reference to Bhutanese religious and cosmological ideas in their abstract patterns. In their virtuoso technique and striking decorative pattern these fabrics are quite comparable to the most elaborate examples of French brocade.

Over the last five years the museum has acquired a number of elaborately embroidered and appliqued wall panels and costume pieces created by Hmong artists. This work documents the profound changes taking place among a people with an old and very strong cultural tradition. The importance of documenting their artistic achievements and cultural change was first recognized by

Charles H. and Lucy W. Bell, John and Lucy Hartwell, and Robert and Gloria Condon. These six individuals have continued to nurture this area of the collection, realizing that as individual pieces are added the value of the whole is greatly increased. Our latest addition to this area of the museum's holdings was made possible through the combined support of eleven generous donors. This segment of the collection shows great promise of becoming one of the finest in the country. It is hoped that through continued growth, especially by the acquisition of older Hmong pieces, the museum will attract additional material which is now in private collections.

The Textile Department is still quite young, and while it cannot grow in all directions at once, we cannot overlook fields in our care. We are committed to the continued growth of our non-Western holdings. We expect to add oriental rugs and related textiles in order to give greater meaning to the already existing material in this area, and to bring in some basic examples of African and Pacific textile arts, now almost entirely unrepresented. Nonetheless we are also committed to increasing our strength in European and American textiles and also to better representing other textile traditions. We want to build strength in specific areas, particularly those well represented in other collections of the museum, and we also hope to achieve sufficient breadth so that there is good comparative material for research use and for the pleasure and enlightenment of the museum visitor.

Lotus Stack
Curator of Textiles

American, 19th century
Crazy quilt
Pieced and embroidered silk
Gift of Eleanor Atwater, Martha Atwater,
Sandra Butler, Ellie Donovan, Suzanne
H. Hodder, Anita Kunin, Laura Miles,
Eleanor W. Reid, and Kathleen Scott,
82.139

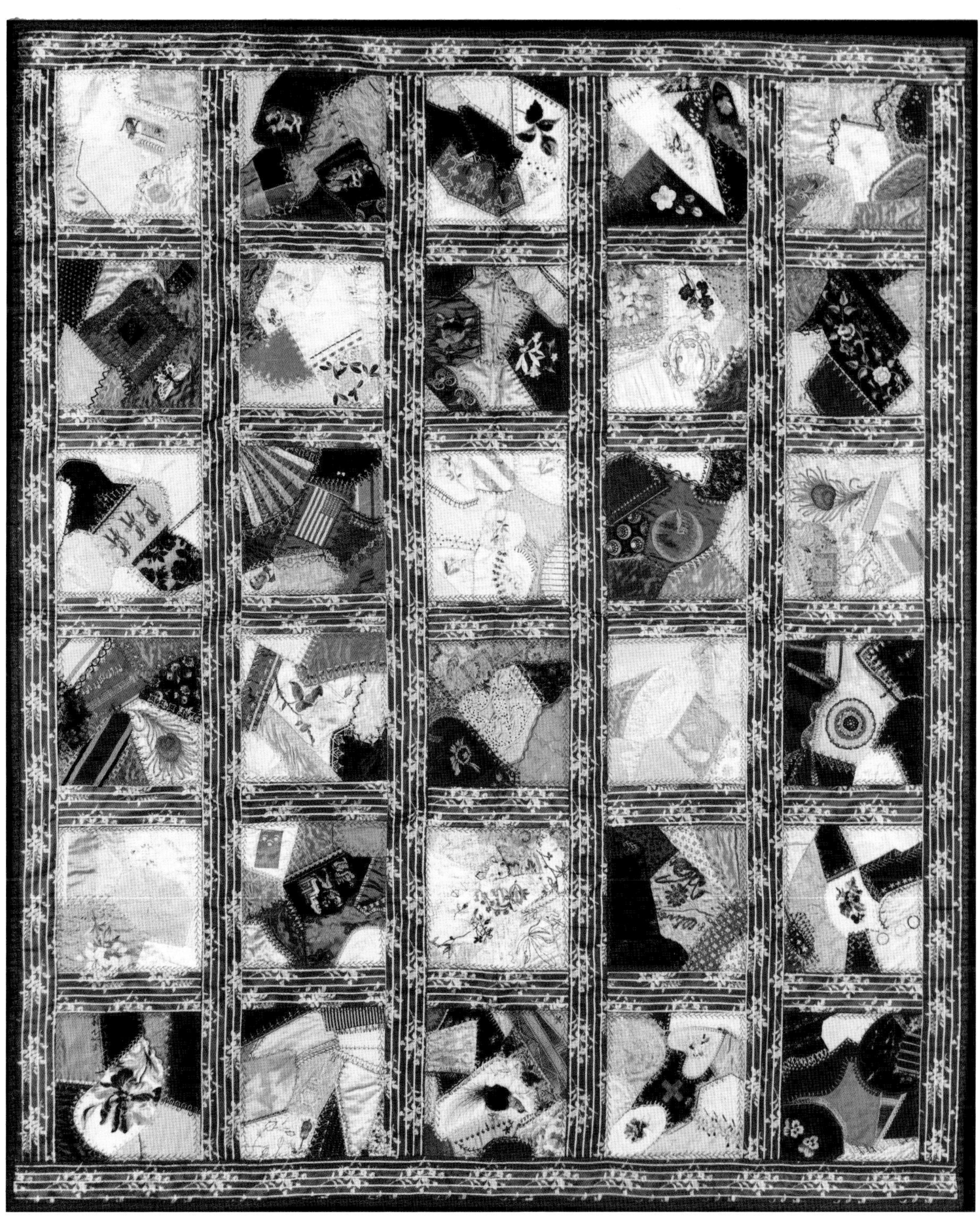

Department of

TEXTILES

American, 19th century
Crazy quilt
Pieced and embroidered silk
Gift of Eleanor Atwater, Martha Atwater,
Sandra Butler, Ellie Donovan, Suzanne
H. Hodder, Anita Kunin, Laura Miles,
Eleanor W. Reid, and Kathleen Scott,
82.139

American, 19th century
Ornamental trim
Silk, cotton and wool
Given in appreciation of Joel S. and
Frances Torstenson, 84.131.1, 2

MARY SIBLEY
American, 19th century
Sampler
Embroidery
Linen and silk
Gift of Carroll Simmons, 81.91

American, 20th century
Bag with flap
Embroidery
Linen and silk
Gift of the Textile Council, 83.105.2

American, 20th century
Dresser scarf
Embroidery
Linen and silk
Gift of the Textile Council, 83.105.1

LYNN KLEIN
American, 1950–
Wool Blind, 1976
Weft ikat
Wool and linen
Anonymous gift, 83.158.3a–g

JACK LENOR LARSEN
American, 1927–
Magnum, 1970
Machine embroidery
Cotton, nylon, vinyl, and polyester stage
curtain
Gift of Charles M. Senseman, 85.26

JAN MYERS
American, 1954–
*A Plane View of Things Past/
Transparent Ideas,* 1984
Quilted and hand dyed cotton
Gift of an anonymous donor and the
Minnesota Quilters, 84.63

CAROL ANN SMITH
American, 1953
Frost
Fabric sculpture
Linen, cotton, silk, and natural materials
Gift of the artist, 84.128

Bhutan, 20th century
Kho (man's coat)
Warp faced plain weave with
supplementary warp patterning
Silk and cotton
Gift of N. Bud Grossman, 82.102.39

Bhutan, 20th century
Kira (woman's dress)
Warp faced plain weave with
discontinuous supplementary weft
patterning
Silk and cotton
Gift of N. Bud Grossman, 82.102.1

Bhutan, 20th century
Kira (woman's dress)
Warp faced plain weave with
discontinuous supplementary weft
patterning
Silk and cotton
Gift of N. Bud Grossman, 82.102.12

Bhutan, 20th century
Yatta Dhen Khep (bed covering)
Plain weave with discontinuous
supplementary weft patterning
Wool
Gift of N. Bud Grossman, 82.102.29

Bokhara, Uzbek, 19th century
Panel
Warp ikat
Silk and cotton
The Ethel Morrison Van Derlip Fund,
81.49.2

Bokhara, Uzbek, 19th century
Panel
Warp ikat
Silk and cotton
Gift of Ellen and Sheldon Sturgis, 84.29

Dutch, 18th century
Panel
Satin ground with supplementary weft
patterning
Silk
The Ethel Morrison Van Derlip Fund,
81.13.14

Egyptian, Coptic, 5th–7th century A.D.
Jewelled cross
Plain weave with tapestry patterning
Linen and wool
Gift of Aimee Mott Butler Charitable
Trust, Mr. and Mrs. John F. Donovan,
the Estate of Margaret B. Hawks, and
Eleanor Weld Reid, 83.126

English, 17th century
Chalice veil
Raised work embroidery
Silk and metallic threads, wire, feathers,
pearls, and beads
The John R. Van Derlip Fund, 85.25

English, 18th century
Gilet
Embroidery
Silk
The Ethel Morrison Van Derlip Fund,
85.53.1

English, about 1700
Coverlet
Embroidered linen fabric with silk
thread worked in satin stitch, long and
short stitch, brick stitch, couched cord,
and French knots
The Ethel Morrison Van Derlip Fund,
80.72

WILLIAM MORRIS
English, 1834–1896
Birds, 1879–80
Jacquard woven double cloth curtain
panels
Wool
Gift of Mrs. Adele Roller, 84.66

European, 17th or 18th century
Fringe
Woven silk, metal and cotton
Gift of Stanford and Phyllis Lehmberg,
85.78.1

European, second half of 18th century
Fringe
Woven and tied silk
Gift of Stanford and Phyllis Lehmberg,
84.112.14

European, 19th century
Ornamental trim
Woven with wrapped appendages
Silk, wood and paper
Gift of Dr. David Bradford, 84.107.10

MARY SIBLEY
American, 19th century
Sampler
Embroidery
Linen and silk
Gift of Carroll Simmons, 81.91

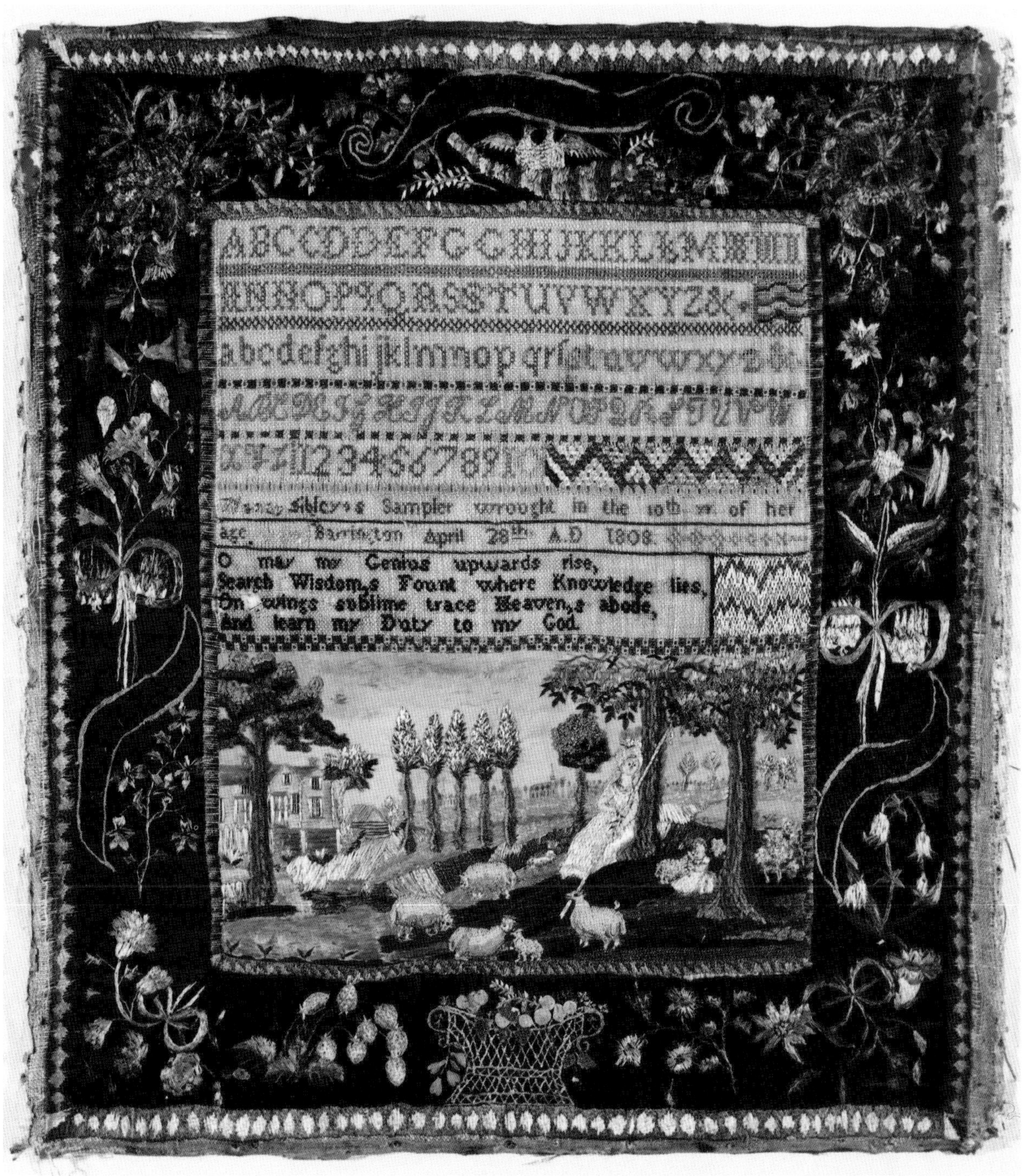

Department of

TEXTILES

European, 19th century
Ornamental trim
Woven silk and cotton
Gift of Dr. David Bradford, 84.107.12

European, 19th century
Ornamental trim
Woven cotton and wool
Gift of Dr. David Bradford, 84.107.13b

European, 19th century
Ornamental trim
Woven cotton and wool
Gift of Stanford and Phyllis Lehmberg,
84.112.1

European, 19th century
Ornamental trim
Woven silk and cotton
Gift of Stanford and Phyllis Lehmberg,
84.112.3

European, 19th century
Tassels and cord
Silk, cotton and wood
Gift of Dr. David Bradford, 84.107.3a

European, 19th century
*Valance with decorative trim and
tassels*
Silk, cotton, metal and wood
Gift of Stanford and Phyllis Lehmberg,
84.112.11

European, 19th century
Velvet trim
Woven, supplementary warp pile
Silk and cotton
Gift of Dr. David Bradford, 84.107.8

French, 18th century
Chasuble
Embroidered silk and metallic threads
The Christina N. and Swan J. Turnblad
Memorial Fund, 85.114

French, 18th century
Embroidery sample for dress
Embroidered silk
The Ethel Morrison Van Derlip Fund,
85.53.3

French, 18th century
Embroidery sample for dress
Embroidered silk, metallic sequins,
buttons and strips of fur
The Ethel Morrison Van Derlip Fund,
85.53.4

French, 18th century
Panel
Satin ground with supplementary weft
patternings
Miscellaneous Funds, by exchange,
84.17.1

French, Lyons, 18th century
Panel
Damask with supplementary weft
patterning
Silk
Gift of an anonymous donor and the
Textile Council, 84.68

French, 1700–10
Panel
Silk and metallic threads
Damask ground with continuous
supplementary weft patterning
The Christina N. and Swan J. Turnblad
Memorial Fund, 82.13.2

PHILIPPE DE LASALLE
French, 1723–1803
Panel, 1770–75
Satin ground with discontinuous
supplementary weft patterning
Silk
The Groves Foundation Fund, 83.36

GASPARD GREGOIRE
French, 1745–1843
after Rubens's *Hours of the Night*
Painted, cut supplementary warp pile
Silk
Gift of an anonymous donor, 82.14

French, Alençon, 19th century
Apron
Needle lace
Linen
The Fiduciary Fund, 81.54.1

French, 19th century
Panel
Chiné, warp printed plain weave
Silk
The Christina N. and Swan J. Turnblad
Memorial Fund, 81.93.4

French, 19th century
Printed trim
Plain weave
Cotton
Gift of Elinor Merrill, 84.111.1.1

French, 19th century
Printed trim
Plain weave
Cotton
Gift of Elinor Merrill, 84.111.1.2

French, 19th century
Printed trim
Plain weave
Cotton
Gift of Stanford and Phyllis Lehmberg,
84.112.6

French, 19th century
Printed trim
Plain weave
Cotton
Gift of Stanford and Phyllis Lehmberg,
84.112.7

French, 19th century
Printed trim
Plain weave
Cotton
Gift of Stanford and Phyllis Lehmberg,
84.112.8

French, 19th century
Upholstery material
Satin with supplementary weft
patterning
Silk and cotton
Anonymous gift and Miscellaneous
Funds, by exchange 84.16.5

French, late 19th–early 20th century
Panel
Chiné and velours sabré
Warp printed with areas of cut warp
floats
Silk
The Christina N. and Swan J. Turnblad
Memorial Fund, 81.93.14

French, 20th century
Panel
Chiné, warp printed plain weave
Silk
The Christina N. and Swan J. Turnblad
Memorial Fund, 81.93.12

French, Lyons, 1913
Curtain tie-back
Made by Bourdon, S.A. Workshop
Silk, cotton, metal and paper
Gift of Michel Bourdon, 85.125.5

Bhutan, 20th century
Kira (woman's dress)
Warp faced plain weave with
discontinuous supplementary weft
patterning
Silk and cotton
Gift of N. Bud Grossman, 82.102.1

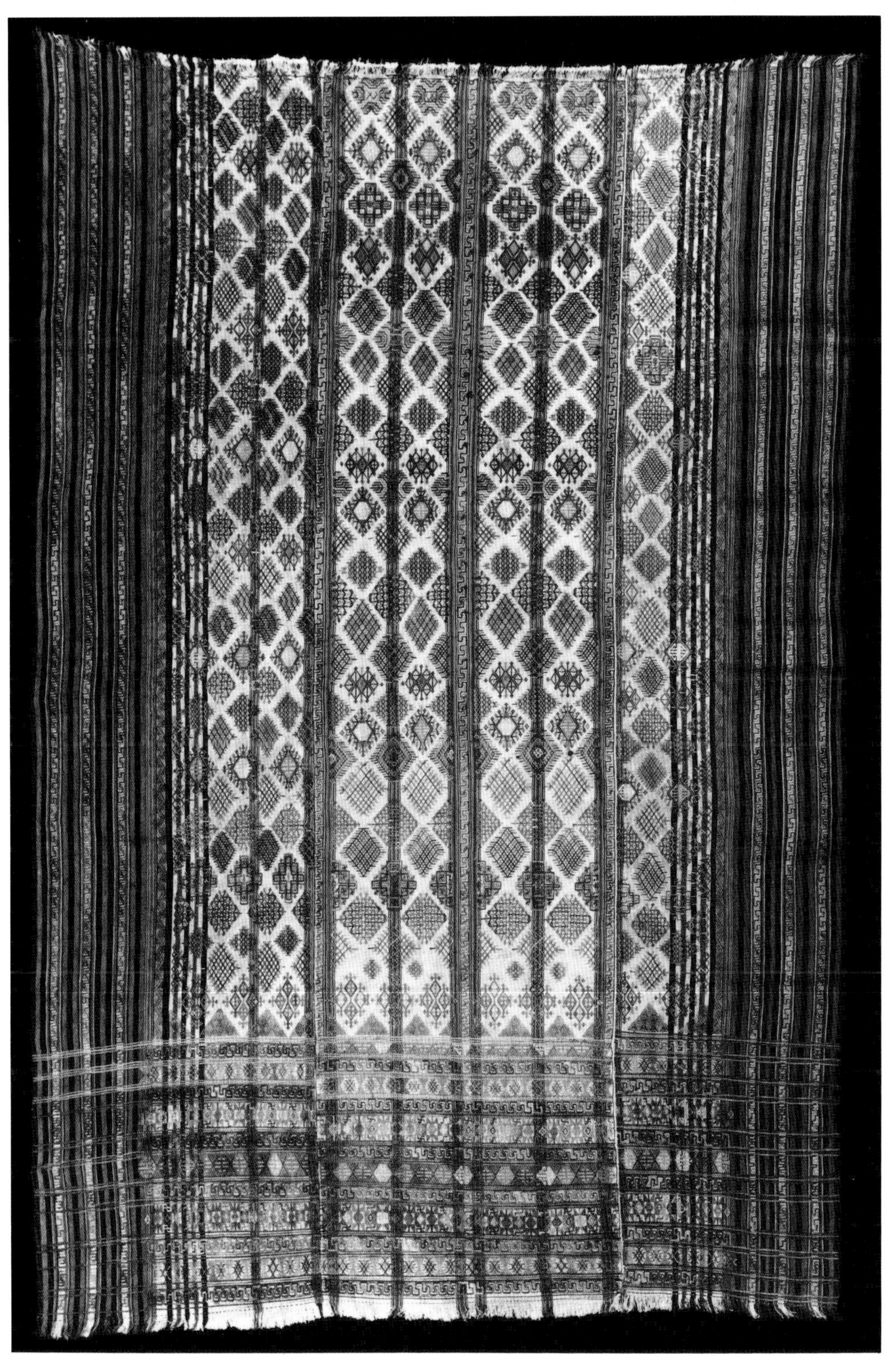

German, 18th century
Panel
Satin ground with supplementary weft
patterning
Silk
Gift of Mrs. Adele Roller, 85.123

Ghana, Asante, 19th century
Kente cloth
Joined narrow band strips
Silk
Gift of Jerome Joss, 84.108.3

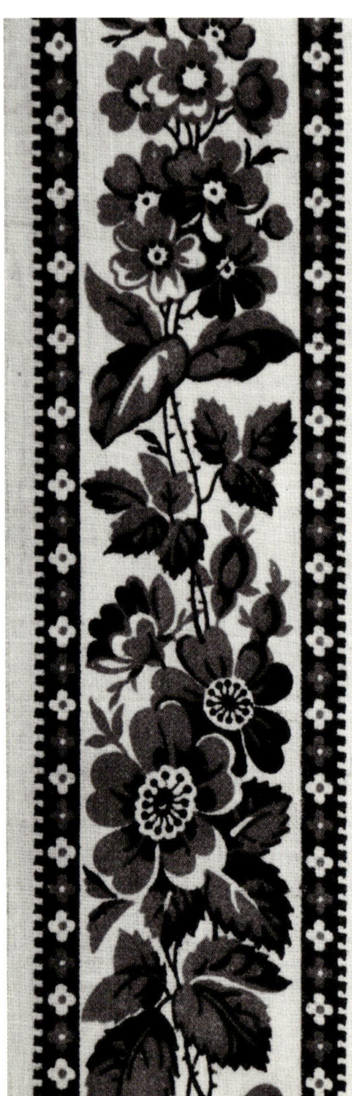

Hmong, 20th century
Ceremonial skirt
Indigo batik, cross stitch embroidery
and appliqué
Cotton, polyester and silk
Gift of funds from Mr. and Mrs. John M.
Hartwell, 82.138

White Hmong
Two belts, 1910–20
Appliqué and embroidery
Silk and cotton
Gift of Robert and Gloria Congdon,
83.70.2ab

TXHIAJ TUB LAUJ
Hmong, 20th century
Story blanket
Embroidery
Cotton and polyester
Gift of Sally Anson, Mary Bowman, Mrs.
Benton Case, Helen Cashman, Margaret
Castor, Thirza Cleveland, Peggy Dixon,
Sue Hodder, Allegra Parker, Topsy
Simonson, Harriet Spencer, and Joan
Truesdale, 85.28

BLIA LEE
Hmong, 20th century
Hanging, 1980–81
Appliqué and embroidery
Poly-cotton blend with silk thread
Gift of funds from Charles H. and Lucy
W. Bell, 82.100

GE LEE
White Hmong, 20th century
Baby hat
Appliqué and embroidery
Cotton
Gift of Robert and Gloria Congdon,
83.70.5

KA ZOUA LEE
Hmong, 20th century
Village story blanket
Fold and tuck appliqué with
embroidery
Gift of Ellen and Sheldon Sturgis, 84.7.1

ZAG VANG
Hmong, 20th century
Jacket patches
Fold and tuck patterning with
embroidery
Cotton
Gift of Robert and Gloria Congdon,
83.70.8ab

DIA XIONG
Blue Hmong, 20th century
Rooster hat
Appliqué with pompons
Cotton
Gift of Robert and Gloria Congdon,
83.70.7

Italian, 17th century
Looped fringe
Tablet woven
Silk and metallic threads
Gift of Mary Heidenreich-Landgraf,
85.74

Italian, 17th century
Tassel
Silk, metal and wood
Gift of Gail Bickmann Balego, 85.70

Spanish, 16th century
Altar frontal
Velvet embroidered with gold metal
threads and polychromed silks
Silk
The Ethel Morrison Van Derlip Fund,
80.73

Spanish or French, 1700–1710
Panel
Silk and metallic threads
Damask ground with continuous
supplementary weft patterning
The Christina N. and Swan J. Turnblad
Memorial Fund, 82.13.1

Zaire, Kuba, 20th century
Musese panel
Cutpile embroidery
Raffia
Gift of Jerome Joss, 84.108.1

Zaire, Kuba, 20th century
Musese panel
Cutpile embroidery
Raffia
Gift of Jerome Joss, 84.108.2

Zaire, Kuba, 20th century
Skirt
Appliqué and embroidery
Raffia
The Ethel Morrison Van Derlip Fund,
84.15

French, 19th century
Printed trim
Plain weave
Cotton
Gift of Elinor Merrill, 84.111.1.2

JAN MYERS
American, 1954–
A Plane View of Things Past/
Transparent Ideas, 1984
Quilted and hand dyed cotton
Gift of an anonymous donor and the
Minnesota Quilters, 84.63

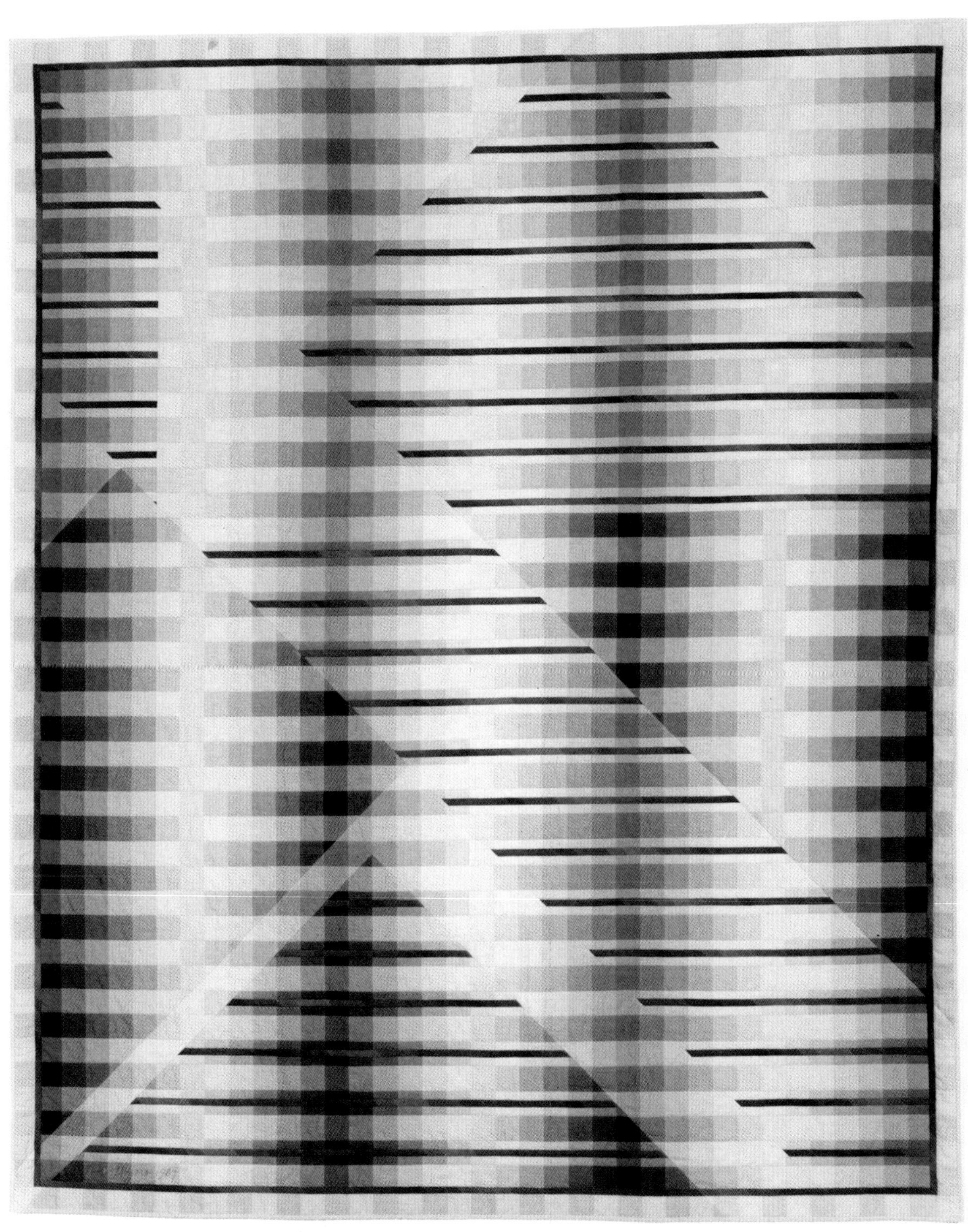

DIRECTOR'S OFFICE
Alan Shestack, *Director*
Timothy Fiske, *Associate Director*
Margaret Olson, Jacquelyn Warner-Hemingson,
Administrative Assistants

DEPARTMENT OF AFRICAN, OCEANIC,
AND NEW WORLD CULTURES
Louise Lincoln, *Associate Curator;
Editor in charge of catalogue*

DEPARTMENT OF ASIAN ART
Robert D. Jacobsen, *Curator*
Catherine Parker, *Curatorial Assistant*

DEPARTMENT OF DECORATIVE ARTS
AND SCULPTURE
Michael Conforti, *Chairman, Curatorial
Division; Bell Memorial Curator of Decorative
Arts and Sculpture; Curator in charge of
exhibition*
Francis J. Puig, *Associate Curator*
William Heidrich, *Curatorial Assistant*
Karen Rigdon, *Curatorial Intern*
Carolyn Scholz, *Administrative Assistant*

DEPARTMENT OF PAINTINGS
George S. Keyes, *Curator*
Rosamond Hurrell, *Curatorial Assistant*

DEPARTMENT OF PHOTOGRAPHY
Carroll T. Hartwell, *Curator*
Christian A. Peterson, *Assistant Curator*

DEPARTMENT OF PRINTS AND DRAWINGS
John W. Ittmann, *Curator*
Richard Campbell, *Associate Curator*
Allyson Hakes, *Secretary*
Suzanne Anderson, *Matting Technician*

DEPARTMENT OF TEXTILES
Lotus Stack, *Curator*
Mary Ann Butterfield, *Assistant Conservator*
Peggy Dorwick, *Secretary*

EXHIBITIONS
Mary Mancuso, *Coordinator*

PUBLIC RELATIONS
Liz Sela, *Director*
Heidi Freerks, *Publicity Assistant*
Alla Litkewitsch, *Administrative Assistant*

DESIGN
Ruth Dean, *Designer*
Anne Knauff, *Assistant Designer*
R. Pat Atherton, *Typesetter*

EDITORIAL
Elisabeth Sövik, *Associate Editor*

PHOTOGRAPHIC SERVICES
Gary Mortensen, *Photographer*
Petronella Ytsma, *Assistant Photographer*

REGISTRAR'S OFFICE
Marilyn Bjorklund, *Registrar*
Karen Duncan, *Associate Registrar*
Claire Ouellette, *Assistant Registrar*
Moira Harris, *Cataloguer*
Roxy Ballard, *Exhibition Designer*
Tom Jance, *Chief, Works of Art Crew*
Nina Chenault, Ken Krenz, Doug Kroeger, Theo
Manzavrakos, Patti Landres, Dennis Grodahl,
Wayne Masterson, Timothy Glaesemann, Mary
Gervais, Michelle Kasimor, John Jance,
Therese Privitera, Kirstin Seterdahl, Lily
Arbore, *Works of Art Crew*
John Black, *Lighting Technician*
Esther Nelson, *Maintenance Technician*

EDUCATION DIVISION
Kathryn C. Johnson, *Chairman*
Tad Park, *Coordinator, Educator Services*
Nancy Malmström, *Educational Resources
Specialist*
Solveig Beckmen, *Education Secretary*
Diane Levy, *Supervisor, Tours and Docent
Training*
Nivin Stott, *Associate, Tours and Docent
Training*
Barbara Sarbach, *Tour Scheduler*
Jean Strommer, *Supervisor, Public Programs*
Susan Jacobsen, *Coordinator, Young People's
Programs*
Cheri Snoddy, *Secretary, Public Programs*
Mary Huber, *Supervisor, Arts Resource and
Information Center*
Jane Hancock, *Supervisor, Media Resources
and Production*
Lisa Nebenzahl, *Video Producer*
Mark Stanley, *Video Producer*

MUSEUM SHOP
Mary Shutes, *Manager*

LIBRARY
Harold Peterson, *Librarian*
Paul Maravelas, *Assistant Librarian*
Michael Boe, *Library Technician*

SECURITY
Gordon Cable, *Chief*